The Faber Pocket Guide to Elizabethan and Jacobean Drama

Simon Trussler is co-editor of *New Theatre Quarterly* and the author or editor of numerous books on drama and theatre, including *Shakespearean Concepts* (1989) and the award-winning *Cambridge Illustrated History of British Theatre* (1993). He was editor of the *RSC Yearbook* from 1978 to 1985, edited and introduced fourteen volumes in the 'Swan Theatre Plays' series (Methuen, 1986–89), and is currently typographical consultant for the 'Shakespeare Folios' series, in which twelve titles have so far appeared. Formerly Reader in Drama in the University of London, he is now Professor and Senior Research Fellow at Rose Bruford College.

D0307754

THE FABER POCKET GUIDE TO
Elizabethan and Jacobean Drama

Simon Trussler

faber and faber

First published in 2006
by Faber and Faber Limited
3 Queen Square London WC1N 3AU

Published in the United States by Faber and Faber Inc.
an affiliate of Farrar, Straus and Giroux LLC, New York

Typeset by Country Setting, Kingsdown, Kent CT14 8ES
Printed in England by Mackays of Chatham

A CIP record for this book is available from the British Library

ISBN 978-0-571-21489-1
ISBN 0-571-21489-4

Contents

Guide to Topics

The section on 'The Historical Context' of each play usually addresses issues which also have wider relevance. The following are the main topics covered.

Preface

As I write, the second of the Royal Shakespeare Company's seasons of work by lesser-known Elizabethan and Jacobean dramatists is in full swing, bringing back to theatrical life yet more plays from that golden age – and showing that this volume by no means exhausts the riches yet to be mined from the non-Shakespearean repertoire. Had the RSC productions of such plays as Middleton and Rowley's *A New Way to Please You*, Fletcher's *The Tamer Tamed* and Massinger's *The Roman Actor* happened when the book was being planned, the task of selection would have become even more difficult. In an age when many professional playwrights evidently had to produce two new pieces a year to earn a living, the original selection was problematic enough; and happily the authors of the plays in the RSC seasons are represented here by other works. For I did want the book to include as many writers as possible besides those whose places in the living theatre have long been secure – notably Marlowe, Jonson and Webster, who all demanded to be fully represented nonetheless. As a result, the volume mixes plays that are quite regularly revived with a number that are all too rarely seen.

This *Guide* differs in several respects from its companion on Shakespeare's plays. Where the plays in that volume are arranged in alphabetical order, here the sequence is chronological; for the book (which, belying its title, also covers the output of the Caroline years) spans just over half a century of political, social and economic change, which the plays directly or indirectly reflect; and it seemed important to trace the changing mood and preoccupations of the times, as I have tried to do in the sections on 'The Historical Context'. An essay on 'The World of the Play' replaces the notes on 'Characters' in the Shakespeare volume. Shakespeare's world is one in which 'character' does indeed begin to take on its modern meaning, of individuals with distinct personalities and a psyche which expresses itself in (or is concealed by) what they do. His contemporaries were perhaps more of their own time in their preference for displaying how action shapes character rather than the reverse (though in thus anticipating the existential sense of selfhood they were arguably no less modern). So in 'The World of the Play', while considering character where appropriate, my aim has been to explore the distinctive ways in which the dramatists create a world which is at once theatrically self-sustaining yet intimately related to that of its audience. Since the analysis in these sections is shaped by the qualities specific to each play, I have added notes on 'The Playwright's Craft' to cover such aspects as form, language, conventions, structure and stage practice where these are not central to the drift of the earlier discussion. A final section, offering a brief overview of each play 'In Performance', is intended to provide enough information to set the interested reader off on his or her own further explorations (for which *Theatre Record* provides an invaluable resource, reprinting complete reviews of all London productions since 1981, and additionally of regional productions since 1991).

I'd like to express my gratitude to Peter Holland, who was kind enough to read early drafts of this book and to make valuable suggestions, and to Nick de Somogyi, who not only proofread with his usual scrupulous care but offered helpful comments from his own deep knowledge of the period. My sincere thanks are also due to Rose Bruford College, for a fellowship which has allowed me that most precious of commodities, time; to my successive editors at Faber and Faber, Peggy Paterson and Dinah Wood, not least for their patience; and to my younger children, Jonathan and Meryl, not least for theirs.

This book is for Sally. Anyway.

Elizabethan and Jacobean Theatre

The most enduring form of late-medieval drama, the great cycles of mystery plays which expressed the civic pride of such towns as Wakefield, Chester and York, celebrated the mid-summer festival of Corpus Christi. This found no place in the calendar of the protestant Elizabethan church, and the last recorded performances took place during the 1570s. Early in that same decade an act for the punishment of vagabonds effectively outlawed companies of strolling players, requiring all acting troupes to obtain noble patronage. Under these convergent pressures, theatrical activity in England became, as it was long to remain, centred on London, where those companies able to find a patron achieved a measure of security which encouraged the building of permanent playhouses. The earliest of note, the Theatre in Shoreditch, opened in 1576.

London, so much smaller then than now, was in effect twin cities: the old and fiercely independent City still largely confined within the Roman walls; and Westminster, with its rambling Palace straddling Whitehall, close by the Hall and Cathedral which symbolised its political and religious centrality. The cities were joined by the umbilical cord of the Strand, off which the streets down to the Thames and around Covent Garden were the earliest location of what we still call the (now farther-flung) West End.

The City authorities were always deeply uneasy about the theatre, and although it enjoyed royal favour and regular commands to play before the Queen, no more than the City did the Court want crowds of unruly theatregoers on its doorstep. So the first theatres were built either to the north of the City in the suburbs of Shoreditch and Finsbury, or south of the Thames, where bull- and bear-baiting arenas and bawdy houses already flourished in the riverside area of Bankside, convenient for London Bridge (still the only river crossing) but beyond the jurisdiction of the City.

The Theatre was built by James Burbage, whose company – first under the patronage of the Lord Chamberlain and after 1603 under that of King James himself – was to include both his son Richard, reputedly the greatest actor of his times, and the actor-playwright William Shakespeare. Theirs was a company of shareholders, each taking a proportion of the risks and the profits; but their main rivals, known as the Lord Admiral's and later Prince Henry's Men, were financed by the impresario Philip Henslowe, who built the first theatre on Bankside, the Rose, around 1587. The Admiral's – whose leading actor was Edward Alleyn – moved north to the newly-built Fortune theatre in 1600, perhaps to avoid the proximity on Bankside of the first Globe, opened in the previous year as a new base for the Chamberlain's (and later rebuilt, after being destroyed by fire in 1613).

Other outdoor theatres, all built between 1577 and 1614, included the Swan and the Hope on Bankside, and the Curtain, the Red Bull and the Fortune to the north of the City. In such playhouses the humblest spectators – the 'groundlings' – stood on three sides of a raised platform stage, while those who could afford to pay for greater comfort sat in the tiers of galleries which formed the perimeter of the generally polygonal buildings, probably accommodating as much as two-thirds of the total capacity. There was no provision for scenery, though special effects might be facilitated by means of trap-doors in the stage and machinery in the roof (or 'heavens') which sheltered the rear part of the stage. Entrances were by means of two doors leading from the 'tiring house' backstage, or via the balcony which provided a second playing level. A curtained space between the stage doors was probably not a functional 'inner stage', but a small area in which a tableau might be revealed – or 'discovered', as stage directions usually have it. If scenery was scant, costumes were lavish, and kept replenished by the cast-offs or bequests of the actors' noble patrons (who otherwise lent little besides their names).

What we do not know is how far, through costume, make-up or other means, attempts were made to persuade audiences that the boy actors who took all female roles were other than boys – not really a necessity for audiences happy to accept that the bare boards of a stage transported them to the field of Agincourt or the sea coast of Bohemia. Bearing in mind not only the limitations of pubescent boys (particularly in imitating women of mature years) but the deeply patriarchal attitudes of the times, the number and frequent prominence of female roles in plays throughout the period is all the more surprising.

Such boy players were in effect apprentices, and often graduated into professional adult actors. There were also companies wholly comprised of children (nominally choristers), which became especially fashionable during the decade after 1600. These had always played indoors, in so-called 'private' houses, for smaller and more select audiences. Thus, although James Burbage had in fact bought and adapted a space for playing within the old Blackfriars priory in 1596, children's companies continued to occupy it until 1608, whereupon the King's Men moved into the Blackfriars for the winter months, returning to the Globe for summer playing. The Cockpit (or Phoenix), another 'private' playhouse (the first in Drury Lane), also housed professional adult companies after 1616.

The open-air playhouses relied on natural lighting, and so performances took place in the afternoons, generally starting at two o'clock – as did those in the private theatres, although these required artificial lighting. Despite Shakespeare's famous reference to the 'two hours' traffic of our stage', performances lasting three hours seem to have been the norm – including a closing jig at the public theatres, and musical interludes between the acts at the private. Dividing a play into five acts was not so much a nod towards a supposed classical rulebook as a practical necessity, since the candles used for lighting needed regular trimming. Outdoor performances appear to have been continuous – no doubt with a good deal of coming and going for refreshments and calls of nature – and the act-divisions in printed texts of plays first staged in public theatres usually represent only the tidy-mindedness of later editors.

In the 'private' theatres, rows of seats in the pit area of the rectangular auditorium (here the most fashionable part of the house) faced an end-on stage, with seating also in the galleries and along the edges of the stage itself. Because these houses were more comfortable (and so more expensive) than the open-air theatres, and also had a considerably smaller capacity, their audiences are thought to have been drawn only from the more privileged classes of playgoers. While some even dispute the point that audiences in the 'public' play-houses constituted a more homogeneous cross-section of the community, a wider debate continues over how far the more limited composition of audiences at the indoor playhouses affected the nature of the repertoire, and how far the more intimate playing-space influenced performance.

What is apparent is that a new word, 'personation', was coined around the turn of the century, apparently to distin-guish the style of such actors as Burbage, creator of many of the great Shakespearean roles, from the likes of Alleyn, whose presumably more presentational acting was more appropriate to the heroes and villains created by Marlowe and Kyd. But, of course, the plays of Jonson required a different style again, perhaps closer to the skills of stand-up comedy, while the works of Chapman, Middleton, Webster, Ford or Brome all make distinctive stylistic demands – as did the now largely forgotten vogue for tragi-comedy, whose leading exponents were Beaumont and Fletcher. No doubt, like good actors in any age, Elizabethan and Jacobean players adapted with pro-fessionalism to whatever demands of style or playing space they encountered, while remaining true also to the changing spirit of their times. For we must remember that although we are dealing with a period of little more than half a century, its beginnings coincided with the defeat of the Spanish Armada and the mood of patriotic fervour which to some extent was compensatory for the economic difficulties of the 1590s, and its sudden end with the beginnings of the Civil Wars – from adulation of a seemingly ageless Virgin Queen to the taking up of arms against an authoritarian King.

The Court had its own theatres, which were of course even more exclusive than the private playhouses. The last of a succession of Banqueting Halls in Whitehall, completed in 1622, was designed by Inigo Jones, as was the more intimate Cockpit-in-Court, which opened in 1630. Here professional companies were frequently summoned to play, but courtly amateurs would themselves perform in the elaborately staged masques upon which Jones as designer collaborated (and often disputed) with Ben Jonson as writer. When the ageing Jonson fell from favour, Jones found William Davenant more compliant in subduing literary content to spectacle, and the last masque to be staged before the Civil Wars, *Salmacida Spolia* in 1640, was evidently most elaborate of all in its allegorical compliment to the wisdom and virtue of the King and Queen. But where the elderly Elizabeth had recognised courtly spectacle (not least the spectacle of herself) as a mode of communication with her subjects, for Charles the masque was a kind of inward-looking wish-fulfilment, no longer symbolising but substituting for the monarch's relationship with his people.

When that relationship finally broke down and military conflict erupted, the order for the closure of the theatres in September 1642 was almost certainly not intended to be more permanent than earlier closures on account of royal deaths or (all too frequently) the plague, but simply as a normal precaution against public disorder. In the event, it was to outlast even the prolonged conflict, remaining in force for eighteen years until the Restoration of Charles II in 1660.

The Spanish Tragedy
Thomas Kyd

c. 1587

Source

None known.

The story

In the outer play which 'frames' *The Spanish Tragedy*, a personified figure of Revenge promises to help the ghost of the Spanish courtier Andrea in pursuing vengeance for his death in battle at the hands of Don Balthazar, heir to the Portuguese throne. Balthazar has been brought honourably captive to the Spanish court, by the Duke's son Lorenzo and Andrea's friend Horatio, son of Hieronimo, Knight Marshal of Spain. The King favours a politically expedient match between Balthazar and Lorenzo's sister Bel-imperia, formerly Andrea's mistress; but her own preference is for Horatio – both as her lover and to seek their joint revenge for Andrea's death. Her servant Pedringano betrays her plans for an assignation with Horatio in Hieronimo's garden to Lorenzo and Balthazar, who hang Horatio from an arbour and abduct Bel-imperia. A distraught Hieronimo discovers his dead son, and vows vengeance upon his murderers. In Portugal, the Viceroy believes the claim of the villainous Villuppo that Balthazar was treacherously slain, but is reassured when a returning Ambassador reports that his son is alive. Back in Spain, Hieronimo discovers a letter in which Bel-imperia names Horatio's murderers – but their high rank forces him to proceed with caution. Lorenzo orders Pedringano to slay an accomplice who might betray the deed – making sure that the murder is observed and the gullible servant hanged. However, a letter from Pedringano to Lorenzo, intercepted by Hieronimo, confirms the old man's suspicions. Bel-imperia pretends to believe Lorenzo's assurance that he acted to protect her honour, and is allowed to return to court, but Hieronimo, crazed by grief, is prevented from taking his accusations to the King. In the framing action, Andrea is furious at the planned match between Balthazar and Bel-imperia, but appeased when a dumb-show conjured by Revenge displays a bloody outcome. This ensues when Hieronimo is asked to stage a tragedy for the wedding of Balthazar to Bel-imperia. Lorenzo and Balthazar are persuaded to take part in the performance, during which Bel-imperia's character slays Balthazar's and then takes her own life, while Hieronimo in role kills Lorenzo. The old man then reveals that the deaths have not been play-acting, and explains his actions over the body of his son. He bites out his tongue before stabbing the Duke and finally himself. In the closing episode in Hell, a delighted Andrea plans tortures for the dead.

The author and his work

Thomas Kyd was born in London in 1558 and educated at Merchant Taylors' School in the City. By 1583 he may have been involved with the newly formed Queen's company of players, and in 1587 with a theatrical troupe under the patronage of either the Earl of Sussex or Lord Strange. He must have shared lodgings with Christopher Marlowe in the early 1590s, for when he was arrested and tortured on the orders of the Privy Council in May 1593 he accused his fellow dramatist of writing the 'vile heretical conceits denying the deity of Jesus' which had been found there. Kyd did not recover from this ordeal, and died in the following year.

Besides *The Spanish Tragedy*, Kyd was probably the author of a Hamlet play (dubbed the *Ur-Hamlet* by later scholars), the lost source for Shakespeare's version; but a 'prequel' to *The Spanish Tragedy*, *The First Part of Jeronimo*, dates from after his death. The full-length version of *Soliman and Perseda* (the 'play within the play' in *The Spanish Tragedy*), published anonymously *c.* 1592, may have been his, and a translation from the French of the Senecan tragedy *Cornelia* appeared under his name in 1594. He may even have collaborated with Shakespeare on *Titus Andronicus*; but the precise extent and nature of his dramatic output remain as elusive as the details of his life.

The historical context

The history plays which were to become so popular in the 1590s drew freely upon England's traditional enmity with the French, spasmodically played out during the Hundred Years War. But since the ending of Mary's childless marriage to Philip II of Spain with her death in 1558, and the moderate protestantism of Elizabeth's religious settlement, the nation's 'natural enemy' was now Spain. The religious differences were real enough, as was Spanish complicity in successive plots to restore England to Catholicism; but the underlying rivalry was imperial, as these two seafaring nations vied for supremacy in the New World. In 1580 Spain went to war with her neighbour to assert Philip's claim to the Portuguese succession, and for the next sixty years Portugal was ruled by Spanish kings. Although the war between Spain and Portugal in *The Spanish Tragedy* is unhistorical, the play's early audiences would have recalled this real-life counterpart – and relished the roll-call of English victories over both nations which closes Act I.

In 1587, a likely year for the play's composition, Drake's raid on Cadiz disabled the Spanish fleet, and Elizabeth finally agreed to the execution of her cousin, the charismatic focus for Catholic dissent, Mary Queen of Scots. Both events enraged Philip, who began to assemble the ill-fated Great Armada to avenge this double affront to his dignity and his faith. But if Kyd's choice of a Spanish setting thus struck a topical note, his theme of revenge was a pervasive preoccupation of his society and times – alike of noblemen demanding the 'satisfaction' of a duel for some supposed affront to their 'honour', and of theologians considering such behaviour in the light of the biblical injunction, 'Vengeance is mine, saith the Lord.'

The world of the play

The main action of *The Spanish Tragedy* takes place in that closed and corrupt society which was how the Elizabethans perceived the Spanish court, as the Jacobeans did the Italian. No tavern scenes in Eastcheap here, or low-life sub-plots. Even the gallows humour of Pedringano is orchestrated by his betters to advance their own concerns – and the single, semi-detached sub-plot merely exchanges the Spanish court for the Portuguese.

While Hieronimo's garden with its deadly arbour is within whispering distance of the resting places of princes and kings, Hieronimo himself is a civil servant, however honoured by a lifetime of wise counsel. From the start, Kyd calculatedly emphasises Hieronimo's inferior social status, in the dispute over Balthazar's custody: the honour goes to Lorenzo because of his high rank, while the ransom – more bluntly, the cash – goes to the civil servant's son. Hieronimo is thus no less at the bidding of his superiors than Pedringano – but it is a nice irony that such bidding includes the mounting of the masque that enables him to dispose of his enemies. Hamlet uses a similar pretence, but merely to put his suspicions to the test, and it is a duel that at last provides the occasion for revenge. Hieronimo must use the play itself to get within a sword's thrust of majesty.

But what is 'the play itself' in *The Spanish Tragedy*? Andrea and Revenge in the outermost play observe and comment on the progress of the 'tragedy' – the closing word of the first scene as it is of the last. This frames a main action which is glimpsed, we are told, through the visionary Gates of Horn – thus becoming a kind of dream in Andrea's mind. And the main action is itself interspersed with the dumb-shows and Hieronimo's stage-managed masque. At other times characters on the same level take on the role of spectators, as when Lorenzo and Balthazar watch Horatio and Bel-imperia making their foredoomed plans; or an additional layer of illusion may be interpolated, as when Revenge conjures a dumb-show for Andrea to show him what is to follow. The stage directions imply that these two observers were continuously present on stage; so the 'real' theatre audience would on occasion have been watching this pair from the underworld watching (or dreaming) a tragedy whose characters were either spying on the actions of their fellows or serving as audience for yet further levels of buried action. When the last of these bursts its boundaries to make a mortal actuality of pretence, we might well feel confused about what is 'actuality' and what 'pretence'.

This pervasive 'theatricalisation' of experience is quite at odds with modern, naturalistic concerns for our suspension of disbelief; but it came to characterise much Elizabethan and Jacobean drama, on which *The Spanish Tragedy* thus exerted a formative influence. Philosophically, it gave expression to the Renaissance concept of a *theatrum mundi*, or 'great theatre of the world', in which a predetermined script is being acted out with God or Fate as its author and stage manager. Calvinistic doctrine – paradoxically as expounded by the puritans who so detested the theatre – offered a not dissimilar view of humankind's 'predestination'.

Such determinism makes puppets of us all, and at one level it is because the characters of *The Spanish Tragedy* are acting out a plot written for them by Fate that they are not 'rounded' in a modern or even Shakespearean sense. But this is also because the age was more interested in typicality than individuality – in how 'character' was a microcosmic expression of generalised behaviour and a play an *exemplum* illustrating a moral point. In this typological sense, Hieronimo is less a grieving father for our empathy than the first in that long line of 'revengers' who agonise their way through the drama of the period to instruct us in the complexities and dangers of that topical, instinctive but most un-Christian impulse.

However, 'decorum' would have denied ignoble characters an honour to defend – the Italian critic Castelvetro declaring in 1570 that 'little men' would always prefer recourse to law over the taking of personal revenge. So it is surely no coincidence that Kyd reveals that his 'little man', Hieronimo, is renowned for his scrupulous fairness in dispensing justice to supplicants – yet when he himself needs to make supplication, the power and influence of his adversaries stand in his way. What drives him mad is not the murder of his son alone, but the impossibility of achieving justice through due process of law. *The Spanish Tragedy* thus dramatises the idea and the enactment of revenge with a resonance that reaches beyond ethical quibbles into the heart of the inequalities and injustices of Elizabethan society. Its conclusion sees not the restoration of social order, but the implosion of the society that occupies the inner play; and Andrea's final line anticipates not Aristotelian catharsis but a cycle of Beckettian despair in that bleakly confident cry, 'I'll then begin their endless tragedy.'

The playwright's craft

LANGUAGE AND RHETORIC   Kyd's use of blank verse – the unrhymed iambic pentameter – for *The Spanish Tragedy* is probably earlier even than Marlowe's. And we may usefully remember that the occasional irregularities or sudden diversions into something closer to a ballad style are not deviations from a norm, but *explorations* of a verse form as yet relatively untested in performance.

The idiom gave Kyd the flexibility to make *The Spanish Tragedy* work successfully for a heterogeneous audience. In a play full of rhetorical devices, classical references and political allusions for its more sophisticated spectators, it is the freedom and fluency of the blank verse which makes it also a thundering good thriller. To label all the figures of classical rhetoric used in the play would be tedious, but we may note in just one exchange between Balthazar and Lorenzo (II, i, 113–38), instances of *anastrophe* (calculated inversion of the expected order of words); *anadiplosis* (the use of a word in one line which is then taken up in the next); and *polyptoton* (the use of the same word in calculatedly different senses). We might also instance the balance Kyd strikes in the play between long set speeches, passages of more fluid, colloquial dialogue, and such recognisably 'rhetorical' but here theatrically pertinent speech patterns as *stichomythia* (exchanges in alternating single lines); or explore the workings of the scene between Belimperia and Horatio at II, iv, 34–49, where the style and tone have the formality of a dramatised sonnet. Appreciation of such devices would not have been limited to the educated in Kyd's audiences, for Elizabethans of all classes delighted in the forceful patterning of language and argument, whether in a sermon at Paul's Cross, a legal tussle in Westminster Hall – or a Bankside play.

STRUCTURE   Influenced by the Roman dramatist Seneca in his use of rhetoric, Kyd also followed Senecan structure in using a chorus between the acts – but since he only requires three interventions from his chorus, he writes four acts rather than the expected five. He also recognises that even the choric characters need to be part of the action as well as commentators upon it. And, most important, in contrast with such earlier and 'purely' rhetorical Elizabethan tragedies as the plodding *Gorboduc*, *The Spanish Tragedy* is virtually the first play of its period in which the word-patterning of the rhetoric is clearly and consciously predicated upon *action* – and the recognition that, even at its most violent, this needs to be seen as well as described. Again, although the play contains its fair share of monologues, these are used not, as formerly, merely to report distant events or gory deeds offstage, but as the means by which a character can *externalise* intense emotions – as, say, in the Viceroy's response to the supposed death of his son at I, iii. Among Kyd's other updatings of Senecan devices, the various 'reporting' scenes do not here serve (at least not often and not primarily) to keep blood and carnage off the stage, but rather to dramatise the variability (or, in Villuppo's case, the calculated fallibility) of points of view. Like his successors in the English drama, Kyd recognised his dramatic inheritance, but refused to be ruled either by classical precedent or neoclassical pedantry.

STAGE PRACTICE   Many of the play's stage directions suggest Kyd's experience in exploiting the full potential of the playing space. The arbour in which Horatio meets his end was evidently among the relatively few properties kept to decorate the otherwise bare Elizabethan stage. Costumes, on the other hand, were often lavish, and opportunities were seized for spectacular display – these ranging in our play from the various masques and dumb-shows to Pedringano's hanging and the Spanish army's triumphal passage over the stage.

In performance

The Spanish Tragedy went through ten editions between 1592 and 1633, and its popularity in print was complemented by stage performance certainly until the turn of the new century, and probably beyond. The circumstances of the earliest stagings are uncertain, reflecting the sparsity of our knowledge of theatrical affairs until, after the plague closure of 1593, the Lord Chamberlain's and the Admiral's Men began their long struggle for supremacy. Henslowe first mentions performances at the Rose on Bankside in 1592 by Strange's Men, for whom Edward Alleyn took the leading roles, though contemporary report had it that Richard Burbage, leading actor for the Chamberlain's Men, also excelled as Hieronimo. The Admiral's inherited Strange's plays, and in 1601 Henslowe paid Ben Jonson to write 'additions' to *The Spanish Tragedy*. Apart from a few student revivals, the play was then lost to the living repertoire until the 1970s, when a fringe production at the little Mercury Theatre in 1973 was followed by a freely adapted version at the Citizens' Theatre, Glasgow, in 1978. Further revivals followed: at the National Theatre in 1982, in which Michael Bryant's Hieronimo never lost sight of the mourning father behind the increasingly desperate avenger; and by the Royal Shakespeare Company at the Swan, Stratford, in 1997, in which the focus shifted interestingly to the tensions between political and erotic imperatives within and for Bel-imperia, played by Siobhan Redmond.

Tamburlaine the Great
Christopher Marlowe

c. 1587

Source

The deeds of the fourteenth-century tyrant recounted in Part One (see 'Historical Context', below) had passed into legend through various accounts, of which Fortescue's *The Forest* (1571) and Whetstone's *The English Mirror* (1586) would have been most accessible to Marlowe – the latter perhaps a recent acquisition. Part Two is collaged from various historical, romantic and military sources unrelated to the historical figure.

The story

In Part One, the shepherd Tamburlaine seizes the crown from Cosroe, whom he has previously helped to usurp the Persian throne, and proceeds to defeat and humiliate Bajazeth, the Turkish Emperor; but he treats with dignity the Soldan of Egypt, whose daughter Zenocrate he takes as his bride. In Part Two, he responds to Zenocrate's death with arbitrary violence, and has her body embalmed to carry in his train. Enraged by his son Calyphas' shirking of battle with Bajazeth's avenging son Callapine, he puts the boy to death and commands his ignoble burial. Further brutal victories see the vanquished kings harnessed to Tamburlaine's chariot before he falls ill and dies, declaring himself to have been the 'Scourge of God'.

The author and his work

Christopher Marlowe was born in 1564, the same year as Shakespeare. The son of a Canterbury shoemaker, he won a scholarship to Cambridge, achieved his BA Degree in 1584, but was awarded his MA in 1587 only at the Privy Council's insistence, probably because he had been absent as a government spy in the Catholic seminary at Rheims. The two parts of *Tamburlaine the Great* were staged around this time, but it is uncertain whether *Doctor Faustus* followed in 1588 or came as late as 1593; and his other plays – *Dido, Queen of Carthage, The Jew of Malta, Edward II* and *The Massacre at Paris* – are also of uncertain date. Their number suggests a young dramatist busily pursuing his stage career; but hints of a darker side to Marlowe's life recur, including brief imprisonment in 1589 for complicity in murder, and a conjectured return to government service three years later when he was in the Low Countries. At that time also came Robert Greene's attack on Marlowe for 'diabolical atheism'; then, in 1593, Thomas Kyd, arrested for possessing atheistical writings, alleged that these belonged to Marlowe, accusing his erstwhile friend of treason and sodomy. Summoned to appear before the Privy Council, Marlowe was examined on 20 May, released on bail – and ten days later stabbed to death in a Deptford inn, his attacker being pardoned following a coroner's finding of 'homicide in self-defence'. On the day of his burial, a note to the authorities from the informer Richard Baines condemned his 'damnable judgement of religion and scorn of God's word'.

The historical context

The historical Timur (1336–1405), nicknamed the Lame, was not a Scythian shepherd but a native of Transoxania, present-day Uzbekistan – just to the north of Afghanistan, which was among the earliest conquests of this ruthless warrior who used his Muslim faith to cloak his ambitions. He embodied, as does Marlowe's Tamburlaine, the combination of personal charisma, capacity for diplomatic subterfuge and ultimate readiness to use brute force which the Elizabethans called *vertu*. This, according to Machiavelli in *The Prince* (1513), was a necessary quality for the successful ruler; and although Machiavelli was prominent in the Elizabethan demonology, the Queen herself displayed *vertu*, as did many of the adventurers and seafaring heroes of her age. *Tamburlaine* dispassionately reflects both admiration for the restless energies of these emergent imperialists and recognition of the cruelties they could inflict. Thus, in the systematic devastation of the Irish province of Munster which followed the rebellion of 1579, some thirty thousand died during six months of famine, disease and by rope or sword – a retribution as ruthless as any devised by Tamburlaine. Lingering ideals of chivalry were giving way before such pragmatic soldiery, and the very nature of warfare was becoming matter for serious debate. To traditionalists, Tamburlaine's upstart origins would have been no less distressing than his textbook professionalism; but Marlowe the cobbler's son appears to have had more than a grudging respect for both.

The world of the play

It is tempting to echo the view of C. S. Lewis, who memorably dismissed Tamburlaine as 'a hideous moral spoonerism: Giant the Jack-Killer'. And (quibble though one may that this giant begins life as a jack) one has to admit the difficulty of finding a way into a play that appears to comprise a plodding succession of triumphs for Tamburlaine and of gory deaths or protracted humiliations for those who oppose him.

Marlowe eases us into Tamburlaine's world by stressing his humble origins and confronting him initially with unsympathetic opponents – the self-demeaning Mycetes, the opportunist Cosroe, the insufferably boastful Bajazeth. But he sets the interior world of his character's certainties in tension with his audience's expectations – of an outcome that will mesh a Christian code of ethics with classical precepts of tragic form. Then he undermines both expectations. So Tamburlaine as Scourge of God – an instrument of divine displeasure, who must himself be scourged – has a place in the Elizabethan moral universe; yet Part One ends in his triumph and marriage, Part Two in a death which is either the happenstance of old age or, if retribution, that of a Muslim God for the burning of the Koran. And though Tamburlaine's character certainly displays the sin of *hubris*, or excessive pride, instead of leading to his tragic fall this only serves to fuel his self-affirmation. It is as if 'fortune's wheel' (a favourite moral emblem of the Elizabethans) has reached its zenith only to blow a puncture.

Elizabethan imperialism and hero-worship are thus made ironic by a sceptical playwright who is nonetheless drawn towards the certainties of selfhood they represent. So, when Tamburlaine aspires to the 'sweet fruition of an earthly crown', the emphasis falls as much on the *earthly* as the *crown*, in transgressive repudiation of the orthodoxy that a heavenly reward is to be preferred. For Tamburlaine, the first materialist hero, even death anticipates only a 'slaughter of the gods', presumably under his own command.

The colours of Tamburlaine's battle tents, which change like traffic lights of doom to alert his victims to ever more terrible retribution, remind us also of his mastery of psychological warfare. He scorns the etiquette of chivalric behaviour whereby (as in *The Spanish Tragedy*) captured noblemen were to be treated as guests until their ransom was paid, preferring to make Bajazeth his footstool than to put a price on his head. Whether in this contempt for an enemy or in his love for Zenocrate, Tamburlaine is thus a proto-capitalist, measuring himself by accumulation: his concern is to *possess* both. He encages the vanquished or uses them as beasts of burden – but he encages his beloved too, embalmed and embellished in her golden hearse. He murders one son because he is not a clone of himself, and to those remaining he bequeaths . . . a map, microcosmic of his conquests and of the territories yet to be taken in his name. Just so a century ago did imperialists look askance in their atlases at faraway lands not tinted red.

We should probably take at its face value Tamburlaine's highly technical lecture to his sons on the arts of war in *Two*, III, ii. Variously understood as a sublimation of his grief for Zenocrate or a recognition of mortality which prompts him to take more seriously the training of his sons, this is perhaps Tamburlaine the tyrant finding solace in art – the only art he knows, the art of war. Certainly, he opens himself to the cadences of war as he seldom does to those of love – except when its object is absent or dead, and so can be objectified.

Thus, when Tamburlaine overhears Zenocrate confess her feelings for him, he 'takes her away lovingly by the hand' without saying a word; and, in the fifth-act reconciliation between her father and Tamburlaine, Zenocrate acknowledges his proposal of marriage in a single, highly formal line – whereas her exchanges with Zabina (*One*, III, iii) show her capable of fluency when she chooses. These characters have few private feelings, and Tamburlaine himself is on more intimate terms with his favourite general, Theridamas, than with the woman he marries and ostensibly loves. (Some read this male camaraderie as homo-erotic, and even fetishise Tamburlaine's kinky armour, but this seems to me to miss Marlowe's point.)

Although Tamburlaine has, by marriage, joined the ruling class he once despised – like not a few Elizabethans of ignoble birth – we know and learn nothing of his qualities *as* a ruler, as distinct from his skills in conquest. Part Two does begin to address the problems of securing an empire once achieved, but military rather than political or economic means are invariably assumed. In the interior world of this conqueror, the struggle is all: and so, while the location of the scenes is constantly changing, instead of using place as an objective correlative – as does Shakespeare in his history plays, cross-cutting between court and tavern and battlefield – here the scene-shifting predicates only pathological restlessness. One place seems much like another as it is reduced or razed to the sameness of Tamburlaine's imperial sway. 'Applaud his fortunes as you please,' the Prologue enjoins us: and in that line is perhaps a key to this purposefully ambivalent play.

The playwright's craft

FORM The first printed version of the play describes it as divided into 'two tragical discourses', and so it is, if we accept an Elizabethan dictionary's definition of *tragical* as meaning 'bloody, deadly, doleful, dismal'. But in the classical sense of tragedy to which a drama was expected to conform, the play resists such categorising. Zenocrate warns that the gods will never allow Tamburlaine to prosper, Bajazeth predicts his certain downfall, and Cosroe curses him with his dying breath – yet neither prophecies nor curses are fulfilled. Tamburlaine continues in his conquests, and dies, if not in his bed, in the bivouac he has always preferred. His death seems to complete not a tragedy but, simply, a biography. The 'new historicist' critic Stephen Greenblatt has even suggested that, far from being a tragedy, the play is *comic*, according to the Bergsonian definition of the comic as the reduction of the human to the mechanical: for Tamburlaine is a kind of military machine which, like a First World War tank, once set in motion is controlled by its own entropic force. Indeed, the play as staged may well have featured more than the few comic moments which remain, since the printer tells us that he omitted some 'fond and frivolous gestures' as unworthy of their author.

LANGUAGE AND RHETORIC   In *Tamburlaine* the language does not simply describe the action: with some notable (and all the more revealing) exceptions, it *is* the action. Many of the play's direst deeds are not seen, but ordered or reported – often with an ironic lack of synchronicity between the elevated language and the awfulness of what it anticipates or describes. And so the rhetoric serves not only as a vehicle for the action, but as a psychopathology of Tamburlaine's drive for power.

Marlowe signals from the start that at one level his play is *about* language, as Mycetes bemoans that he is 'aggrieved' at his own inarticulacy – for his cause requires 'a great and thundering speech'. He is thus doomed as much by linguistic as military incompetence. In this scene (I, i, 95–7) occurs one of the rare instances of a character being interrupted in mid-flow, when Mycetes' brother Cosroe tells him, in effect, to kiss his arse, undercutting an already bathetic attempt to impress. Zabina's broken prose over Bajazeth's body (V, ii, 245–53) is another, very different departure from the rhetorical norm.

But it is as if Marlowe demonstrates this ability to write in more colloquial vein only to recollect his promise of the 'high astounding terms' to which he reverts for the bulk of the play. What Jonson described as 'Marlowe's mighty line' is readily distinguishable from even the earliest Shakespearean style, as it is also from Kyd's. For where Shakespeare from the first integrates the idiomatic into the flow of his verse, and Kyd's gains flexibility from the sheer variety of its rhetorical modes, the great speeches here work rather as a sequence of exhortations, which build line by mighty line to acquire their cumulative force; and even purportedly conversational dialogue transforms into balanced exchanges of more or less equal length, as if part of a formal debate. If Shakespeare's language has the ease and flexibility of dance, Marlowe's is acrobatic – sometimes, confessedly, on stilts, but also capable of astonishing leaps and jumps and somersaults (which make recovery more difficult if an actor wrong-foots himself).

STRUCTURE The Prologue to Part Two suggests that it was a sequel exploiting the success of Part One, and this seems probable, since the latter exhausts the source material, and in staging achieves a coherent self-sufficiency – driving Marlowe, in the second part, largely to retread the plot motifs of the first. The act of individual cruelty that was Agydas' death in Part One is thus echoed in the murder of Calyphas; the sadistic humiliation imposed on Bajazeth becomes the yoking of kings to draw Tamburlaine's chariot; and the last-act sieges of Damascus and Babylon are alike followed by the slaughter of their defenders – the fate of the virgins of Damascus mirrored also in that of the Turkish concubines.

Both parts observe the neoclassical five-act structure, but seem unconcerned with the tragic imperative it assumes, and Marlowe closes his play as it began, *in medias res*. There is a solipsistic climax in Tamburlaine's death, but whether his sons will drive his conquests further west or face defeat by Callapine is left unresolved. There was no Part Three – and Marlowe did not write *Sons of Tamburlaine* instead of the Part

Two we have, though for that there would have been sources enough. He is no more interested, it seems, in the posthumous consequences of Tamburlaine's career than in his childhood, or in that great swathe of his mature life that is, like Faustus', simply taken as read. As in his later works, the overreaching individual *in extremis* is both focus and fulcrum of the action. And, tellingly, in both parts of the play Tamburlaine himself speaks no less than one-third of the lines.

STAGE PRACTICE   From the opening set-piece in which Tamburlaine's soldiers enter weighed down with plundered treasure, the stage directions are replete with demands for ambitious effects, not the least being the caging of Bajazeth in Part One, and the entrance of Tamburlaine in *Two*, IV, iii, 'drawn in his chariot' as he scourges the harnessed kings.

In performance

The plays were clearly already popular when the first printed edition of 1590 appeared, but we have no record of performances before Henslowe's *Diary* records numerous revivals in 1594–5. The play was thought old-fashioned by the turn of the century, and dropped out of the professional repertoire until 1951, when Tyrone Guthrie directed a compressed version of both parts at the Old Vic. 'A royal, god-defying protagonist of a mad dream,' wrote *The Times* critic of the bravura and widely acclaimed performance by Donald Wolfit. Further productions followed, aptly at the Marlowe, Canterbury, in 1966, and the Citizens', Glasgow, in 1972, before the play was chosen to open the Olivier stage of the National Theatre in 1976, with Peter Hall directing and Albert Finney in the lead – 'all armour and no chink,' in Michael Billington's words. A pub theatre revival in 1991 bravely took on both parts, but Terry Hands compressed the plays into one for an RSC production at the Swan, Stratford, in the following year. Antony Sher's Tamburlaine, in Benedict Nightingale's view, was 'a sort of feral Faustus, at once poet and predator'.

Doctor Faustus
Christopher Marlowe

c. 1588

Source

The anonymous *Historia von Doktor Johan Fausten*, published in Frankfurt in 1587. The English translation, *The History of the Damnable Life and Deserved Death of Doctor John Faustus* (1592), is generally known as the English *Faustbook*.

The story

The learned Doctor Faustus is discovered in his study in the University of Wittenberg. Bored with orthodox scholarship, he conjures the Devil's servant Mephostophilis, who acts as an intermediary with Satan in the signing of a pact whereby Mephostophilis is to serve at Faustus' bidding for twenty-four years, after which he will render up his immortal soul to Hell. Despite the Good Angel who urges his repentance, Faustus attends instead to the Bad Angel's persuasions – although, in the event, his interrogations of Mephostophilis teach him little that he did not know, and his adventures offer more spectacle than fulfilment. Having been entertained by the cavortings of the Seven Deadly Sins, Faustus is transported to Rome to play tricks on the Pope, and then visits the Emperor's court, where he humiliates the sceptical Benvolio. Returning to Wittenberg, he conjures up the silent form of Helen of Troy and is so enraptured by her beauty that, despite the pleas of an Old Man to save his soul, he demands her simulated spirit, or succuba, as his mistress. As the end of his contracted term approaches, Faustus bids farewell to his fellow scholars, and ekes out a final, desperate hour, unable to implore the divine mercy of which he remains lingeringly aware. As the clock strikes midnight, he is carried away by devils to Hell.

The author and the text

For Marlowe's life, see under *Tamburlaine*, p. 9. My assign-
ment of *Faustus* to the earlier possible date of writing is on the
grounds of a dramaturgy that I find to be less well developed
than that of *The Jew of Malta* and *Edward II*. But any decision
is complicated by the fact that we have two very different
texts of this play, both posthumously printed – the 'A-text'
of 1604, often thought closer to the original than the 'B-text'
of 1616, which is longer by over a third. This second text
amplifies the scenes at the papal court, and introduces the
Emperor's rival nominee for the papacy, Bruno, who is freed
by Faustus from the Pope's clutches. At the Emperor's palace,
an elaborate retaliation is planned by Benvolio, only to be
thwarted by the omnipotent Faustus. And a great deal is made
of the cheating of a Horse-Courser and the frustration by
Faustus of his attempts at revenge. Shifts in bibliographical
emphasis over the years have seen one text preferred to the
other, alongside critical debate over whether our aim should
be to reconstruct the text as first conceived by its author or as
most fully embodying the collective choices of a theatre company. Theatrically, however, the decision may rather depend
on whether a director feels that the added high-jinks diminish
or amplify what is perceived as the 'meaning' of the play. What
follows is based on an eclectic conflation of the two texts, with
preference generally given to the fuller version.

The historical context

Some seventy years before *Doctor Faustus* was written, Martin
Luther proclaimed in the city of Wittenberg in Saxony the
theses from which sprang the protestant Reformation. Hamlet
in Shakespeare's play returns to Elsinore from the University
of Wittenberg, where Luther had lectured, to be confronted
with a Ghost from a Purgatory that no longer had a place in
protestant theology. *Faustus* starts and ends in Wittenberg, a
city which was thus emblematic of the social tensions which

arose from the abolition of the old certainties. For now that the 'magic' of Catholicism (whether miracles wrought by saintly relics or the mystery of transubstantiation) was denied to worshippers, 'unofficial' superstitions took its place – while among the better educated scepticism was growing, in a world where religion seemed subject to monarchical whim, and an investigation of nature that could almost be called scientific was casting doubt on biblical verities. So in the late Elizabethan period we see on the one hand an increase in trials for witch-craft and interest in demonology (on which, a few years before his accession, James I had written a pamphlet); on the other a spirit of intellectual enquiry which had to proceed very cauti-ously lest it seem to bring into question the prime causality and hence the omnipotence of God – though it was no less reprehensible, in terms of the function of religion as a sanc-tion, to deny the existence of the Devil. Those who cast doubt on a literal interpretation of the scriptures fell under suspi-cion of atheism – as did Marlowe and others associated with the so-called 'School of Night', though its numbers included devout Christians intent only on scientific advancement. The school's 'leader', Ralegh, could, typically of his times, at once bring a keenly analytical mind to biblical analysis – yet also set out in all seriousness on a voyage to discover El Dorado, the mythic land of inexhaustible gold.

The world of the play

In the study of a respected but now disenchanted academic figure, *Doctor Faustus* opens with what is essentially a critique of a university system still rooted in medieval scholasticism. This condemned intelligent men on the cusp of the scientific revolution to 'live and die in Aristotle's works'. Yet Faustus is not – and Marlowe, for all his freethinking, dared not be – an advocate of the kind of reforms which would have brought academic study into the modern world. He can only conceive of knowledge beyond the bounds of the syllabus as illicit – and seeking it as (quite literally) consorting with the Devil. So he knows the limitations of his studies, yet proceeds to work within them – his world view circumscribed by the strait-jacket of scholasticism and all the hierarchies of the Ptolemaic universe. Despising the worldly rewards of the law, his ambitions yet hinge only on wealth and power. Knowing that medicine cannot confer eternal life, he yet seeks no more than a twenty-four year guarantee from Mephostophilis in return for his immortal soul.

His world is a very lonely one. Beyond the conjurings of Mephostophilis, there lie only his servant Wagner and a few scholars of Wittenberg. Even Tamburlaine had a family – and family relationships, intermeshed with sexual, are at the centre of most Elizabethan drama; yet when Faustus, at the end of the play, returns home to die, his 'home' is his office. The clichéd taunt thrown today by the gregarious at such lonely figures is 'get a life' – by which is meant, have a bit of fun. And that, having realised how perfunctory are the intellectual rewards for which he claimed to be selling his soul, is what Faustus does: he has twenty-four years of fun. Modern purists who would discard the fun are reminiscent of the puritans of Marlowe's day, who approved what has come to be called the 'protestant work ethic' as a sign of grace, but were embarrassed by the worldly profits it tended to generate. Hence the belief in the delayed gratification of desire – a delay which should preferably extend until the reaping of one's heavenly reward.

Faustus cashes in his heavenly reward in exchange for the immediate gratification of desire. But desire for what? Arguably, what Faustus is seeking is not so much knowledge as power – and power as *energy* rather than dominion. It is thus doubly ironic that probably the best remembered line in the play is Faustus' rhetorical question at the sight of Helen of Troy: 'Was this the face that launched a thousand ships?' At one level the irony is that Faustus is eulogising not so much Helen's face as the energy it generates – to launch ships, and to burn 'the topless towers of Ilium' (his own intention being that 'Instead of Troy shall Wittenberg be sacked'). But the more significant, often overlooked irony is that the question is not as rhetorical as it seems: this is *not* Helen's face, but that of a succuba – Satan's holographic reconstruction, its reality as virtual as Lara Croft's (played, of course, by a boy actor in drag). Faustus thus sells his soul for a twenty-four year subscription to Satan's shopping 'n' fantasy channels – anticipating our own recognition that the mask of benevolence worn by modern capitalism is in the self-interest of encouraging the desire to consume: 'The god thou servest is thine own appetite.'

In this sense, *Faustus* is a very modern play – so modern, indeed, that we have only recently felt confident in answering the complaint that it is not really a play at all but a dramatic poem, because, in the conventional sense, it lacks dramatic conflict – it is a play in which nothing much *happens*. And it is true that all the comic conflicts are predetermined by Faustus' omnipotence, while the only 'serious', spiritual conflict is within Faustus himself. Interventions from the old morality figures – the Good and Bad Angels and later the Old Man – are there only to be repudiated, and Mephostophilis knows he has his man as soon as the contract is signed. As he tells Faustus at their first meeting, Hell is an existential state of mind: 'Why this is hell, nor am I out of it.'

Yet the assumption that a play requires conflict is actually of quite recent origin – and refuted by such a modern work as *Waiting for Godot* no less than by *Doctor Faustus*. Both portray the human condition as at once tragic in its stasis and comic in its absurdity. Godot never comes; Faustus' ambitions remain unfulfilled. In *Godot* the waiting begins all over again; and in *Faustus* time simply but inexorably runs out. However we may quibble over generic labels, neither play can be denied its place or its power on the living stage.

This many-faceted play is also very much of its own time, in that Faustus' ultimate failure is to pass the protestant test of justification by faith – for his faith is insufficient to believe in the possibility of his own salvation. Yet no less is it rooted in medieval tradition, in that the yoking of pride with despair was seen as constituting the one unforgivable sin – the sin against the Holy Ghost. And this is a play which fits neatly within the 'comic strip' frames so often employed by medieval art – as displayed in stained-glass windows, or along Chaucer's tale-strewn road to Canterbury, or in mystery plays trundling one after another through city streets. It is along such an axis that Marlowe's procession of ancient and modern morality figures is plotted, ringmastered by an existential devil who knows that Hell is all about us. Straddling the worlds these figures predicate – comic and tragic, heroic and hedonistic, Christian and satanic – is Faustus himself, at once profoundly alone and yet, in the mythic status he has since assumed, the very archetype of the latter-day Everyman.

The playwright's craft

FORM Morality plays, in which personified representatives of good and evil contend for the soul of an average man, culminated in the redemption of their Everyman figure, whereas this 'anti-morality' ends with the damnation of an exceptional character – whom we might rather expect to find in a tragedy, such as the original title-page claims *Faustus* to be. Yet selling one's soul to the Devil is more serious than the flaw of character said to distinguish the heroes of classical tragedy, and eternal damnation scarcely induces a sense of closure, let alone catharsis. There is a sense in which Marlowe seems to be testing here the potential and the limitations of both these older forms – incidentally provoking an audience to thought by raising expectations he refuses to meet.

LANGUAGE By contrast with *Tamburlaine*, Marlowe is now better able to extract poetry from less than hyperbolic language, whether in the quiet, precisely analytical terms of the opening soliloquy or in the pacing out of Faustus' last hour at the close. For all their awful ring of mortality, here the words are simple, concrete and urgent, rising to the hopeless despair of the unmetrical but unforgettable, 'See, see where Christ's blood streams in the firmament' – before descending into despair and the intended bathos of the final, futile, 'I'll burn my books! Ah, Mephostophilis!' In a play whose dominant imagery is of gluttony and consumption, Eliot spoke of Marlowe's 'gain in intensity' and 'new and important conversational tone' – which one would qualify only with the reflection that the most important 'conversations' in this play are those that Faustus has with himself; and that the subtext of the 'intensity' is the ever more pressing sense of his own damnation.

STRUCTURE In a play which largely conceals its own complexity of structure, one is struck by an often unnoticed congruity between the tragic and comic scenes. While Faustus is chopping logic over whether Mephostophilis was or was not compelled to answer his summons, his servant Wagner discovers in the following scene how much easier the Devil is to raise than to dismiss. After Faustus and Mephostophilis steal from the Pope, so do Robin and Dick from the Vintner. Then, towards the end, the levels merge as Faustus himself gets involved in the 'low' action with the Horse-Courser: the scholar who has demeaned himself by playing the clown at last becomes one.

CONVENTIONS Critics who have exercised themselves with the theological niceties of the pact which Faustus signs with Satan, and whether it is theologically enforceable, overlook the fact that Elizabethan audiences would have taken such a contract at its face value, as a theatrical 'given', unless (as in Shylock's case) the play itself hinged on its terms.

STAGE PRACTICE With its requirements for a Hell's Mouth, all the paraphernalia of magic and attendant displays of devilry, its parade of sins and its pageantry of Helen's conjuration, *Faustus* made extensive but by no means unacceptable calls on the capacity of Elizabethan stagecraft. Interestingly, it has been argued that the shorter text is the more 'serious' not because it comes closer to Marlowe's original conception, but because it was reconstructed from a touring version in which the comic incidents would have called for resources less adaptable to a 'fit-up' stage.

In performance

The first references to performances of *Doctor Faustus* do not occur until 1594, by which time the play was in the repertoire of the Admiral's Men at the Rose, with Edward Alleyn in the title role. The Admiral's may have purchased the prompt-book from Pembroke's Men, thought to have performed the play at court at Christmas 1592. *Faustus* was in the Admiral's repertoire at least until 1597, and a revival in 1602 restored the piece to popularity almost until the closure of the theatres in 1642. The play survived in its original form for only a few years after the Restoration, before being drawn into the services of early English pantomime and by the nineteenth century even burlesque versions drew mainly on Goethe's *Faust*. In 1896 William Poel gave Marlowe's original the 'authentic' staging to which his Elizabethan Stage Society aspired. The Phoenix Society next presented the piece in 1925, with a company which included Ion Swinley as Faustus and John Gielgud as the Good Angel; but the play only began to see regular, full-scale revivals after the Second World War, the first of which was Walter Hudd's production at the Memorial Theatre in Stratford in 1946, with Robert Harris in the lead. An Old Vic production with Cedric Hardwicke as Faustus and Harry Andrews as Lucifer followed in 1948, and in 1961 the Old Vic again presented the play, in Michael Benthall's production with Paul Daneman as Faustus. Burton famously eulogised Taylor's Helen in Nevill Coghill's OUDS production of 1966. Revivals by the RSC included Clifford Williams' in 1968, with Eric Porter in the title role; Gareth Morgan's with David Waller in 1970, and John Barton's with Ian McKellen in 1974. The 1980s saw a surge of interest, with productions by Actors Touring Company in 1987; Contact Theatre at the Young Vic in 1988; the Medieval Players at the Riverside Studios in 1989; and in the same year a further RSC revival at the Swan in Stratford, directed by Barry Kyle with Gerard Murphy. Jude Law took on the title role in David Lan's production at the Young Vic in 2002.

Friar Bacon and Friar Bungay
Robert Greene

c. 1589

Source

Greene drew mainly on folk legend, probably adapting a tale
from one of the popular stories, or chapbooks, hawked by ped-
lars; but the first such version surviving dates only from 1627,
so the extent (and even direction) of the influence is uncertain.

The story

Out hunting in Suffolk, Edward, son and heir of Henry III,
lusts after a chaste country girl, Margaret, who virtuously
spurns his advances. Leaving his friend Lacy, Earl of Lincoln,
to woo the maid on his behalf, the Prince travels to Oxford to
seek the help of Friar Bacon, a famous magician who has been
working for seven years on a 'brazen head' to protect England
against her enemies. Meanwhile, the King is planning the
betrothal of his son to the beautiful Eleanor, daughter of the
King of Castile. The royal visitors, along with the Emperor of
Germany, plan to journey with the King to meet the Prince at
Oxford, where the skills of Vandermast, a necromancer in the
Emperor's train, are to be pitted against those of Friar Bacon.
At Edward's urging, Bacon agrees to conjure a vision of
Margaret in his 'perspective glass'; but this reveals that the
girl has fallen in love with Lacy, and is about to be married
to him by the aged Friar Bungay. Bacon prevents this just in
time by striking the old man dumb and transporting him to
Oxford astride a devil. The Prince hastens back to Suffolk
meaning to kill his rival, but Margaret reconciles the pair and
Edward gives his blessing to the match. The King's party has
now reached Oxford, whence Edward returns with Lacy to
meet his intended bride. Though Vandermast betters Bungay

in magical displays, Friar Bacon proves himself the German's superior, by raising a devil to carry Vandermast back home. But Bacon's servant fails to wake him at the crucial moment when the 'brazen head' first speaks, and the head is destroyed before the Friar can harness its powers; then, when he is asked by two scholars from Suffolk to conjure a vision of their fathers, the former friends are seen fighting a duel in which both are killed. The despairing Bacon vows to abandon magic and devote himself to God, while Margaret, believing herself deserted by Lacy for a courtly bride, plans to enter a nunnery. But the King is so taken with Lacy's description of her that he orders Margaret to be summoned to court. Lacy restores himself to the girl's favours, and their wedding is celebrated along with that of Edward and Eleanor. Bacon prophesies happiness for the couple and for England.

The author and his work

Robert Greene, born in 1558, was the son of a Norfolk tradesman, and educated at Cambridge University. Because of his humble origins, he was all the keener to be counted among the 'university wits' – who felt superior to grammar school boys such as Shakespeare. Between his graduation in 1583 and early death in 1592, poverty forced him to become one of the first men to seek a living (rather than a reputation) from writing. His prolific output varied from fictional romances to 'autobiographies' (couched as the cautionary tales of a profligate), and from elegant 'euphuistic' imitations to popular 'cony-catching' pamphlets, designed to titillate with secrets of the tricksters against whom they warned. His dramatic output – relatively modest in comparison – included *Alphonsus, King of Aragon* (*c.* 1589), which adds love interest to the theme of endless conquest it shares with Marlowe's closely contemporary *Tamburlaine*; *Orlando Furioso* (1591), a dramatised adaptation of Ariosto's romantic epic of the days of Charlemagne; *A Looking-Glass for London* (with Thomas Lodge, *c.* 1591), which parallels the sins of the biblical citizens of Nineveh with those of present-day usurers; and the misleadingly titled *James IV* (*c.* 1592), whose pastoral-romantic heroines cast the mould for Rosalind and Celia in *As You Like It*. There also exists a sequel to *Friar Bacon* called *John of Bordeaux; or, The Second Part of Friar Bacon* (*c.* 1590), which may or may not be by Greene. This shows Bacon renewing his magic skills in order to vanquish the Turks and to win a return match with Vandermast.

The historical context

The late-Elizabethan nerve-endings of Greene's play show in Friar Bacon's preoccupation with building a wall of brass to protect England from her enemies. Greene's audience would have relished such an idea, for while the Spanish Armada had been defeated in 1588, anxious expectations remained of others to come. To add to invasion fears, England was getting bogged down in its military support for the Dutch against Philip of Spain's imperial sway, while seeking to extend its own imperial sway over Ireland. The mood was thus of solidarity rather than celebration – which makes more understandable the lack of popular unrest in the 1590s, despite continuing inflation, incoming 'asylum seekers' from Catholic persecution, and high unemployment, blamed on vagabonds and 'masterless men' (among them crippled soldiers returned from the wars). Bacon's closing prophecy, like Cranmer's in Shakespeare's *Henry VIII*, is both a reminder for the audience of glories past and a prayer for good fortune ahead.

The world of the play

The world of *Friar Bacon* is, like that of *Twelfth Night*, both timeless and recognisably of late-Elizabethan England. Its folkloric characters – fools and clowns, a fair rustic maiden, a clumsy sorcerer's apprentice and 'jolly friars' – are of all times and of none. The son and heir of Henry III, later Edward I, did indeed marry Eleanor of Castile. (They were apparently a devoted couple, and Edward was stricken with grief by her death, as the last of the 'Eleanor crosses', marking her funeral route, testifies on the forecourt at Charing Cross Station.) Roger Bacon and Thomas Bungay were indeed Franciscan friars and renowned Oxford scholars, who came under suspicion of heresy in the late thirteenth century. And at that time a brass nose was indeed to be seen above the gates of Brasenose College, Oxford, of which Bacon is here made Master.

The brass nose still existed in Greene's day, exiled to Stamford. Was not its survival evidence that it was once attached to a 'brazen head' which had been shattered by a supernatural hammer? In mundane truth the name Brasenose derived from the college's origins as a brewhouse, or *brazen-huis*, and what enhanced an Elizabethan audience's conviction of truth was thus based on false etymology. So also was Bacon's belief in Britain as the New Troy, a fanciful vision of the past still affirmed by many antiquarians and shared by most laymen of the time. In such ways were fact and fable often casually intertwined for the Elizabethans. Just so did 'modern' science in the popular imagination merge imperceptibly into magic – chemistry into alchemy, astronomy into astrology – and women wise in herbal lore become feared and burned as witches. An audience's attitude to Bacon's necromancy, as to that of Faustus in Marlowe's play, was probably a mixture of protestant scepticism and deeply ingrained superstition.

Greene's world is more bustling and quotidian than Marlowe's, and though it rubs shoulders more familiarly with Shakespeare's the two men's views of life differ as often as they converge. Prince Hal's youth as drawn by Shakespeare in *Henry IV, Part One* was in many ways more dissolute than Edward's – yet Shakespeare drops no hints of *sexual* misbehaviour on Hal's part, whereas Greene makes quite clear that Edward's intentions towards Margaret are dishonourable. Lacy is well aware that she is desired only as 'concubine unto the Prince of Wales', and Margaret herself puts it well: 'Be what he will, his lure is but for lust.' Even Edward's highflown eulogising in the opening scene is undercut not only by the fool Rafe's sly counterpoints but by the Prince's recognition that it is 'marriage or no market' with this fair maid.

In *The Winter's Tale*, on the other hand, Shakespeare was to show us a princely heir more constant than Edward in his love for a country girl – though conveniently she turns out to be not a shepherd's daughter but a real princess. If Greene's is an inconstant prince, his Margaret remains true to her origins as daughter of a gamekeeper. In making her choice between a noble match and a nun's 'marriage' to God, she prefigures Isabella in *Measure for Measure*; but while Isabella famously remains silent when the Duke more or less requires her to marry him, here Margaret accepts the call of the flesh with open arms. As for Friar Bacon, besides being a theatrical contemporary of Marlowe's Faustus, he anticipates Prospero in Shakespeare's *The Tempest* both in his willingness to meddle in matters of love and in the redemption he seeks from abandoning magic: but Bacon's intentions and his spiritual fate remain altogether more ambiguous. In the ways that such different emphases mark him out from Shakespeare, Greene shapes a world that is perhaps franker in its worldly wisdom, if closer to the surface of the human heart.

To all this the fool Rafe is incidental – but he is central (as a clown always was) to the play's performing company, and enjoys an insistent presence around the edges of the action. As so often, he tends to act as an intermediary between the audience and the play, whether representing the 'common man', drawing the stand-up comic's nudging attention to his own jokes, or finding other ways to remind us that what we are watching is make-believe. Thus, during an extraneous but entertaining episode when he disguises himself as the Prince, Rafe warns the Oxford scholars that he will 'make a ship that shall hold all your colleges, and so carry away the Niniversity with a fair wind to the Bankside in Southwark'. And that, of course, is precisely what happens, for proud though Greene was of being a 'university wit', he is happy enough to mock the 'Niniversity' for the pleasure of audiences at the Rose on Bankside.

The playwright's craft

FORM   We tend to associate the turn of the 1590s with the emergence of high-sounding tragedy as practised by Marlowe and Kyd. Greene here rejects such 'bombast' in favour of his own pacy idiom in a comedy that, like many of Shakespeare's, is 'romantic' in its sentiments but which touches us also with its 'realistic' sense of human frailty. But it is difficult to pin down the play generically with a neat neoclassical label. Though 'comic' in its plot devices and climactic nuptials, it is 'tragic' in the weight and implications of its necromantic theme; for that matter, it is a 'history' play too, in that it draws upon actual figures from a few centuries past. As with the late plays which are hard to categorise in Shakespeare's canon, perhaps 'tragi-comedy' or 'romance' best describes how the play's mood reflects its matter.

STRUCTURE   Like most plays of the time, *Friar Bacon* has no act-divisions, and its sixteen scenes, changing along with location and characters, make their natural lengths. Greene's intricate plotting has been both enthusiastically praised (by no less a critic than William Empson) and dismissed as two stories which keep bumping into each other. There has been no recent opportunity to test the play's mechanics on stage, but a receptive reading of the text tends to support Empson's view that events develop and intermesh seamlessly, and with a semblance of clarity. The two plots on occasion elide with an irony we can take as we choose. For instance, no sooner has Bacon quit the stage intent on 'pure devotion' to the service of God than Margaret appears in nun's apparel ready to do the same: but 'the flesh is frail', and Margaret is quickly converted to the charms of courtly life.

LANGUAGE   'Decorum' usually required noble characters to speak in verse, lesser mortals in prose. The newly favoured idiom of blank verse here prevails, with largely end-stopped lines that scuttle along in brisk pedestrian fashion, often easier on the modern ear than Shakespeare's precisely because of their lack of subtlety. (Few passages soar like Shakespeare's either, but since they do not aspire to such heights neither do they descend into bathos.) Miles' mock-Skeltonics apart, among the rustics Margaret alone speaks in verse, littered with classical allusions, as if in anticipation of her future station. Or perhaps it reflects her 'innate' nobility. Or perhaps, as one critic has suggested, it's because she has read too many of Greene's courtly romances.

CONVENTIONS There are moments in *Friar Bacon* which we may find uneasy, but which would have presented few difficulties for audiences familiar with the conventions they reflected. In the scene in which Margaret dissuades Edward from duelling with Lacy and he resigns the girl to his friend, disappointed expectations of 'psychological realism' are exacerbated by the perfunctory rhetoric with which the Prince swings swiftly from revenge to blessing, then to acceptance that he must marry as dynastic needs dictate. But the Prince feels Lacy's betrayal of close male friendship more strongly than Margaret's rejection, just as in Shakespeare's nearly contemporary *Two Gentlemen of Verona* Valentine offers up his beloved Silvia to Proteus in token of that bond. Then, when Margaret has to endure her lover's rejection and later accept that this was only a test 'to try sweet Peggy's constancy', she is taking on the mantle of 'Patient Griselda', whose legendary resignation had already been depicted by both Chaucer and Boccaccio. Greene's audience would have enjoyed recognising such conventions as an emotional shorthand which did not need what we would call 'motivation'.

STAGE PRACTICE Perhaps the 'fearful dragon' summoned by Bungay reappropriated Mephostophilis' first guise in *Faustus* – and might the Tree of Hesperides have been thrust through the trap to sprout from its throat? This is only one of many interesting questions of stage practice raised by a play with unusually detailed directions as to what is required, but silent on how it is to be done. Of course many Elizabethan plays, from *The Spanish Tragedy* to *Twelfth Night* and beyond, require 'overlooking' scenes, and one must assume that Bacon's 'perspective glass' merely 'conjured' real actors to enter on the opposite side of the stage; but the 'brazen head' was clearly real, was clearly required to 'make a great noise' and then to speak, and clearly had to be broken up with a hammer before the audience's eyes.

If one considers such 'magical' devices in modern terms, what is Bacon's 'perspective glass' but a closed-circuit security monitor ahead of its time? Is his scheme to 'girt fair England with a wall of brass' so very different from an American president's hope of quarantining a continent against missile attack? And what is the brazen head but a proto-computer, its shattering the equivalent of a software virus melting down its motherboard? We cannot yet whisk a pub landlady from a tavern kitchen to an Oxford college; but we accept the future scientific possibility of 'teleporting' every time we watch *Star Trek*. Thus do the most 'improbable' aspects of Greene's play interface with the actualities of our present as of his.

In performance

The play is now generally dated 1589, though it could be a year or so either side – at the latest 1592, when Henslowe records seven performances by Strange's Men at the Rose on Bankside. At that time Strange's included the famous clown Will Kemp – creator of Shakespeare's early clowns, and perhaps also the first Falstaff – and it is tempting to cast him in the role of the King's fool Rafe in *Friar Bacon*. The play reached print posthumously in 1594, and in 1602 Henslowe notes a payment of five shillings to Thomas Middleton for adding a prologue and epilogue for a Christmas performance at Court, making it likely that this was one of the last plays seen by the Queen as she sought distraction from the imminence of death. The play failed to engage much interest in the twentieth century, but there are records of two amateur performances in Cambridge by the Marlowe Society, directed by John Barton and Michael Bakewell, in 1954 and 1960.

Arden of Faversham
Anonymous

c. 1590

Source

The *Chronicles* (1577) of Holinshed – who interrupts a largely
political account of the reign of Edward VI to record in detail
the actual murder in Faversham, Kent, in 1551 of a former
mayor of the town, Thomas Arden, by his wife and her lover.

The story

Arden's friend Franklin congratulates him on his grant of title
to the lands of the former Abbey of Faversham; but Arden is
distracted by his wife Alice's affection for the upstart steward
Mosby. Franklin advises caution, and Alice persuades him of
her innocence. Soon, however, she is using a local landlord as
go-between to her lover, and bribing Arden's servant Michael
to kill his master in return for the hand of Mosby's sister
Susan, who is her serving maid. A rival for Susan's hand, the
painter Clarke, is offered the same reward to poison Arden,
but Arden rejects a tainted bowl of broth. Alice next enlists
an aggrieved tenant, Greene, with the promise that his lands
will be restored, and Greene hires two ruffians, Black Will and
Shakebag, to murder Arden during a visit to London with
Franklin – Michael becoming reluctant accomplice to the pair
in the botched attempts on Arden's life which follow. When
Arden returns home, the would-be assassins are again thwarted,
this time by fog. Arden contemptuously spurns another dispossessed tenant, Dick Reede, before Alice and Mosby taunt
him into a duel in which Arden overcomes his rival, but is yet
again persuaded of his wife's innocence. Finally, Black Will and
Shakebag entrap and murder Arden in his own home, while he
and Mosby play at backgammon before a supper planned to

celebrate their reconciliation. Arden's corpse is dragged behind the Abbey, but the suspicions of the other guests lead to its discovery and to the punishment of those complicit in the crime.

The authorship

Many Elizabethan plays (*The Spanish Tragedy* and *Tamburlaine* among them) were, like *Arden of Faversham*, printed anonymously. Contemporary allusions or later scholarship give us authors for many of these, but *Arden of Faversham* remains unattributed, though claims have been made on behalf (jointly or severally) of Marlowe, Kyd and Shakespeare. But the play was not even among those other 'apocryphal' works included in the 'Third Folio' of Shakespeare's plays in 1663, and when he was first proclaimed author in 1770 it was by a citizen of Faversham. The scholarly debate reveals less about whether Shakespeare had a hand in the play than about our own bardolatry – the implicit belief that such an ascription would instantly make the play somehow 'better' than it was before.

The historical context

Arden of Faversham opens as Franklin presents Arden with the deeds to the lands of the dissolved Abbey of Faversham – granted him by the Duke of Somerset, as Lord Protector to the young Edward VI. Our author is thus concerned from the outset to locate the action with chronological as well as geographical precision. The surname 'Franklin' denotes a holder of land, the state which Arden now enjoys; and Mosby, too, is upwardly mobile – a despised 'botcher' who has risen to the stewardship of a noble estate. Such social mobility was characteristic of the period; but since the actuality of emergent capitalism was in tension with a theoretically stable, still semi-feudal hierarchy, it was viewed with suspicion by those who did not enjoy its benefits. The play thus touches on public issues as well as private woes – and while the upheavals caused by the dissolution of the monasteries, from which Arden profits, were now past, the enclosure of common land was continuing to deprive the poor of time-honoured rights. Many thus became vagabonds and 'masterless men' – their ranks swollen by discharged soldiers such as Black Will. When Franklin speaks the epilogue, he points the irony of Arden lying in the plot of ground he had 'by force and violence gained' from Dick Reede – whose sole dramatic purpose has been to reveal Arden as a ruthless landlord and to pronounce a curse upon him. Arguably it is this curse which at last enables the murderers to seal Arden's fate.

The world of the play

Generic boundaries in Elizabethan drama were looser than we are often led to expect, not least by the editors of the 'First Folio' of Shakespeare's plays, with its careful division into his *Comedies, Histories and Tragedies*. So critics seeking to classify *Arden of Faversham* have variously dubbed it the first domestic or 'bourgeois' tragedy, a 'realistic satire', a 'tragic melodrama', an attempt at 'documentary realism', an antecedent of what we would today call 'black comedy', and even an 'early detective mystery'. But this very profusion suggests we should allow the play its own identity – just as, in the Epilogue, Franklin insists it should speak for itself, since the 'simple truth' does not need the 'glozing stuff' of sententious commentary or homiletic postscript.

Many recent plays, notably of the so-called 'in-yer-face' school of the 1990s, but going back at least to Joe Orton's *Loot* (1966), if not actually glorifying criminality, have made petty criminals their central characters. Less pettily, so does Shakespeare in *Macbeth*, which our play prefigures in a number of respects – not least Alice's inability to wash away her victim's blood, and the use of hired assassins as surrogates for her guilt. In such company, Shakebag and Black Will do not appear over-ruffianly. Despite Will's fancying himself Warden of a Worshipful Company of Murderers (since his old comrade Bradshaw is now a goldsmith), in the real business of murder the pair appear out of their depth. Black Will's own tally of twelve years of wrongdoing in Scene xiv amounts to no more than the bullying of prostitutes and the taunting of tapsters and constables. Now, a threat from an apprentice to summon his mates is enough to outface him, and a sympathetic lord sends Will packing with a crown and a caution. (Imagine Kenneth Williams as Will and Charles Hawtrey as Shakebag in *Carry on Murdering*.)

This pair trail behind a veritable posse in vain pursuit of Arden – Michael the lovelorn servant; his rival Clarke, the painter of poisoned portraits; and Greene, who 'had rather die than lose my land' (i, 518). After Arden has six times escaped death, an Elizabethan audience may well have been inclined, like followers of the hunt, to join in baying for his blood. The sudden change of tenor when the murder does occur thus becomes all the more shocking – and by then Alice and Mosby are no longer lovers seeking a desperate freedom, but seem entrapped in a nightmare of predestination, almost welcoming the exposure and condemnation that follows.

Tynan saw Alice Arden as prefiguring not so much Lady Macbeth as Strindberg's Miss Julie – her innate strength sapped by being yoked to a social inferior to whom she is attracted as much as anything out of boredom. And certainly class, like cash (or its equivalent in land), lies at the heart (or lack of heart) of this play. Mosby, of course, is anxious to clamber further up the social ladder. Arden mocks his ambitions, and is careful to warn him against wearing a sword, forbidden by the dress code of the day – even protecting one's honour thus being a matter of class. (No wonder the later duel at first attracts Mosby, then humiliates him.) Yet Arden himself has enhanced his status by marrying Alice, and her dowry has presumably added to his riches. Significantly, children of this marriage are mentioned only once in the play – as the reason Arden 'hoards up bags of gold'.

Arden is proto-capitalist to his bootstraps – or the galoshes that his servant Michael loses while daydreaming about Susan, whereupon he is berated for daring to abuse his master's time.

Arden *owns* his servant. He also owns his wife, as did all Elizabethan husbands, just as he owns the Abbey lands – the former
to be defended against Mosby, the latter against Greene's
pleas and Reede's curses. He glories in the social standing his
wealth bestows, yet rejects its obligations – by contrast with
Lord Cheyne, whose only real purpose in the play is to embody the 'true' nobility which condescends as easily to Black
Will as to Arden. Even murder is here subject to market forces,
with Alice repeatedly reduced to haggling over the price to be
put on her husband's death.

One thing that unites the main characters is that all believe what they want to believe, and readily argue themselves
out of any self-doubt. Black Will and Shakebag believe they
are murderous desperados, despite the near-farcical failure of
their villainies. Arden is recurrently persuaded that his wife is
faithful, despite the evidence of his own and others' eyes. Alice
and Mosby are convinced that they can murder him with
impunity and live happily ever after, despite Alice's brief mid-
play repentance and frequent tiffs with her lover – and despite
the doubts expressed by Mosby in his soliloquy at the start of
Scene viii, when brief regret at having risen above his station
gives way to the recognition that accomplices in evil must be
disposed of in their turn, and that Alice, having betrayed her
first husband, may well betray a second. The emotional mood-
swings are products not of uncertain dramaturgy (nor even of
stage convention, which nodded at such instant transitions) but
of the characters' solipsistic reshaping of their inner worlds.

The playwright's craft

FORM   Since, in the Epilogue, Franklin describes *Arden* as a
'naked tragedy', it is worth adding to what has already been
said of its generic labelling that it both fulfils and disappoints
more rigid expectations of tragic form. Arden's death is based
on historical fact, and is also in fulfilment of a curse – but he
and his murderers lack the expected noble birth (as, for that
matter, do Hieronimo and Tamburlaine).

STRUCTURE The play begins *in medias res*, with Alice and Mosby already in love and already intent on Arden's murder. After a masterly exposition – some twenty lines telling us all we need to know – with careful but unobtrusive craftsmanship the author intermingles scenes of social exchange, of verbal or physical conflict, of intimacy real and fractured, and of intro-spection or soliloquy. Formal scene-divisions, useful for nota-tion, are superfluous to an action whose fluency transcends its discontinuities of time and place. A few continuity gaffes aside (such as Michael's apparent previous acquaintance with Black Will and Shakebag when only a few hours earlier Greene had had to identify them), the play is beginning to flex and exert all the muscles of the Elizabethan drama.

LANGUAGE As befits *Arden*'s structural variety, its language (despite the rigid end-stopping of the blank verse) achieves a far greater tonal range than *Tamburlaine*, without employing the rhetorical formality, dressed with classical allusions, of *The Spanish Tragedy*. The distinctive imagery is of dismemberment and disintegration, of animal instincts driven by the struggle for survival – motifs made most explicit in Arden's remarkable account of his dream in Scene vi (reminiscent of Clarence's dream in *Richard III*, I, iv). The thieves and lackeys employ blank verse no less than those who come closer to nobility – though some original prose may have been refashioned into verse by the 'memorial reconstruction' from which the printed text of 1592 is thought to derive. But such passages as Michael's soliloquy in Scene iv (58–86) unquestionably show a servant in full command of the idiom – while Shakebag's bombastic outbursts mock the 'high-astounding terms' of *Tamburlaine* well before the parodies of Shakespeare's Ancient Pistol.

STAGE PRACTICE The stage directions demand a practical shutter, for breaking Will's head in Scene iii; and the eventual murder at the gaming table would have needed careful orches-tration – not only of its commission, but also when the drag-ging away of the body prompts Shakebag into a soliloquy that distracts attention from its return, to be 'discovered' in a different place. Other apparently complex demands – the ditch in the fog, the business with the ferryman – were well within the enlarging scope of an Elizabethan audience's imagination. The stage doors and who enters through which are the main concern of other directions – and were all that would have been needed for the attempted murder at the Nag's Head.

In performance

No records of contemporary performances exist, but the new printed editions called for in 1599 and 1633 suggest a continuing if unspectacular stage life. The play's location ensured that in Faversham it remained 'ever popular', and during the eighteenth century there were also adaptations for the London stage by Eliza Haywood (1736) and George Lillo (1759), whose version was generally preferred until 1852 – though some Kentish revivals remained loyal to the original. William Poel's abridgement for the Elizabethan Stage Society in 1897 was apparently a near-disaster, but he did fuller justice to the play for the Renaissance Theatre in 1925, when Ernest Milton was 'amazed at the elasticity' of the staging – the 'constant lapping over of times and places' providing 'continual movement and excitement'. When Joan Littlewood directed the play with her recently formed Theatre Workshop company in 1954, Kenneth Tynan described Harry Corbett's Mosby as played 'with a dark, cringing bravura that recalls the Olivier of *Richard III*'; while in the view of *The Times* Susan Engel's 'sense of urgency' as Alice redeemed a production by Bill Gaskill in 1961 at the Cambridge Arts which 'made it difficult to take the murder seriously'. A first RSC revival in 1970 was marred by dissension, but when Terry Hands directed the play for the company in 1982 he found a style described by Michael Billington as 'Elizabethan Expressionism': it was as if the characters were 'living though a signally bad dream', with even the thwarted murders capturing 'the precise quality of nightmare, in which every alley turns out to be a blind one'.

The Jew of Malta
Christopher Marlowe

c. 1590

Source

The Christian island of Malta had famously repulsed a siege
by the Turks in 1565; but the characters and detail employed
in Marlowe's play appear to have been entirely his invention.

The story

Having allowed their tribute to the Turks to fall into arrears,
the Christian rulers of Malta levy an extortionate tax upon
the Jews of the island to raise the sum. The rich Jew Barabas
is reluctant to submit to the demand for half his wealth, and
is consequently deprived of all his possessions – including his
house, which is converted into a nunnery. Barabas persuades
his daughter Abigail to pretend conversion to Christianity, and
by this means she is able to restore to Barabas the treasure he
had concealed about the house. Meanwhile, Del Bosco, vice-
admiral to the King of Spain, has arrived in harbour with a
shipload of Turkish captives. He promises Spanish assistance
to the governor Ferneze against the Turks if he is allowed to
sell his slaves in the market. The boastfully villainous Ithamore
is purchased by Barabas to help him revenge himself upon
the Christians. In pursuit of this, the Jew provokes rivalry
between Don Mathias and the governor's son, Don Lodo-
wick, for his daughter's hand; but when the suitors slay each
other in a duel the despairing Abigail becomes a true convert
to Christianity – and her father wreaks his vengeance against
her and the entire nunnery by poisoning the food he sends as
'alms'. Two friars, Jacomo and Bernardine, violating the secrecy
of Abigail's dying confession, threaten to proclaim Barabas'
guilt, whereupon the Jew, by professing himself willing to

give his wealth to whichever priest converts him, provokes an avaricious dispute between them. After strangling Bernardine, Barabas manages to make Jacomo appear guilty of murder. The slave Ithamore is now persuaded to blackmail Barabas by the courtesan Bellamira, with whom he is besotted, and her pimp Pilia-Borza. The Jew responds to the threat by disguising himself as a French lute-player, and poisoning all three with a bouquet of flowers – but not before they have accused him to the governor. Arrested, he manages to feign death, is thrown from the city walls – and betrays the island to the Turks, for which service he is made governor. However, the exultant Barabas now promises to betray the Turks in turn if the Christians can muster a sufficient bribe. His plan to blow up the common Turkish soldiery succeeds, but the Christians reveal to the Turkish generals his scheme for their deaths in a boiling cauldron, into which Barabas himself is duly plunged. Ferneze praises heaven for the deliverance of the island.

The author and the text

For Marlowe's life, see under *Tamburlaine*, p. 9. No records of early performances exist, and the play did not appear in print until 1633, so the date here assigned is conjectural, being based on my subjective judgement that it employs a fuller range of theatrical resources than *Doctor Faustus*, but is less dramatically complex than *Edward II*. Some scholars argue that the published text was as revised by Thomas Heywood.

The historical context

After two centuries of persecution and exploitation, all remaining Jews were expelled from England in 1290, and by the reign of Elizabeth the few Jews to be found in London were (at least nominally) converts to Christianity, mostly of Portuguese origin. One of their number, Roderigo Lopez, physician to the Queen, was executed in 1594 for complicity in a plot to assassinate her; and while there were simply not enough Jews in the country for racial intolerance to spring from fear of a ghettoised minority, such as the Jews of Venice (from whom Shakespeare plucked his Shylock a few years later), the happenstance of the Lopez affair was enough to reignite a fear rooted deep in the Christian mindset. For Jews were not only held collectively guilty for the death of Christ, but were, like Barabas, supposed to garner great wealth from the practice of usury, long forbidden to Christians. Yet usury – the loaning of money at interest – was a prerequisite and enabler of emergent capitalism. John Calvin was the first of the protestant reformers to lift a ban so inimical to the 'work ethic', and the secular (but not religious) authorities recognised the practice in England in 1571. *The Jew of Malta* enjoyed a flurry of revivals after the Lopez affair; yet if Marlowe on one level was exploiting the typology of the rapacious, conspiring Jew, in also displaying the Christian society on which he depends as greedy and hypocritical he hints at an historical complexity submerged or sentimentalised in *The Merchant of Venice*. In part that complexity derives from Barabas as a representative of any alien 'other' – including all those foreign exiles, ironically mostly protestants driven from their homelands for their faith, whose presence in late-Elizabethan London was widely resented. One contemporary lampoon actually singles out the 'Machiavellian merchant' for special obloquy.

The world of the play

The Jew of Malta opens with a Prologue spoken by Machevil, misrepresenting the historical Machiavelli as an embodiment of unprincipled cunning. This sets the equivocal tone of a play which shows Christians and Turks as more truly Machiavellian than Barabas – whose successes, however ingenious, are temporary, expedient, and reactive to events. In Barabas' opening eulogy to 'infinite riches in a little room', the evocation of the riches is remarked more frequently than the littleness of the room, with which Barabas is quite content: and in the following soliloquy he desires only the 'peaceful rule' needful for business – disavowing force, since 'nothing violent . . . can be permanent' (I, i, 101–38). In all this, he resembles rather the merchant than the Jew of Shakespeare's Venice.

Critics have complained that so rational if materialistic a man of business should metamorphose into the mad conspirator of the later play. Yet if King Lear, dispossessed of his kingdom, his daughters, his retinue, and even shelter from the storm, descends into madness, why should not Barabas, in a comparable plight, do likewise? Inarticulately, Lear threatens, 'I will do such things – / What they are yet I know not, but they shall be / The terrors of the earth.' One feels that his enfeebled mind is reaching for such revenges as Barabas here attempts – a younger but no wiser defender of his dignity. The difference between the plays lies, of course, in Marlowe's calculated equivocation, which extends to the formal expectations he arouses – or fails to arouse. *King Lear* is a tragedy. What is *The Jew of Malta*?

T. S. Eliot wrote of the 'terribly serious, even savage comic humour' of the play, describing it as 'a farce of the old English humour'; and in seeking the spirit in which an Elizabethan audience would have received this play, it is certainly helpful to remember not only the cheerful brutalities of Tudor farce but the bull- and bear-baiting arenas close by the theatres on Bankside. We may also think forward, to such a modern 'savage farce' as Joe Orton's *Loot* – staged in 1966, two years after an RSC revival of *The Jew of Malta* had shocked many by being played for laughs. Yet Marlowe cannot but have meant Barabas to evoke laughter, whether in his outrageous retributions or in his climactic plunge into that Heath Robinson cauldron.

Marlowe invites an ironic rather than a comic response to the Jew's declared depravities, catalogued for the benefit of the avid Ithamore (II, iii, 176–203). Here, perhaps, Marlowe's equivocation is more cynical, rehearsing the folkloric libels of Jewish ritual murders and poisoned wells while also letting Barabas draw a self-portrait which is entirely at odds with his earlier self. The speech thus becomes a criticism of the likes of Ithamore (and of those among the audience) who find such rantings credible. This is a Marlowe whose 'mighty line' is now adapting to the need not only for more idiomatic interchange between characters, but for a modulation of their 'tones of voice' – from the objectively reasonable to the inwardly reflective, from the uncontrollably angry to the subtly ironic.

But the play's pervasive irony is that, whereas in *Tamburlaine* and *Doctor Faustus* God is defied but his existence is never in doubt, in *The Jew of Malta* none of the three religions represented appears to acknowledge a God. The absence of invocations has been attributed to a revision of the text in the light of the Act against profanity of 1606; yet the emptiness of the religiosity is dramatically consistent – not so much with the Machevil of the Prologue (who proclaims religion a 'childish toy') as with the historical Machiavelli, who viewed religion as an instrument of statecraft. To sustain our keynote of equivocation, that this is how Christians, Jews and Turks are alike presented might equally reflect a playwright's atheistic scepticism or his devout despair.

Ferneze saves Malta for Christianity, but does so through unscrupulous duplicity – in Machiavellian terms, the 'policy' so often called on in this play, which has no character of true moral probity. Abigail alone appears to struggle with a conscience, and her death is the most conventionally tragic; yet she dies with an entirely misapplied faith in the confessors from her new-found Christianity – and even her wish to 'die a Christian' is instantly undercut by Friar Bernadine's 'Ay, and a virgin too, that grieves me most' (III, vi, 40–1). Such snappy, cruel comebacks or asides help to give the play its characteristic quality of being on constantly shifting ground, with every apparently secure foothold sinking one further into the moral quicksand.

The playwright's craft

FORM   In addition to what has already been said concerning the play as tragedy, farce, or hybrid, it is pertinent to note, in the light of the title-page's assertion of tragic dignity, that after

Kyd's civil servant, Marlowe's earlier shepherd and university lecturer, and the wicked landlord of *Arden of Faversham*, we now have a character of even ignobler status, a money-lender, as would-be tragic hero.

STRUCTURE   Critics were once inclined to doubt Marlowe's authorship of the third, fourth, and even much of the fifth act of *The Jew of Malta* on the grounds that they lacked the impressive set-speeches of the opening two. One might respond that the change marks an appropriate movement from establishing characters and relationships to the pell-mell action that has thus been anticipated; or assert that the episodic discontinuity of these scenes reflects the play's questioning of ideological orthodoxies. Yet both of these 'answers', while sensible enough, implicitly accept that the charge *needs* an answer. In practice, the plots and stratagems and the counter-plots that foil them simply mark the play's characteristic *modus operandi*. If this structural ebb and flow *works* in the theatre, as it does, it needs no defence, but reflects Marlowe's increasing assurance that a play may best be permitted to find its own shape. 'Plotting' is of course here an aspect of character as well as of dramatic construction, making the succession of twists and reversals of the last act both a confident feat of theatrical showmanship and a comic *exemplum* of 'the biter bit'.

LANGUAGE   What distinguishes the use of blank verse in *The Jew of Malta* and *Edward II* is that the characters are no longer so much engaged in *making speeches* at each other as in actually conversing – or quarrelling or lamenting or cursing – in shorter, more reciprocal and essentially colloquial exchanges. These make the more reflective passages – such as Barabas' opening soliloquy (which itself gains colloquial fluency from beginning in the middle) – stand out more purposefully, as likewise do those passages where he is speaking in any tongue but his own. The oft-criticised shifts of tone are thus consistent not only with the Jew's own changing preoccupations, but with the faces he needs to assume (perhaps for this reason, although Barabas speaks almost half of the play's lines, his dominance is less noticeable than that of Tamburlaine or Faustus). Marlowe takes delight in the sheer range of effects that dramatic language can achieve – whether offering narrative background, as in Del Bosco's evocative account of the battle with the Turks (II, ii); providing a black comic interlude such as Barabas' mock-confession (IV, i); or indulging in self-parody, as in Ithamore's wooing of Bellamira, which burlesques Ovidian and pastoral modes to conclude with his own invocation in *The Passionate Shepherd*, 'Come live with me and be my love' (IV, ii, 91–101). And just as such 'low' characters break into verse, so may the 'high' descend to prose – as in Barabas' curtly casual excuse for an old adultery: 'That was in another country: and besides, the wench is dead.'

CONVENTIONS Some see Barabas as a Vice – the minor devil of the morality drama whose antics made him laughable, and so insidiously attractive. But Marlowe individualises Barabas by giving him frequent 'asides', through which the character, having constructed himself as he wishes to be perceived, readjusts our vision to his own. This use of the 'aside', which by the nineteenth century had dwindled into melodramatic bathos, was for the Elizabethans a flexible means of dramatising the multiple levels of a character's consciousness, or, as here, of distinguishing between self-presentation and self-knowledge.

In performance

Lord Strange's Men probably first performed *The Jew of Malta* around 1590. A performance at the Rose on 26 February 1592 garnered Henslowe fifty shillings, and some 36 further performances are recorded in the following four years, peaking in the summer and autumn of 1594 after the Lopez incident. When the original Barabas, Edward Alleyn, died in 1626, the play passed into the ownership of the Red Bull theatre; reputed to attract vulgar audiences; but by 1632 (according to the title-page of the first printed edition of the following year)

Queen Henrietta's company were presenting it in the fashionable Cockpit and at court, with the role of Barabas now played by the protean actor Richard Perkins. Although the play was apparently still in print after the Restoration, there are no records of revivals in the later seventeenth or eighteenth centuries. Samson Penley adapted the play for Kean's revival at Drury Lane in 1818, which he took to the Park Theatre, New York, in 1821, but it was not until 1923 that the play again reached the London stage, when the Phoenix Society gave two performances at Daly's Theatre with Baliol Holloway in the lead, Isabel Jeans playing Abigail, and Ernest Thesiger as Ithamore. Apart from a handful of university and amateur productions, interest in the play then lapsed until the quatercentenary of Marlowe's birth in 1964, when the Victoria Theatre at Stoke-on-Trent presented Bernard Gallagher as Barabas, and there were also productions at the Marlowe Theatre, Canterbury, and Unity Theatre on Merseyside. In the same year, Clifford Williams' production for the Royal Shakespeare Company began its run at the Aldwych Theatre, with a cast that included Clive Revill as Barabas, Michele Dotrice as Abigail, Ian Richardson as Ithamore and Glenda Jackson as Bellamira. Eric Porter took over as Barabas when the production transferred to Stratford in 1965. Little-noticed revivals by the Marlowe Society in 1975 and at the Donmar Warehouse in 1984 were followed in 1987 by a further RSC production at the new Swan Theatre in Stratford, directed by Barry Kyle. Here Machevil proved to be a disguised Ferneze in what Jim Hiley described as a 'hypocritical world, addicted to corruption and betrayal, which Barabas exemplifies rather than stands beyond'. Steve Grant was among several critics worried by the production's 'knockabout anachronism', but Hiley found Alun Armstrong's Barabas 'a tour de force of affected histrionics and ad-libbing slapstick villainy', and in Michael Billington's view the production showed how Barabas 'is driven into the role of a venomous chameleon simply in order to survive'.

Edward the Second
Christopher Marlowe

c. 1592

Sources

Holinshed's *Chronicles*, probably in its second edition of 1587. Incidents in the play suggest Marlowe's diligent reading of other historical sources, including Fabyan's *Chronicles* of 1557 and Stow's *Chronicles of England* of 1580.

The story

The newly crowned Edward II rejoices at the return of his favourite, Gaveston, from the banishment imposed by his dead father. He lavishes honours and offices upon his minion, and when the barons force the low-born Gaveston back into exile Edward's Queen, Isabella, so pities her bereft husband that she intercedes on his behalf. The barons' disquiet flares into open rebellion when Edward refuses to ransom Mortimer Senior from capture by the Scots in the King's service, and Gaveston is seized and executed. Edward pursues vengeance against the rebels, and with the help of the elder Spencer, father of his new favourite, defeats them in battle. He orders the execution of the ringleaders, the banishment of his own brother Kent, and the imprisonment of the younger Mortimer in the Tower. Edward dispatches Isabella and their young son as emissaries to France – where Mortimer, who escapes from the Tower with the aid of Kent, also flees. Joining forces with the now disenchanted Queen, Mortimer lands at Harwich to renew the rebellion. The King's army is defeated and, despite seeking refuge in disguise, the King, Young Spencer and his companion Baldock are betrayed to the Earl of Leicester and imprisoned at Kenilworth Castle. Here the King is forced to abdicate in favour of his son, and Mortimer declares himself

Protector to the infant heir. Fearing that the Commons are sympathetic to the deposed monarch, Mortimer instructs the murderer Lightborn to dispose of him. Lightborn discovers Edward starving in a pool of foul water in the dungeons of Berkeley Castle, and pretends sympathy for his plight before revealing and fulfilling his intentions. He is then himself murdered by the King's jailers, Gurney and Matrevis. Despite his tender years, the young Edward III declares Mortimer a traitor, and wins the nobles' support in having him beheaded, while his mother, suspected of complicity, is sent to the Tower.

The author and the text

For Marlowe's life, see under *Tamburlaine*, p. 9. The play, now generally agreed to have been Marlowe's last, was first published in 1594, along with others owned by Pembroke's Men (probably reflecting their need to raise ready money), and bears indications of originating from the playhouse copy.

The historical context

Despite the new historiography of Renaissance Italy, which began to give a humanist slant to its subject, there remained in Elizabethan treatments of history the sense so pervasive in medieval culture of a simultaneity (and certainly a correspondence) between past and present – a simultaneity which sets Shakespeare's *Henry V* at once on medieval battlefields and in a very Elizabethan London. Yet the defeat in 1485 of Richard III by the man who made himself Henry VII changed not only the course of history but the writing of history – for Tudor power had to be asserted by more than force of arms if the cycle of civil war was to be broken. Edward Hall's *Union of the Two Noble and Illustrious Families of Lancaster and York* (1548) thus interpreted the Wars of the Roses as at once a warning against insurrection and a validation of the new dynasty. The line he pursued is summed up as the 'Tudor myth' – a myth which was duly sustained in the later, partly derivative *Chronicles* of Raphael Holinshed, as in Marlowe's other sources, noted above. Also influential were such collections of cautionary tales from history as the *Mirror for Magistrates* (1559), which invited rulers to learn from the mistakes of the past how they should respond to analogous events in the present. The drama often drew upon such sources, but by the time of its flowering, relatively late in Elizabeth's reign, the introspective concern with lessons to be drawn from the past was often complemented by an outward-looking pride in England as a thrusting nation-state. In the history plays of Shakespeare – of which the *Henry VI* trilogy probably preceded Marlowe's play by a year or so – these twin impulses are at times seamlessly merged, at times interestingly in tension. But in his English histories (as very distinct from his Roman plays) sexuality is invariably a sideshow, whether in bluff King Harry's bluffing his way through proposing marriage to Kate in *Henry V* or in Gloucester's serpentine seduction of Anne in *Richard III*. Marlowe, however, well recognised that for better or worse the sexual drive is among the impulses which determine the rise and fall of kings. Elizabeth, after Henry VIII's obsessive treatment of her own mother, Anne Boleyn, and her cousin Mary Stuart's heedless mingling of passion and politics, had reason to make an almost mystical moral virtue of her own (by now pragmatic) virginity. As for homosexuality, this was a term unknown to the Elizabethans, for whom sodomy was a capital offence, but intimate male bonding (as in Shakespeare's *Two Gentleman of Verona*) a respected, ostensibly platonic virtue.

The world of the play

For Tamburlaine, the world is a map to be coloured-in with his conquests; for Faustus, it is a laboratory for metaphysical experiment; for Barabas, its essence is that little room in which he can hoard his wealth. While some would similarly schematise *Edward II* as the quest of a king to reduce government to self-gratification, Edward – unlike even Barabas, to whom all the peripheral characters are in some way reactive –

is alone in being subject to the independent ambitions and desires of others. Mortimer – himself the central character of other contemporary plays – is politically no less pivotal than Edward; Gaveston has an agenda of his own, as do his successors, the Spencers and Baldock; Isabella and even Kent feel the tugs of conflicting loyalties and interests; Lightborn's appearance is a cameo of brief authority wielded with relish; and at the end a child king seizes the initiative, asserting the authority as well as the symbolism of his crown.

This is the more remarkable given the centrality of the King to Shakespeare's *Richard II*, with which Marlowe's play is often compared (as influential but inferior). And while the world of the play is socially less heterogeneous than that of, say, *Henry IV, Part One*, it is also (the barons' xenophobia aside) less homogeneously 'English'; for the few commoners – three poor men, a mower, and a murderer – are either incidental or emblematic to this sequence of power struggles among the powerful. Their ever-shifting allegiances may make it difficult for actors to find a psychological 'throughline'; but politicians will not be so unfamiliar with such constant jugglings between personal loyalties and political choices. In the sexual politics of *Edward II*, the lust for power outweighs the power of lust: even after Gaveston's death, the King is less concerned to mourn his personal loss than, with the instant preferment of Young Spencer, to fill the power vacuum it has created.

Of the figures struggling to control others, Gaveston gets the opening scene, and makes his intentions clear – good, in that he clearly loves Edward in his way; bad, in that he intends to 'draw the pliant king which way I please'; and indifferent, as in the courtesy he shows to the three poor men – not from compassion, but because 'it is no pain to speak men fair' (as, later, he deals more diplomatically with his wife than Edward ever does). Yet, except in the King's eyes, Gaveston clearly lacks the charisma of a Machiavel, and is a willing accomplice in the taunting of the barons. The modern debate as to whether his psychological dominance over Edward reflects his active role in their sexual partnership is of little concern either to

Marlowe or the nobility – as Mortimer Senior pragmatically acknowledges, 'The mightiest kings have had their minions' (Sc. iv, 392). Their anger is not with Gaveston's penetration of the physical body of the King but with his penetration of the body politic. This has drained 'the treasure of the realm' – and the last straw, significantly, is also financial: the rejection by Edward of Mortimer's demand that his uncle be ransomed from the Scots.

If Gaveston is profligate of his lover's treasury, this is in part because he lacks resources of his own – hence his jibe at the parasitic nature of the peers' own wealth: 'Base leaden earls, that glory in your birth, / Go sit at home and eat your tenants' beef' (Sc. vi, 74–5). Conversely, the barons despise Gaveston's low birth as much as his effeminacy (for an Elizabethan audience, too, an aspect of his foreign ways). It is a measure of our own preoccupations, not of Marlowe's, that Gaveston is presumed glad to be gay while his equally latter-day striving for upward mobility goes largely unremarked.

As for Edward, his fatal weakness is not his sexuality but his inability to simulate the simplest of evasive politenesses towards either his wife or his peers; and far from being unaware of this incapacity, he appears to relish and even cultivate it. This is all of a piece with a character one is tempted to diagnose (however unhistorically) as sado-masochistic. Gaveston knows his lover well enough to choose the tearing apart of Actaeon by his own pack of hounds as the sort of spectacle he fancies; in the humiliation of the Bishop of Coventry (politically inept in its alienation of the spiritual as well as the temporal peers) he has to be restrained by his lover from casting the cleric into the gutter; in the lavishing of honours upon his favourite, the King realises that this only puts him in greater danger ('If for these dignities thou be envied, / I'll give thee more,' Sc. i, 162–3); and even in the passage between Lightborn and Edward there is a sado-erotic charge – a promise and a threat poised between a feather-bed and a red-hot spit.

Edward believes that the role of kingship gives him the right to treat the nation as his plaything. He is asserting not the divine right of kings as preached in Marlowe's time, but the proprietorial primacy of a feudal overlord. In this, as in the play's outbreaks of violence – not structured and chivalric, but instinctive, brutish scuffles – Marlowe is probably closer than Shakespeare to the rawness of medieval life. The crucial problem dramatised in the play is, in Moelwyn Merchant's phrase, 'the disparity between status and person' – and this is a problem which touches the whole hierarchical system, not just the king who is at its apex.

As so often, Marlowe's authorial stance is equivocal. Said to be himself homosexual, he gives us an overtly gay monarch whose popular image as a weak link between a lawgiving warrior father and a brave if often baffled son is (for an Elizabethan audience, if not for us) more effectively dramatised than problematised. And he permits, arguably encourages, yesterday's righteous (and today's self-righteous) to see the King's fate as a hideously apt punishment for his sins. Yet, as the parentheses in this paragraph suggest, what a liberal, modern audience sees is a liberal, modern play, which is acceptive of the full spectrum of sexuality without gloss or special pleading.

The playwright's craft

FORM   *Edward II* falls outside the time-limits of the 'Tudor myth', and cannot readily be interpreted as a cautionary tale (though a decade later the bisexual James I might have learned a few survival tactics). It is nonetheless of that peculiarly late-Elizabethan genre (though some claim Aeschylus' *Persians* as a precedent) – a 'history play', and not a tragedy. The generic nicety matters only because it is symptomatic of the interest prevalent in the 1590s in the mechanisms of whole societies, drawn from recorded behaviour, as much as in the uniqueness of particular 'tragic falls'. (Though some find Edward – the noblest by birth of Marlowe's central characters – aspiring to tragic dignity as he nears death, he still clings blindly to the rights of his lost kingship, even trying to bribe Lightborn with the jewel that is its remaining vestige.)

STRUCTURE   The play was not originally divided into acts and scenes, and apologies if my references to scene numbers (as restored in recent editions) do not conform to the text you are using. But they do better reflect what may be paradoxically described as the episodic ebb and flow of Edward's power – in whose current Gaveston first bobs up, then disappears, then re-emerges, only to be swept away as the Spencers dive in, while Mortimer catches the tide. The weakest swimmer of all is swept away at the end because he loses the lifebelt of his crown. So Gaveston's removal does not, as some have claimed, leave the play broken-backed, because its fluidity defies such fractures. When Brecht cast his adaptation of the play (1924) into his own kind of 'epic' mould, carefully defining the passage of nineteen years, he more closely reflected historical actuality – since Gaveston was Edward's companion and bedfellow for nine years, not the few months that here seem snatched; while ten years intervened between his death and Edward's defeat of the barons. Our theatrical perception is that by the end of Marlowe's play perhaps a year or so has elapsed – a 'double time' that only matters in that it conveys Marlowe's wish to give the action its impulse and its urgency.

LANGUAGE   Marlowe employs a leaner, cleaner idiom in much of the dialogue, while allowing Edward and Gaveston their voluptuous passages, and the King his climactic lamentations. His greater assurance in reflecting character through language is perhaps most marked in Isabella, whose pitiable expressions of her pain in the early parts of the play become harsher as her own sensibilities harden, finally breaking down into the drained despair of the ending.

CONVENTIONS   Mortimer refers to the medieval emblem of 'fortune's wheel', as bearing him up only to cast him down; but his is not a life in which fortune appears to play much part, unless we suppose the gods to be driving him mad for power while they drive Edward mad with desire – or, in our terms, make Mortimer a case-study for Jung, Edward for Freud.

STAGE PRACTICE   The dungeon from which the imprisoned Edward ascends was probably situated beneath a stage trap; but a 'discovery' behind an upstage traverse curtain, or even a normal entrance through one of the stage doors, would not have disturbed the audience. While the crown is here the most basic of the few specified 'props', we should remember that, despite its perfunctory scenery, the Elizabethan theatre made lavish use of costume, and the sumptuary laws made audiences well aware of the distinctions symbolised by dress: so Gaveston's finery was offensive not only for its flamboyance but for outraging social decorum. As to the 'hot spit' that Lightborn requires, no further instructions for its use appear in the text: only in Holinshed do we find the details of anal insertion which many directors now feel it necessary to follow.

In performance

Though the play was first performed by Pembroke's Men, probably in 1592, we know little more of its stage history than the title-page claim that it was 'sundry times publicly acted', but its continuance in print suggests it also remained in the live repertoire, at least into the 1620s when it was being played at the supposedly rowdy Red Bull. It was not rediscovered until the early twentieth century, when William Poel directed Granville Barker as Edward for his Elizabethan Stage Society, perhaps inspiring Frank Benson to bring a version to Stratford-upon-Avon two years later. Alan Wade directed another 'little' theatre production for the Phoenix Society in 1923, before Joan Littlewood's in 1956, for her Theatre Workshop company at Stratford East, became the first of a string of major revivals later in the century, including Clive Perry's production at the New Arts in 1964; Toby Robertson's touring Prospect Theatre production, which opened at the Edinburgh Festival in 1969 with Ian McKellen in the title role; Nicholas Hytner's production at the Royal Exchange, Manchester, in 1986, with Ian McDiarmid; and Gerard Murphy's at the Swan, Stratford, in 1990, with Simon Russell Beale.

Every Man in His Humour
Ben Jonson

1598

Source

None known.

The story

Accompanied by his foolish country cousin Stephen, Edward
Kno'well sets out for the City from his home in Hoxton, to
meet his witty young friend Wellbred at the Windmill tavern.
His anxious father, Old Kno'well, has intercepted the invitation, and wants to keep an eye on whatever develops. No less
suspicious of Wellbred's ways are his brother-in-law Kitely,
with whom he lives, and his half-brother, Squire Downright.
They particularly deplore Wellbred's acquaintance with the
plagiaristic poet Matthew and the incurably boastful swords-
man Bobadill, who lodges with the water-carrier Cob and his
wife Tib. Brainworm, Kno'well's wily servant, meanwhile puts
on the disguise of an old soldier, and, having fooled both his
old and young master, decides to turn events to his advantage.
Kitely fears for the virtue of his young wife and his sister
Bridget in a house frequented by such gulls and gallants. His
watchful servant Cash duly dispatches Cob in search of Kitely
when the party from the Windmill arrives. Cob tracks down
Kitely at the house of the quirky but fair-minded Justice
Clement, and takes his chance to obtain a warrant against
Bobadill, with whom he has disputed the virtues of tobacco.
Matthew has meanwhile been making poetical overtures to
Bridget, which Young Kno'well and Wellbred mockingly
encourage to Downright's disgust – and the distraction of the
returned Kitely, who assumes that Edward has made him a
cuckold. But Edward has set his sights on Bridget, and while

he and Wellbred depart to arrange a secret marriage, Brain-worm diverts attention by making Cob's house the focus of Kitely's suspicions. The resulting mix-up leads the party to Justice Clement's, where Bobadill and Matthew are seeking revenge on Downright after the beating he has inflicted on them both. In spite of the compounded deceptions which Brainworm now confesses, Clement commends him on his wit, and chirpily dispenses his own brand of justice. The newly married Edward and Bridget are reconciled with their various relations, as are Kitely and Cob with their wives, and all adjourn for a celebratory supper.

The author and his work

Ben Jonson was born in 1572, a month or so after the death of his father. His mother remarried in Ben's early childhood, and although 'brought up poorly' the boy received a good education at Westminster School under William Camden, his lifelong friend. But instead of going on to university (a lack he always regretted) he was reluctantly apprenticed to his stepfather's bricklaying trade. He escaped by volunteering to fight for the Dutch against the Spanish in the Netherlands. He had returned to London by 1597, when he appeared as an actor and playwright under the manager Philip Henslowe – though he later worked entirely as a freelance. He suppressed much of his early output, and although *Every Man in His Humour* survived to reach print in 1601, around 1610 Jonson rewrote the play – transplanting the action from Florence to London – for the version used in his collected *Works* (1616), on which our own discussion is based. Though several times imprisoned – once for killing a fellow-actor in a duel, twice for overstepping the bounds of permissible satire in his plays – he nonetheless established himself at court following the accession of James I in 1603; and during his long subsequent career he alternated between creating elegant masques and entertainments for the King's circle and roistering comedies of city life for the public playhouses. In 1616 he was granted an annual pension, becoming in effect the first Poet Laureate. He found himself less favoured at court after the accession of Charles I, and in 1628 a paralytic stroke confined him to his chambers; but although his later work for the theatre was not much enjoyed, he kept on writing – and entertaining his 'tribe' of disciples – to the end. After some years of increasing destitution, he died in 1637 and was buried in Westminster Abbey. (Fuller biographical background to Jonson's later plays in this volume will be found under their individual titles.)

The historical context

Elizabethan London was a proud and self-confident city – or rather two cities, linked by Fleet Street and the Strand. The City of Westminster was the seat of government and the law, close by the Court in Whitehall, around which clustered courtiers and their hangers-on in the already fashionable 'West End'. The City of London was populated rather by merchants, tradesmen and craftsmen, who both lived and worked 'within the walls'. The jealously guarded independence of its citizens was respected by a monarch who needed their moral and financial support – but was viewed with at best condescension, at worst scorn by many whose status as 'gentlemen' was defined by their not needing to work at all. While Londoners had not yet become the ridiculed 'cits' of Restoration drama, Elizabethan dramatists still preferred to locate their comedy within the 'court' or 'country' – in Shakespeare's case, often shunting the characters symbolically between the two, or if a mercantile context was needed (as for *The Merchant of Venice*) choosing an Italianate or otherwise 'romantic' location. Yet it was Shakespeare who, in the *Henry IV* plays of 1596–7, drew upon the taverns of Eastcheap for his low life, and Jonson who in the same year set the first version of *Every Man in His Humour* in Florence. It is ironic that the impression we receive in the revised version of the bustling life of Elizabethan London was the afterthought of a maturing author, who, with the exception of *Volpone*, was never again to stray far from his native city for comic inspiration. When it came to tragic rather than comic intrigues, it was as much a sensible precaution as a convention to portray these in faraway courts or faraway times. Yet it was the historically distant *Richard II*, supposed to legitimise the deposing of a monarch, which the Earl of Essex ordered to be played at the Globe in February 1601, on the eve of his rebellion. It was the City of London that Essex sought to raise against the Queen – and it was the City of London's rebuttal which sealed his fate. Jonson's reworking of our play thus acknowledges not only the wellspring of his own comic genius, but the City's increasing importance as a repository of political as well as economic power.

The world of the play

The pacing of the play by the hands of the clock brings not *order* but a sort of well-made anarchy to the proceedings. The difference is between my plot summary, which I fear may make the action appear tortuous to a reader, and a stage world tying itself in knots in 'real time' while its audience goes with the flow. For the plot and its mechanisms are but the vehicle for the timescape of this day, in which – in the words of the Prologue – characters 'such as comedy would choose' reveal their foibles through 'deeds and language such as men do use'.

The climax to the day and the play is supper, and Jonson punishes the worst offenders as if they were naughty children, by denying them this treat. And most of these characters are, indeed, more childish than villainous – like Don Quixote in musical modern dress, just dreamers of impossible dreams. Cervantes (publishing his novel at the same time as Jonson was revising his play) no more approved the original Quixote than Jonson validates his own self-deluded fantasists. But these are not Machiavels – simply, they are living their secret lives with rather less secrecy than Walter Mitty.

As Freud recognised, in naming his Oedipus complex after the tragic hero of Sophocles' play, artists have often delineated neuroses long before they have been medically acknowledged.

Medieval medicine, in attributing varieties of human temperament to the four bodily fluids known as 'humours', did recognise, though it misattributed, an imbalance which causes what we now call obsessive-compulsive behaviour. Jonson dramatises this kind of behaviour, which is driven by overriding preoccupations or anxieties, in his 'humours' comedies. It may be a mere affectation, as Matthew affects to be a poet, or it may take over and control one's whole existence, as the pretence to swordsmanship has taken over Bobadill. It may be no more than keeping up with the latest craze, as in Stephen's yearning to master falconry; or it may threaten the stability of a marriage – as in what one recent editor diagnosed as Kitely's 'sexual neurosis of repressed voyeurism'.

Less solemnly, Kitely's concern with the temptations to which a younger wife is prey is as traditional in comedy as Old Kno'well's fretting over the shortcomings of youth, and should not be over-psychologised. Brainworm's ancestry also stretches back to Roman comedy, in a line of 'clever servants' which continues to Molière, to Shaw's Enery Straker in *Man and Superman*, and to Barrie's eponymous *Admirable Crichton*. However, such latter-day Jeevesian lackeys disdain the delight in intrigue for its own sake which makes Brainworm so insidiously attractive – but which also makes him a control freak, a comic counterpart to Iago, who has wormed his way even into Justice Clement's brain by the end of the play.

Though the results of Brainworm's schemings are largely tangential to the action – where those of Mosca in *Volpone* are of its essence – his trick of assuming a lowlier status than his own works better than the pompous pretensions of Bobadill or Matthew. Yet if he escapes punishment at the end of the play, so surely should Bobadill; for Brainworm is self-aware in his cunning, and so is potentially the more harmful of the two, while Bobadill is most concerned with convincing himself. He does not really deceive even Cob, though the latter complaisantly allows people to be what they want to appear – where his opposite, Downright, makes it his 'humour' to distrust all appearances.

No less important than the individual 'humours' of these characters is their social range – from Old Kno'well, who as a gentleman of leisure ranks highest in the scale, and Kitely, a well-to-do merchant with a business to run, down to Cob and Tib, who eke out meagre livings by taking lodgers; and from hangers-on like Matthew and parasites like Bobadill, through superior servants such as Brainworm with time for mischief on their hands, to harassed clerks like Cash. These characters live in places like Hoxton and Clerkenwell, and their talk is of the familiar sights of Elizabethan London and its northern suburbs – of the archery practised in Finsbury Fields, of the prostitutes of Picket Hatch, of the wounded soldiers who gather in Moorfields, of the Dad's Army of ageing territorials who exercise in the Artillery Garden.

Matthew and Bobadill even exchange views on *The Spanish Tragedy* (I, iv), with Bobadill enthusing over its old-fashioned hyperbole. And the dispute between Bobadill and Cob over the 'precious weed' was as topical in Jonson's time as in ours. Elsewhere, touches of Jonson's off-the-wall humour abound, as when Stephen, given the use of Matthew's study, anxiously asks, 'Have you a stool there, to be melancholy upon?' or Cob, grateful for the warrant he has been granted by Justice Clement, wants to 'honour the very flea of his dog'.

It has to be admitted that Jonson is not very good at his women characters, though the proletarian Tib gets a more distinctive voice than either Dame Kitely or Bridget. Nor is he much better at suave gallants like Wellbred, who, while they may appear to win the battle for intellectual and amorous dominance, make little theatrical impression – Wellbred does not even appear (in III, i) until a third of the play is over. Some suppose Wellbred and Young Kno'well to represent the 'norm' from which the 'humours' characters deviate: if so, it appears to consist in condescension towards others and in manipulating them for one's own self-interest. We may feel more sympathetic (as did Jonson in his later plays) towards those who, though they may be a little mad, at least live relatively harmlessly inside their own heads.

The playwright's craft

THE REVISION   A comparison between the two versions of
the play allows us insights into the dramatist's changing perception of his subject, his audience and his craft, as Jonson
transforms a nebulous and artificial Florence into an intimately detailed London. He preserves his neoclassical five acts,
but it is now the irregular ebb and flow of action that dictates
their pattern. The play's first version also made much more of
the dispute between the Know'ells over the value and function of poetry; its curtailment is for the better, but the pair are
not given compensatory work to do, and so never achieve the
significance that their presence in the opening scenes and the
elder's long soliloquy at II, iii, 1–66, seem to anticipate.

STRUCTURE   With a side-swipe in the Prologue against the
discursive structure of Shakespeare's history plays, Jonson takes
care to set his own play within a single city during the waking
hours of a single day. Given that we are well into the action
by the time that Cob remarks on its being six o'clock (I, iii),
it's clear that Old Kno'well has risen with the sun on this
'fresh morning'. By the time Kitely reaches his warehouse, it
is 'Exchange time', or ten o'clock (III, ii) – and so the day ticks
on, towards its suppertime climax. Unity of place and time
are not, however, matched by unity of action, for Jonson's
mastery lies precisely in teasing out a plot-line from a loosely
linked sequence of comic turns and double-acts.

LANGUAGE   Unusually for Jonson, the play mixes the colloquial prose which predominates with the blank verse spoken
by Old Kno'well and Kitely – ironically in both cases, since the
former ostensibly despises poetry, while the latter appears all
the more pompous for elevating his jealousies into iambics.

CONVENTIONS   Brainworm's disguises, like so many of the
period, would have lost their point had the audience not been
able to recognise the same actor underneath. The costume

transformed the man, though the face remained the same – the strict sumptuary laws of class-coded dress making the convention less arbitrary than it may now appear.

In performance

Anecdotally, Shakespeare recommended this work by a little known playwright to the Chamberlain's Men for its first performance in 1598, and is said to have taken the part of Old Kno'well, with the clown Will Kemp a likely Bobadill. Continuing popularity is suggested by records of a court performance in 1605 and another as late as 1631. The Restoration preferred Jonson's later work, but James Quin appeared as Old Kno'well in 1725, and Garrick's version of 1751, with himself as Kitely and the great clown Harry Woodward as Bobadill, brought the play back into the regular repertory. It was absent from the stage of Drury Lane for only two seasons out of the next twenty-five, and was still being regularly performed there or at Covent Garden until 1802. Edmund Kean played Kitely in 1816, as did Macready in 1832 and 1838, but the most renowned revival of the century was an amateur production of 1845 – with the novelist Charles Dickens hugely acclaimed in the role of Bobadill. Since then the play has been less in favour, though there were productions at the Shakespeare Memorial Theatre in Stratford in 1903, and again in 1937 (to celebrate the tercentenary of Jonson's death), directed by Ben Iden Payne, with Donald Wolfit as Bobadill. Later revivals came in 1960, when Joan Littlewood directed the play for her Theatre Workshop at the 'other' Stratford, in the East End, with Victor Spinetti as Brainworm and Brian Murphy playing Bobadill. The play was revived by the RSC for the opening season of its new Swan Theatre in Stratford in 1986, in a production by John Caird which was brought to the Mermaid in London the following year. Pete Postlethwaite was Bobadill and Young Kno'well was played by Simon Russell Beale – his resemblance to 'the accepted likeness of Jonson' serving, in Martin Hoyle's words, as a 'framing device' for the action.

The Shoemakers' Holiday
Thomas Dekker

1599

Source

Three distinct prose tales in Deloney's *The Gentle Craft* (two
parts, *c.* 1597, 1598), blended by Dekker into an original whole.

The story

The Earl of Lincoln disapproves of his nephew Lacy's love
for Rose, daughter of the Lord Mayor of London – who is no
better pleased at the prospect of a spendthrift courtier as son-
in-law. Lincoln persuades the King to put Lacy in command
of the London troops mustered for the French wars – among
them the newly-married Ralph, a shoemaker who works for
Simon Eyre of Tower Hill. Despite the pleas of Ralph's master,
his fellow-craftsmen Hodge and Firk, and his wife Jane, Lacy
declares it beyond his powers to release Ralph – though Lacy
has himself bribed his cousin Askew to take over his command so that he need not leave London. In pursuit of Rose,
Lacy disguises himself as the Dutch shoemaker Hans, joins
the journeymen employed by Simon Eyre – and helps his
master make a shrewd investment in the cargo of a recently
docked Dutch vessel. In consequence Eyre rises to become a
well-to-do merchant, and is chosen first as an alderman and
then as Sheriff of the City of London. The Lord Mayor has
meanwhile been encouraging the wealthy Hammon as his
daughter's suitor, but when she rejects him Hammon becomes
enamoured of Jane, who is now working as a seamstress after
quarrelling with Eyre's wife Margery. Hammon has a list of
the war dead on which Ralph's name appears – but in truth
he has only lost a leg, and, returning home, seeks the help of
his fellow journeymen in finding his wife. The disguised Lacy

elopes with Rose, and the couple's wedding is planned for the same morning as Hammon and Jane's. But Ralph recognises a shoe he made for his wife, sent to be matched for a wedding pair, in time to join with his comrades and prevent the marriage. Hammon tries to bribe Ralph to forego his wife, but, shamed by his refusal, gives the money to the reunited pair. The angry fathers pursuing Lacy and Rose are deflected by Firk to the wrong wedding, but give their reluctant blessing to the couple at the behest of the King, who is honouring the banquet hosted by Simon Eyre for all apprentice shoemakers to celebrate his own election as Lord Mayor.

The author and his work

Little is known of the life of Thomas Dekker, beyond his prolific output and evident tendency to live beyond the means this secured – which landed him in debtors' prison from 1613 to 1619. Even his assumed year of birth, 1572, depends only on a reference to his 'threescore years' in a dedication published in the probable year of his death, 1632. He is first heard of as one of the many playwrights writing for Philip Henslowe, and between 1598 and 1602 had at least a hand in well over forty plays, of which a bare half-dozen survive. Unsurprisingly, many of these were collaborative works with fellow hack dramatists; but throughout his long career Dekker also wrote in collaboration with the greatest of his contemporaries: perhaps even with Shakespeare, in revising the long-unpublished *Sir Thomas More* (*c.* 1594), and certainly with Jonson, on *Page of Plymouth* (1599) and other lost plays; with Marston on *Satiromastix* (1601); with Middleton on *The Honest Whore* (1604) and *The Roaring Girl* (1608); with Webster on *Westward Ho!* (1604) and *Northward Ho!* (1605); with Massinger on *The Virgin Martyr* (1620); and with Ford and Rowley on *The Witch of Edmonton* (1621). Such a range of compatibilities suggests the spirit of humanitarian empathy which pervades even his more commonplace work – notably, an extensive journalistic output and entertainments for the Lord Mayor's

Show and other civic celebrations of the city he loved. *The Wonderful Year* (1603) is a vivid prose account of the year which began with the Queen's death and ended with an outbreak of plague, and *The Gull's Hornbook* (1609) a satirical put-down of affectations in the form of a primer for fashionable gentlemen. His other plays include *Old Fortunatus* (1599), a comedy in which morality and vulgarity characteristically overlap, and an historical allegory, *The Whore of Babylon* (1606). For *The Roaring Girl* see p. 139, and for *The Witch of Edmonton* see p. 217.

The historical context

The mutual dependence and respect shown by the craftsmen of *The Shoemakers' Holiday* offers a romanticised but not entirely misleading view of the craft system as it functioned during the fifteenth century. An apprentice, unpaid but for his keep, was bound to his master's household for seven years or more, after which he became a journeyman, working at his craft as a day-labourer; he could then aspire to mastership by presenting, precisely, his own 'master-piece'. This term was not applied exclusively, as now, to a work of 'high art', but to any piece consummately crafted after its kind – as it might be, a pair of shoes. Simon Eyre is thus 'master' of the journeymen Hodge and Firk not only in the economic sense (that he pays their wages), but also in the aesthetic sense – that he has demonstrated his superior skill, having risen from the ranks of the apprentices, whom he now rewards with a feast and (anecdotally but not historically) the annual pre-Lenten holiday of Shrove Tuesday. As skills became more specialised, and the range of experience to complete a product extended beyond a single craftsman's capacity, such a proof of 'mastery' became ever harder to fulfil – and less relevant to the needs of an emerging capitalist system. As with many aspects of the Tudor ideological inheritance from the medieval world, the theory was honoured, but in a state of tension with the harsh reality of apprentices exploited and journeymen condemned never to rise above that station – while mastership increasingly depended on purchase or inheritance rather than craft pride. Dekker's play lacks the cynicism of later 'city comedies' such as *Eastward Ho!* because its historical setting, in what appears to be the reign of Henry V, allows it to celebrate the integrity of a system rather than bemoan its corruption.

The world of the play

The Shoemakers' Holiday was written in the summer of 1599 – a year or two after Shakespeare's *Henry IV* plays, but about the same time as his *Henry V*. This was the summer of Essex's ill-fated expedition to Ireland and of strong rumours of imminent Spanish invasion. Many thousands of men were mustered in August at Mile End (a month after Lacy, in Scene i, describes just such a muster there) and elsewhere on the outskirts of London. Yet where Shakespeare unhesitatingly travels between London and the 'vasty fields' of France, Dekker is concerned not with the politics of nations but the politics of community. For ordinary people, the impact of war was relatively slight and secondhand – though devastating for the casualties among its conscripts, who were often reduced to vagrancy as 'masterless men'. Shakespeare simply ignores this issue, and arguably Dekker fudges it by giving the crippled Ralph such supportive workfellows – but where Shakespeare's commoners blend the eccentric and the emblematic while seeming untouched by the economic, Dekker's have to earn their livings in a play-world which sets its 'holiday' or carnival mood very firmly in a context of workaday normality.

For all the apparent social harmony and economic equilibrium of *The Shoemakers' Holiday*, the social classes of which Dekker presents so broad a spectrum are in tension as well as in balance. The Earl of Lincoln and the Lord Mayor of London, though warily polite, distrust each other's role in society – the Earl fearing the egalitarian implications of an alliance with a citizen's family, the Mayor suspicious of the parasitic indolence to be expected from the nobility. It is Dekker's romantic fancy that Lacy, forced to learn a trade to rescue himself from youthful improvidence, can pass for a shoemaker, just as it is that a rich citizen like Hammon would stoop to contemplate marriage with a mere seamstress. That social mobility is possible outside marriage is shown by Eyre's turning capitalist entrepreneur – but by thus thriving on the surplus value created by others, he betrays his declared belief that advancement can come only through hard work. Ralph has not the means to bribe his way out of military service, where Lacy is able to do so – arguably displaying cowardice as well as cunning thereby: and he gets his girl, while the more deserving Ralph loses his leg and nearly loses his wife.

It is needful to stress Dekker's awareness of such inequities, for in performance the play's darker corners can as easily be overlooked as those of *Twelfth Night* – probably written within a year of our play. Indeed, *The Shoemakers' Holiday* might aptly have been subtitled *Shrove Tuesday*, for it shares that festival's dedication to the topsy-turvy spirit of carnival – and feasting is a recurrent motif. The Lord Mayor's banquet at the beginning is for the likes of Lincoln and 'many courtiers more' (for whom it is an obligation rather than a treat); midway through, Eyre has his journeymen join him for the feast at Old Ford, more or less obliging the Lord Mayor to offer hospitality to all; and at the close Eyre lays on a fine repast for mere apprentices, with their liveried masters waiting at table.

Sidestepping the issue of whether such a brief, carnivalesque inversion is truly subversive or merely a licensed release of energies, Simon Eyre deftly combines the offices of Lord Mayor and Lord of Misrule – for in both roles he presides over the festivities rather than participating in them. Ironically, in a synopsis of the play his role can thus appear relatively minor, since the substantial action mainly involves and is initiated by the other characters (not least his irrepressible sidekick Firk), even his wealth deriving from Lacy's inside information. Like Falstaff, Eyre thus encompasses the play while remaining distanced from its harsher realities: yet all the characters are infected by his spirit, from the journeymen at the start to the King himself at the close. Significantly, the single character who never encounters him, the twice-spurned Hammon, remains to the end a formal, friendless figure.

To call *The Shoemakers' Holiday* a democratic play would be anachronistic, for to the Elizabethans 'democracy' meant mob rule – as displayed by apprentices in their sporadic riots, for which Shrove Tuesday was a favoured occasion. Yet Dekker does dare to present the underlying equality of humankind as a positive and energising force rather than a threat. And in having Eyre prematurely don the garb of an alderman to enable his first merchant venture, he is both employing a familiar disguise convention yet also – and more daringly in an age of sumptuary laws – suggesting the irrelevance of dress as a signifier of status. Even his choice as subject of 'the gentle craft' carries a 'democratic' double meaning – the implication being that cobblers are as 'gentle' as any gentleman.

Yet the King breaks off from feasting with the reminder that there are still wars to be fought, which will require more hapless Ralphs as fodder. And one critic's complaint that Simon Eyre is 'Shylock masquerading as Falstaff' might with more justice have dubbed him a proto-capitalist employer promoting his own enlightened self-interest. More clear-sightedly than most of his contemporaries, Dekker thus recognises and dramatises the complexity of his society, without aspiring to understand or analyse it. Shakespeare – his setting the neverland of Illyria rather than London – does not address these issues, though he shares Dekker's sense of the need to defeat puritanism. *Twelfth Night* embodies this in the humiliation of Malvolio, *The Shoemakers' Holiday* in its celebration of feasting and carnival. But both plays end with a song of the wind and the rain, as if in recognition of their own optimism.

The playwright's craft

STRUCTURE In seamlessly merging three plot sources which have nothing but shoemaking in common, Dekker creates a microcosm of the social structure of his city which is gradually suffused by the benign spirit of Simon Eyre. Strictly, the duration of the play must accommodate Ralph's departure and loss of his leg, his return, and his master's amassing of a fortune; yet our *sense* is of the passage of days rather than of months – a 'double time' which Dekker's episodic sequence of self-determining scenes better allows than the strict act-divisions imposed by later editors.

LANGUAGE Though Dekker observes the 'decorum' that the nobility should speak in verse and commoners in prose, his blank verse, like its speakers, seems merely to be going through the motions, and at times comes close to bathos – as when Hammon reflects on the fortunes of the hunt in Scene v. Even the doggerel couplets in the wooing scenes (vi and xii) have a livelier feel. But the prose is both vivid and hugely varied, from Margery's harassed harangues and compulsive catch-phrases to the proliferating double-meanings by which Firk lives up to his name and the pidgin Dutch which 'Hans' makes his own. And, like Falstaff, Simon Eyre is virtually self-created through his own verbal stream-of-consciousness – an entirely original mix of the idiomatic and the inventive, not least in a resonant and often bawdy nomenclature which invokes Cicely Bumtrinket, Mistress Figbottom and Master Bellymount, not to mention a 'barley-pudding full of maggots' and a 'bombast-cotton-candle quean'.

CONVENTIONS The spirit of camaraderie in the play is entirely male – Lacy's good fellowship with the other shoemakers amply demonstrated, but his love for Rose mostly taken as read. Eyre's wife Margery is constrained within the typology of the nagging shrew – while Rose, conversely, has the fresh innocence expected of the 'madonna'. Jane becomes the more interesting when, supposing herself a widow, realism wins out over romance in her acceptance of Hammon: and even when she rejects him in favour of her restored husband, she remains astute enough not to return his gifts or refuse his twenty pounds (while Dekker spurns such a conventional reward of comedy as discovering the humble lover to be a long-lost heir).

STAGE PRACTICE Eyre lives 'over the shop', and Hodge and Firk probably inside it. Scene xiii opens with 'Hodge at his shop board' – a counter by day which could be swung closed to form a shutter at night. And in Scene xii Jane is 'discovered' in her seamstress's shop. The fluidity of Elizabethan stage locations would have permitted all such scenes to flow from workshop to street as required, with perhaps one of the stage doors hinged horizontally to provide a practicable counter.

In performance

Henslowe paid Dekker £3 for the play in July 1599, and it was probably first performed at his Rose theatre that same autumn, though the title-page of the first printed text of 1600 records only a court performance before the Queen on the previous New Year's Day. Five new printings by 1657 suggest a continuing stage life – which was then interrupted until 1919, when an amateur, all-female production at the Birkbeck Theatre proclaimed itself 'the first recorded performance of the play in London for over three hundred years'. Cedric Hardwicke was the first professional Simon Eyre of the century when the Birmingham Repertory Theatre staged the play in 1922, and the role was taken by Baliol Holloway when the play joined the Old Vic repertoire in 1926, with Edith Evans making, in James Agate's words, a 'complete woman' of Margery. ('The audience at this theatre,' condescended Agate, was made up of 'simple middle-class people', and 'here is the play for them.') Revivals followed in 1938 at the Playhouse, directed by Nancy Price; in 1944, at the Lyric, Hammersmith, directed by Walter Hudd; and in 1948 at the Oxford Playhouse, directed by Nevill Coghill; while in 1964 David William's production for the Mermaid memorably brought Cicely Bumtrinket to cantankerous life. In 1981 the play reached the Olivier stage of the National Theatre, where Alfred Lynch's Eyre was described by Milton Shulman as more 'bossy and ambitious' than 'madcap jester', but Brenda Bruce's Margery was, in Michael Coveney's judgement, 'a brilliant study in harmless snobbery'.

The Malcontent
John Marston

1603

Source

None is known.

The story

Pietro, Duke of Genoa, swears vengeance when he is warned
by Malevole that he is being cuckolded by his trusted minion
Mendoza. Malevole enjoys a 'fool's licence' at court; but when
he consults with his faithful friend Celso we learn that beneath
this malcontent disguise he is the banished Duke Altofront,
overthrown when Pietro entered into alliance with the Duke
of Florence and married his daughter Aurelia. Mendoza has
indeed won Aurelia's favours, but she spurns him for another
admirer, Ferneze, who has bribed the old bawd Maquerelle to
tell her that Mendoza prefers one of her own waiting women.
Mendoza turns this to his advantage when challenged by the
Duke, promising to prove that his real rival is Ferneze – who,
surprised that night with Aurelia, impales himself on the Duke's
rapier. Mendoza, now proclaimed as heir by Pietro, makes his
peace with Aurelia and befriends Malevole, who, left alone
with the 'corpse', finds Ferneze stirring back to life. The
foolish old courtier Bilioso preens himself for being given the
diplomatic mission of telling the Duke of Florence of his
daughter's infidelity. Mendoza now conspires with Malevole,
who pretends disaffection, to seize power by murdering the
Duke and marrying Altofront's imprisoned wife Maria. But
Malevole alerts Pietro and, persuading him to disguise himself as a hermit, astounds the court with news of Pietro's death,
which the 'hermit' confirms. Mendoza, succeeding to the dukedom, sends the penitent Aurelia to share the hermit's lot and,

fearing to be beholden to such allies, separately instructs hermit and malcontent to poison each other. But Bilioso returns with orders from Florence that Aurelia must die and Altofront be restored. Pietro now renounces his own claim, and Malevole reveals to him his true identity. Sent by Mendoza to woo Maria on his behalf, Malevole finds his wife resolved to defend her honour. He tells Mendoza that the hermit is poisoned, and feigns death when the same innocuous mixture is used on him. At the masque celebrating Mendoza's succession, Pietro and Altofront reveal their identities, and Altofront, acclaimed as Duke by the company, shows mercy to his former enemies.

The author and his work

John Marston was born into a well-to-do Oxfordshire family in 1576. After graduating from Oxford in 1594 he was meant to follow his father into the law, and shared his chambers in the Middle Temple from 1595. He came into his inheritance on his father's death in 1599, though he had evidently disappointed his parent by showing more interest in the social than the professional life of the Inns of Court. His earliest published work included fashionable imitations of Ovid and numerous satires, notably in *The Scourge of Villainy* (1598) – among the works banned and burned by order of the Archbishop of Canterbury in 1599. He then turned to the theatre, writing the satirical romance *Antonio and Mellida* (1599) and its sequel *Antonio's Revenge* (1600) for the Children of Paul's. This was one of the elite 'private theatre' companies of boy players which specialised in satire – not least the internecine satire of the so-called 'war of the theatres', of which the first shot was fired by Marston in his caricature of Jonson in *Histriomastix* (1599), to which Jonson retaliated in *Cynthia's Revels* (1600) – Marston (and Dekker) returning to the fray with *Satiromastix* (1601). Possibly the 'war' had more to do with mutually beneficial publicity than strong hostility, because by 1605 Jonson and Marston were collaborating with Chapman on *Eastward Ho!* (see p. 95) and Marston had dedicated *The Malcontent* to

Jonson. This play was first performed in 1603 by a boy's company, but in the following year it was revised, with additions by John Webster, for performance in a public theatre, the Globe, by the King's Men (to which status James had elevated the Chamberlain's company). Marston himself took a share in the Children of the Chapel Royal, now known as the Queen's Revels, performing at the indoor Blackfriars; and for them he wrote the satirical *Parasitaster* (1604), the earthy city comedy *The Dutch Courtesan* (1604; see p. 102) and the stoic tragedy *Sophonisba* (1606). His committal to Newgate jail in 1608 may have been connected with his theatrical activities, since he then sold his share in the Queen's Revels and wrote no further plays. He was ordained in 1609, and seems to have lived uneventfully thereafter until his death in 1634.

The historical context

The year 1603, when the first version of *The Malcontent* probably reached the stage, witnessed what Dekker in *The Wonderful Year* described as the 'general terror' which followed the death in the spring of the old Queen – who had cultivated her seeming immortality as she had once made a political virtue of her virginity. Relief at the bloodless succession of James was soon tempered by horror at a visitation of the plague – its brooding threat heightened by the belief that it also betokened divine displeasure. Numerous plays were well-tuned to the uncertain temper of the times. Even Shakespeare turned with the new century from romantic comedies and patriotic histories to those works which critics label 'problem plays' – including *Measure for Measure*, with its own disguised Duke putting all to rights in a disordered court; *Troilus and Cressida*, with its sour view of the way in which sexuality goes hand in hand with political ambition, expressed through the railing Thersites (anecdotally modelled on Marston himself); and, of course, *Hamlet*, whose central character at once embraces and transcends the typology of malcontent. *Troilus* may well have been first staged at the Inns of Court – equally renowned as a 'third university' for legal training and as a finishing school for the sons of the wealthy – where Marston's own ideas and style were formed. Certainly, he helped to shape the fashion for irony and paradox which characterised the shift from the consciously balanced style of the Elizabethans to the 'metaphysical' asymmetry of the early Jacobeans. The tastes and extravagance of a bisexual monarch, the prevalence not only of the plague but of the more insidiously endemic venereal disease, and an increasing awareness that the values of emergent capitalism were no aberrations but marks of the breakdown of belief in intrinsic value and 'degree, priority and place' – such were the thematic concerns of the new writers and the forces which shaped their everyday lives.

The 'augmentations'

Theatre companies, not playwrights, owned the plays they produced, and we do not know how *The Malcontent*, written for a private theatre, came into the possession of the King's Men. The Induction claims it was in retaliation for the boys' company having stolen a King's play (the now venerable *Spanish Tragedy*): but the Induction is itself a fiction, designed – along with eleven other additional passages scattered through the text – to increase the play's length to that expected by a Globe audience. The Induction was not, however, merely compensating for the 'not-received custom of music' (which extended the playing time in private theatres). Boy players simulating adult behaviour had a 'distancing effect' appropriate to satire – and the Induction achieves a similar distance by having adult actors become stage simulcra of themselves – one of their number, Will Sly, even playing an audience member who proceeds to call for Harry Condell, Dick Burbage . . . and Will Sly, who, of course, is already there. Such multi-levelled personation also anticipates the theme of the play, whose characters both are and are not what they 'present'. In the title role, Burbage, recently celebrated as Hamlet, thus 'plays' in the Induction an actor of his own name who is about to play a deposed duke who is himself playing at being a malcontent; while the character whose speech ends the play proper is a duke who has just been playing Malevole taking the role of another character in the masque, now putting on the mask of benevolent ruler – and who turns out, in the Epilogue, to be an actor named Burbage seeking the audience's applause.

The world of the play

In tragedy, the ending, though (and because) it is replete with mortality, effects a closure: antagonisms are resolved in death, with some semblance of a moral order restored. And comedy affirms our sense of everyday proprieties through marriage or feasting. Tragi-comedy, of which *The Malcontent* is often cited as an early example, thus stands accused of a hybridity which appears to raise issues of tragic import, but leaves us dissatisfied by resolving them through the moral short-circuitry of comedy. Certainly, the play-world of *The Malcontent* allows us none of the 'givens' of the regular genres: we are not only more aware of it as a construct, but of Marston's – and Malevole's – role in the construction. The intention, however, is to offer not the moral soft-landing of tragi-comic reconciliation, but the self-awareness needful for satire to achieve its bite.

Marston purposefully leaves us uncertain of his attitude to his central character. How far does Malevole keep his distance from what he censoriously observes, and how far is he concupiscently obsessed by it? In his absorption in the 'humour' of the malcontent, is he taking his revulsion to such humorous excess that it becomes comic – or is he rather expressing what one critic calls a 'profound existential nausea' with what he sees? In theatrical terms, he appears to be 'playing the role' of malcontent less in relation to his alter-ego Altofront than to an audience's expectations of his character-type – and by thus heightening an audience's sense of the play as fiction inviting them to share the joke. Supposedly 'difficult' moments, such as Ferneze's return from the dead (II, v, 136–61), as also the recurrent occasions when 'high' and 'low' characters converge,

lose much of their problematic quality if an audience recognises with Malevole that absurd events and contingencies *are*
absurd – both in the comic *and* existential senses of the term.

Hence the action of *The Malcontent*, though complicated,
is driven forward without deviation or sub-plot. While the
Bilioso–Passarello–Maquerelle strata at court is socially and
functionally subordinate to the Pietro–Mendoza level, both are
caught up in the same entanglements – with Malevole usually
present both as participant and commentator. The very isola-
tion of the Ferneze–Aurelia affair suggests that its purpose is
not to forward the plot, but rather to illustrate a particular
kind of behaviour. The action thus unfolds as a sequence of
exempla – more or less self-contained episodes intended to
illuminate satirical or moral points – with Malevole acting as
a connecting link between them.

There is no 'psychological' consistency in the characterisation of the leading villains – Pietro being transformed from
cruel usurper to penitent and Mendoza from sensual opportunist to cold Machiavellian intriguer. But their behaviour
'works' dramatically within this exemplary world – in which
most of the characters are occupied in playing roles: Pietro
not simply when he assumes the covert role of a hermit, but
in his very usurpation of the dukedom; Bilioso in his fawning
adjustments of his behaviour to the requisites of royal favour;
Maquerelle as supplier of sexual fantasies; Mendoza whether
play-acting in his manipulation of the Ferneze–Aurelia affair
or in the deceptions which lead to his little brief authority;
and, of course, Passarello – added to the Globe version not
only to provide a role for their resident Fool, but to serve for
a public theatre audience as a more familiar intermediary between their own world and the world of the play.

Like Claudius in *Hamlet*, conspiring against his nephew,
Mendoza is ultimately destroyed by himself – except of course
that in this case only his ambitions are destroyed (his own fate,
the stage directions tell us, the absurd one of simply being
'kicked out'). Malevole, like Hamlet, seizes rather than creates
his opportunities for revenge, attributing his own ascendant

fortunes to the 'tumbling' of fate (V, iv, 90–2). But while Hamlet fails to kill Claudius when he is at his prayers lest he should save his soul, Malevole fails to kill Pietro because he *wants* to save his soul.

Marston leaves unresolved the question of whether Duke Altofront can now survive without Malevole – for in revenge tragedy turned revenge comedy, the question of 'what happens next' looms larger than in the regular forms. But that – as in the similar predicament at the close of Brecht's *The Good Woman of Setzuan*, when Shen Teh casts off her worldly-wise persona Shui Ta – is again for the audience to decide.

The playwright's craft

FORM   To what has been said above, it may be added that the play was described as a 'tragi-comedy' when entered in the Stationers' Register, while Marston in his dedication talks of his *'asperam . . . Thaliam'*, or harsh comedy – and in his preface of taking 'the freedom of a satire'. The Induction calls the play 'neither satire nor moral, but the mean passage of a history'.

STRUCTURE   Since it originated as a private theatre play, *The Malcontent* was from the first divided into five acts to indicate the placing of intervals for music. Its scene-divisions follow the practice of marking changes by the entrance of major characters or significant regroupings, rather than following a complete clearance of the stage.

LANGUAGE   The shifts between the verse and prose in *The Malcontent* do not distinguish between scenes of 'high' and 'low' action – indeed, they occur not only within scenes of both kinds but within the speeches of individual characters. Marston's style nonetheless has its own jagged fluidity, here nicely summed up by his editor G. K. Hunter: 'Verse often grows out of prose as a point of view crystallises out of disordered facts and then breaks down into prose again when passion overcomes the ordered vision of verse.' Though much criticised and satirised for his alleged clumsiness of style, Marston was helping to expand the boundaries of what blank verse as a medium could encompass as it, too, passed from the quest for synthesis which characterised the Elizabethan style to the Jacobean probing and questioning of moral certainties.

CONVENTIONS Besides the type of 'the malcontent' himself and the addition of the fool Passarello, the 'foolish old gentle-man' typified by Bilioso was in a much more venerable 'line', stretching back to the plays of Plautus – and, of course, most recently exemplified by Polonius in *Hamlet*. Marston also follows the expected typology which separates sexually desir-able women into immaculate madonnas (such as Maria) and whores (such as Aurelia).

STAGE PRACTICE As its easy transition from private to public staging suggests, *The Malcontent* made few special demands on either. But the Induction, apart from its functionality within the play, highlights some notable differences between the two forms of theatre – as in the opening denial of 'Will Sly's' attempt to sit upon the stage at the Globe, a form of self-advertisement permitted in the private houses.

In performance

The Malcontent appears to have remained in the repertoire of the King's Men, and a surviving diary reference confirms a per-formance as late as 1635. A six-night revival at the Olympic Theatre in 1850, where G. H. Lewes declared the play to have been 'mercilessly murdered', was followed, after a further century of neglect, by university productions, at Southamp-ton in 1964 and by OUDS in 1968. Jonathan Miller directed the play for the Nottingham Playhouse in 1973, with Derek Godfrey as Malevole, and it was staged for the first time by the Royal Shakespeare Company at its Swan Theatre, Stratford, in 2002, with Antony Sher in the role of Malevole.

Thomas Heywood
A Woman Killed with Kindness

1603

Source

A free conflation of several *novelle* as translated in William
Painter's *Palace of Pleasure* (1566–67).

The story

At the wedding of John Frankford to Anne, sister of Sir
Francis Acton, Frankford's servants celebrate with country
dances while their betters discuss how ideally matched are the
happy couple. But the sobriety of the bride contrasts with the
careless spirit of her brother, who readily accepts a wager
from Sir Charles Mountford for a contest at falconry on the
morrow. Acton and Mountford quarrel over the outcome,
and when a brawl ensues Sir Charles kills two of Acton's men.
Immediately repenting his 'heat of blood', he rejects the pleas
of his sister Susan to take flight and surrenders himself to the
Sheriff summoned by Sir Francis. The news is brought to
Frankford by his friend Wendoll, who is invited to make himself free of the household – though Frankford's servant Nick
intuitively distrusts the man, and eventually overhears him
seducing Anne in her husband's absence. Although Mountford
manages to clear his name, he loses everything but a single
farm, which he and Susan are forced to work themselves –
until his false friend Shafton forecloses on a loan in order
to seize the land. Sir Francis, arriving to gloat as his enemy
is returned to jail, finds himself enamoured of Susan, and
determines to possess her. Though her pleas to Mountford's
relatives and former dependents fall on deaf ears, she spurns
Sir Francis' offers of help – but her defence of her honour so
impresses him that he arranges privately to discharge Sir

Charles' debts. Mountford cannot bear such an obligation to
Acton, and begs his sister to repay the debt by satisfying Sir
Francis' lust. Susan agrees, but plans suicide to redeem her
honour. When Nick tells Frankford all he knows, his master
plans to put his suspicions to the test by pretending to be
called away. He surprises the embracing lovers, but is held
back from killing Wendoll, and sends Anne to a distant dower
house, never to see him or their children more. Acton is so
moved by Susan's readiness to sacrifice herself that he agrees
to take her without dowry, as his bride. The reconciled friends
visit Anne and, finding her close to death from self-inflicted
starvation, send for Frankford, who forgives Anne and renews
their marriage even as she dies.

The author and his work

Thomas Heywood was born in Lincolnshire around 1574,
and was at Emmanuel College, Cambridge, between 1591 and
1593, though he never took a degree. In the following year he
published an epic poem, *Oenone and Paris*, and his first known
play, *The Four Prentices of London*, was performed by the Lord
Admiral's Men. From then until his death in 1641 he was
probably the most prolific author of the three reigns spanned
by his working life: indeed, eight years before its end he claimed
to have 'had either an entire hand or at the least a main finger'
in 220 plays. Like Shakespeare, he was unconcerned about seeing these in print, and barely two dozen have come down to
us; but the survival of other works in prose and verse affirms
his astonishingly prolific output. A stalwart journeyman, he was
no doubt open to whatever commissions came his way, in a
long career which began as a hack for the Admiral's Men under
Henslowe; for this, a contract survives from 1598, but nothing
of his output other than a two-part chronicle play, *Edward IV*
(1601). By the turn of the century he had evidently prospered
sufficiently to become a sharer as well as an actor and writer
with Worcester's Men, which (under Queen Anne's patronage
from 1603) staged most of his theatrical work in the decade

that followed. This included domestic comedies such as *How a Man May Choose a Good Wife from a Bad* (1602) and *The Wise Woman of Hogsdon* (1604); tragi-comedies such as *The Royal King and the Loyal Subject* (1602) and *The English Traveller* (1625); the two-part Elizabethan chronicle, *If You Know Not Me You Know Nobody* (1605–6); a hybrid Roman ballad drama, *The Rape of Lucrece* (1607); and collaborations with Webster on *Appius and Virginia* (1608) and Rowley on *Fortune by Land and Sea* (1609). His work in other forms included a translation of Ovid's *Art of Love* (1600) and the long quasi-historical poem, *Troia Britannica* (1609). An outline of Heywood's life continues in our consideration of *The Fair Maid of the West*, which probably reached the stage in 1610 (see p. 154).

The historical context

A noted feminist critic has taken Anne's qualities as described in the opening scene of *A Woman Killed with Kindness* as typifying Elizabethan male expectations – that a wife should show Christian modesty (or, in Mountford's words, be 'meek and patient . . . pliant and duteous'); gifted in feminine accomplishments (as is Anne in music and foreign tongues); and a true partner to her husband (in this case, 'both scholars, both young, both being descended nobly'). The new opportunities open to Renaissance women were, it is argued, constrained by their use – to set off the supposed superiority (and legalised authority) of the male. Many men assumed that a baser, 'truer' womanhood lay beneath such a veneer, ready to reveal itself in such actions as Anne Frankford's adultery. While traditional Catholic doctrine followed St Paul in viewing marriage as a necessary evil, protestant reformers remained equivocal about the nature of women. Luther believed them fit only for childbearing, and Knox was vituperative against the *Monstrous Regiment of Women* (which, on that book's appearance in 1588, included the Catholic rulers of Scotland and France as well as England's Elizabeth); but they did agree that marriage was a desirable state, which should be rooted in mutual affection, not financial or dynastic convenience. Such was, increasingly, the accepted view, but for the middle classes (and above) the economics of marriage remained important. Owing to the 'wild blood' of Acton and his father, Anne has 'to her dower her mother's modesty' and perhaps not much else; yet it is later assumed that Susan's lack of dowry rules out other than an illicit relationship with Sir Francis. That he is persuaded otherwise is less probable than it is morally appropriate.

The world of the play

The world of *A Woman Killed with Kindness* is one of bound-aries – around landed estates and protecting hearth and home. Sir Charles is readier to sell his sister's virtue than the last remnant of his property – the farm from which his family began its ascent from yeomanry to gentry three hundred years before. And though Frankford describes his estate as 'mean', he is able to exile his wife to a 'manor seven mile off'. The farm workers at his wedding feast are never seen again, but they and his tenants' rents so well supply his needs that he has to invent a lawsuit in York as excuse to leave home. In an ironic, bourgeois inversion of overreaching, his tragedy is precipi-tated by the very excess of his domestic contentment – and his misplaced confidence in those that share it (Sc. iv, 1–14).

Within these provincial boundaries are played out sexual passions and jealousies which Shakespeare was soon to set in wider if less realistic worlds. A brother's life saved in return for a maidenhead is what Claudio in *Measure for Measure* asks of his sister Isabella, who appears to have no more say in her climactic marriage to the Duke than does Susan in accepting Acton's honourable proposal – although the feelings of both women towards their suitors are rather of gratitude than of affection. And in *Othello*, as in our play, a husband's joy over his marriage gives way to jealousy aroused by a trusted servant which causes the wife's eventual death – though Othello's trust in 'honest' Iago is ill-judged, where Frankford's eventual confidence in the 'blunt, yet . . . honest' Nick (Sc. viii, 72) is only too well placed. And in both plays there is a problem of 'double time' – though where in *Othello* it is of insufficient hours for all the dalliance alleged, in *A Woman Killed with Kindness* it is of a seemingly continuous action which conceals the passage of years, during which two children are born to the Frankfords.

Both husbands demand what Othello calls 'ocular proof' – which takes the flimsy and misleading form of a handkerchief for the gullible Othello, where for Frankford it is the sight of the lovers 'lying / Close in each other's arms'. Yet Desdemona is murdered, Anne is by 'her husband's kindness killed' in a play notable for the absence of ostensible violence – other than the affray after the falconry contest which sets the sub-plot in motion. The terrible consequences of Sir Charles' impetuosity contrast with Frankford's scrupulous care over thinking before he acts – his single moment of being ruled by his emotions restrained by the maidservant, who 'clasps hold on him' with what he likens to an 'angel's hand'.

Despite that, there is something disquieting about Anne's deathbed scene, in which a double murderer who would have prostituted his own sister and a profligate who is also a would-be ravisher join a husband whose cool and calculated punishment of his wife has proved a sentence of death perhaps more cruelly lingering than a rapier's thrust. This exhibits, as we might say today, a desire for 'control' similar to Acton's 'kindness' towards Sir Charles and his sister – or Shafton's 'kindness' in making a loan with the sole intention of foreclosing. The dilemma caused when Sir Charles offers his sister to discharge his obligation to Acton can conveniently be resolved by marriage, but Anne can only repay her own 'obligation' by death – thereby, despite her confidence in heaven, mortally sinning twice over in orthodox eyes, by committing suicide as well as adultery. Heywood hints at the hypocrisy of Frankford capping the forgiveness of his wife with a clearly rhetorical 'I'll wish to die with thee', dutifully echoed by the onlookers, when Nick, in an aside, pleads exemption: 'So will not I! / I'll sigh and sob, but, by my faith, not die' (Sc. xvii, 99–100).

It would be unhistorical to suggest, as have some recent critics, that Anne is the real 'victim' of the play, beset on the one hand by her husband's need for control, on the other by a lover's concupiscence. Yet we must also recognise that the converse of Heywood's admiration for active and proactive women (which will be further discussed in relation to *The Fair Maid of the West*) might well be sympathy for those forced by circumstances and upbringing into a passive role – and that this enforced passivity is as much Anne's burden as a wife as it is conducive to her compliance as a lover.

This is a play-world as rich in texture as in incident. So much happens in the twin plots that it is easy to overlook the background to the events which Heywood fills in, notably in giving a more vivid realisation of bourgeois life than is to be found in either *Arden of Faversham* or *A Yorkshire Tragedy*, from the subtle gradations of servitude which are the subtext for the country dancing (Sc. ii), and the way that the domestic servants form part of the middle-class extended family, to the presence of the self-effacing Cranwell as a second house guest or the laying out of a carpet for the games of cards. With the harmonious interruption of the dancing at the play's beginning may be contrasted Anne's plaintive farewell to her lute near its close. And there are unexpected encounters such as Susan's with the procession of those who spurn her brother's pleas, and Anne's with Nick on her journey into exile, as he struggles with the temptation to pity. All illuminate without in any pedantic sense forwarding the action.

Wendoll remains enigmatic to the end. Introduced as a minor character, of recognised gentility but in reduced circumstances that force him to depend on the hospitality of wealthier men, he is allowed an extended soliloquy of real moral torment – albeit undercut by Jenkin's unrecognised presence – before giving way to his desires (Sc. vi). When he returns towards the end, apparently to make what amends he can, Anne recognises him only as the Devil, and he anticipates a future of wandering exile, like an apprentice malcontent in hopes of preferment as a courtly parasite (Sc. xvi, 125–37).

The playwright's craft

FORM Those who stress the didactic (or 'homiletic') nature of domestic tragedy find this exemplified in a Christian, redemptive reading of the play, though as we have seen this is open to question. Also, the plot is based not on a topical occurrence but adapted from fictional sources – though this would seem to leave it more rather than less open to didactic shaping.

STRUCTURE As we have discussed, the main and underplot interweave more by inference than direct connection; and it is notable that there is no 'low' sub-plot as such, the role of the servants, notably Nick and Jenkin, being fully integrated into the main action.

LANGUAGE The very occasional attempts at poetic flight, as in Frankford's likening of his sweating brow to 'morning dew upon the golden flowers' (Sc. viii, 62), threaten bathos; and the passages in rhyming couplets are also problematic, since their effect of closure is seldom justified by their sense. But the movement between blank verse and prose is assured and almost imperceptible, both being notable for colloquial ease and flow rather than high-flying hyperbole or elaborate metaphor. The more prosaic similes reflecting middle-class concerns – as when Sir Charles compares a well-matched couple to a 'well-made suit' – are rather happier, as are the scenes of extended double-meaning, playing on the sexual implications of country dances in Scene ii and of card games in Scene viii.

CONVENTIONS An Elizabethan audience's capacity to live comfortably in its own world alongside that of the play is evidenced when Jenkin responds to Sisly's request to start serving dinner by reminding the spectators, 'though it be afternoon with you, 'tis but early days with us'. And at a moment of far higher seriousness after the discovery, Anne breaks off to address the audience with the little invocation which begins, 'O women, women . . .' (Sc. xiii, 141–5).

STAGE PRACTICE   The unusually full stage directions are less concerned with the practicalities of performance (as we might expect from a prompt copy) than with amplifying the author's own intentions, suggesting the play was put into print from Heywood's own papers. But stage practice is reflected in the recurrent concern with costume as a signifier of status: in Scene x, Sir Charles is in irons, 'his feet bare, his garments all ragged and torn', but his entrance in Scene x is declared 'gentlemanlike'. His presumed dress as a working yeoman in Scene vii goes undescribed in the directions since his condition is made quite clear from his opening speech.

In performance

Henslowe's records indicate a first performance of *A Woman Killed with Kindness* at his Rose Theatre on Bankside in February 1603, a month before the old Queen's death (for which two payments totalling £6 to Heywood compare with over £8 for costumes). Three quarto editions between 1607 and 1617 and various contemporary references suggest the play's continuing popularity in the new reign; but it was then lost to the stage until 1887, when the Dramatic Students Society presented a revival at the Olympic. The French director Jacques Copeau opened his Théâtre de Vieux-Colombier with the play (minus the sub-plot) in 1913. It was then revived at the Birmingham Rep in 1922, directed by H. K. Ayliff, and at the Malvern Festival of 1931, when the cast included Robert Donat and Ralph Richardson. In 1971 the National Theatre revived the play at the Old Vic, directed by John Dexter, with Anthony Hopkins as Frankford and Joan Plowright as Anne; and in 1991 Katie Mitchell directed it for the RSC at The Other Place, with Saskia Reeves and Michael Maloney as the unhappy couple. 'Reeves,' commented Benedict Nightingale, 'suggests a genuine artlessness and vulnerability, and makes a most touching end in the arms of Maloney, a warm, decent man who has won the battle against his blacker emotions.' A production by Northern Broadsides went on tour in 2003.

Bussy D'Ambois
George Chapman

1604

Source

The historical Bussy, born *c.* 1550, was a hanger-on at the French court, known for his intemperate bravado. No account of Bussy's life was published until 1609, so Chapman must have drawn on gossip and anecdote. Bussy was never poor, but he was murdered on account of his adultery.

The story

Bussy D'Ambois, an impoverished but haughty adventurer famed for his duelling skills, is taken under the protection of Monsieur, brother to King Henry III of France, as an instrument of his ambitions for the crown. Most courtiers despise the arrogant arriviste, but the King himself is impressed by Bussy's sturdy spirit, and at Monsieur's urging even pardons him when a violent quarrel involving six courtiers leaves Bussy the sole survivor. Although Bussy is supposedly paying courtly attentions to the wife of the Duke of Guise, while Monsieur woos Tamyra, chaste wife of the Count of Montsurry, Tamyra spurns Monsieur's attentions and develops an attachment to Bussy, in which her confidant, the Friar Comolet, acts as go-between. Monsieur, already jealous of his protégé, learns of the affair with Tamyra from her maid Pero, and joins forces with the Guise to plot Bussy's downfall. In an encounter midway through the play, the two exchange frank opinions of each other, and are apparently reconciled to a friendship free of illusions; but, after a banquet given by the King to reconcile Bussy to the Guise, Monsieur taunts Montsurry with being a cuckold, and tells him to send for a secret paper in which he will reveal all. Tamyra persuades her husband of her innocence, and offers to write to Monsieur for the paper. When Bussy and Tamyra meet, the Friar conjures up Behemoth and other spirits, who reveal a vision of Monsieur, Montsurry and the Guise cloistered over the paper. Bussy leaves to try to smooth matters over. Montsurry, failing to elicit from Tamyra the name of the go-between, resorts to torture, which proves a fatal shock to the watching Friar – whereupon Tamyra admits his role in the affair, and is forced to write in her own blood an invitation to her lover. Bussy ignores the warnings both of Behemoth and the Ghost of the Friar, and goes to meet his mistress – and his death, at the hands of Montsurry's hirelings.

The author and his work

Born in 1559, and thus older by five years than Shakespeare and Marlowe, George Chapman is probably best known for a work which few have read, but to which Keats gave vicarious immortality in his sonnet, 'On First Looking into Chapman's Homer'. His *Seven Books of the Iliad* was published in 1598, a completed revision in 1611, and a translation of the *Odyssey* three years later. He also added his own ending to Marlowe's unfinished *Hero and Leander* (1598). Little is known of Chapman's early life, but he was writing comedies for Henslowe in the mid-1590s, and for the Queen's Revels at the Blackfriars early in the new century. These included *A Humorous Day's Mirth* (1597), said to have influenced Ben Jonson's theory of 'humours comedy'; *May Day* (1601); *All Fools* (1601); and the ill-fated collaboration with Jonson and Marston, *Eastward Ho!* (1605; see p. 95). *Bussy D'Ambois* is his first extant tragedy, and was followed by a sequel, *The Revenge of Bussy D'Ambois* (1610). But *Charles, Duke of Byron* (1608) offended the French Ambassador, and got Chapman into further trouble, perhaps causing his subsequent abandonment of the theatre. Following the premature death of his first patron, James' eldest son Prince Henry, and the disgrace of his second, the Earl of Somerset, his later years appear to have been spent in poverty. He died in 1634.

The historical context

Although set in the recent past, the play ignores the very real brutalities of the religious wars in France – notoriously, the St Bartholomew's Day massacre of Protestants in 1572 (two years before Henry's accession), when the historical D'Ambois is said to have murdered his own cousin. Chapman's interest is limited to struggles for political and sexual dominance within the hothouse atmosphere of the court. Bussy has won fame as a duellist: he is sole survivor of the three-a-side duel (which is fought offstage, but reported in detail at II, i, 25–103), possibly suggested by an actual encounter between supporters of the King and the Guise in 1578; and at the close he proves himself a man of honour by sparing Montsurry when he 'hath him down' – only to be 'ignobly' shot from offstage by a hired assassin. This early modern sense of 'honour' perverted the medieval ideal of chivalry, turning its ideal of service to others into a mere vindication of self-image – when necessary, by issuing a challenge to a duel. Duelling was already in vogue in England when Shakespeare made it a determining theme of his *Romeo and Juliet* around 1594, and the practice reached its peak during James' reign – requiring, in 1613, the issue of a royal proclamation to stamp it out. This proved fruitless, and asserting machismo through the threat of violence has found its way down the ages and even through the class system – where it survives in today's streetwise demand for 'respect'. Shakespeare's *Henry IV* personifies the change – whether in Hotspur's self-aggrandising perception of honour or in Hal's belief that he can leave his rival to 'engross up glorious deeds on my behalf' and then 'tear the reckoning from his heart' – a metaphor of a man's honour as subject to takeover bids which aptly reflects the rise of capitalist individualism.

The world of the play

Chapman, an admirer of Marlowe, here creates a figure half way between Tamburlaine and Gaveston – a low-born hero, truculent in a court where he is an unwelcome minion, who can even, like Faustus, conjure spuriously helpful spirits. Yet Bussy is not only an Elizabethan overreacher but a very Jacobean malcontent, in a line that leads to *The Revenger's Tragedy* and *The White Devil*. His object, however, is not revenge – unless it be revenge for his own poverty, which is a 'given' of the action signalled by the opening stage direction that he is discovered 'poor'. His first condition for agreeing to serve Monsieur is thus for 'high naps' to replace his 'threadbare suit'. And Bussy, in the course of the action, puts on Machiavellian policy along with his courtly garb.

Critics tend to create a Bussy in line with their own prejudices or their knowledge of Chapman's – as an exemplar of humble virtue betrayed by aspirations to Marlovian *vertu*; as a Christian corrupted by the ways of the world; or as a stoic giving way to the lures of passion. But Bussy has no pre-existence, no life beyond the play – and offers us little even by way of retrospection. There *is* no 'essential' Bussy to become untrue to itself. Like so many Jacobean tragic figures, he is no more – and no less – than the sum of his own dramatic actions.

His self-construction is plotted between three extended passages in which his vision of himself shifts under the force of his own rhetoric: the soliloquies which precede and follow his first encounter with Monsieur (I, i, 1–139); the 'flyting' (or structured exchange of abuse) with his patron (III, ii, 312–412); and his dying speech (V, iii, 123–93). Despite Bussy's initial declaration that, 'Who is not poor, is monstrous,' he sidesteps from contempt for courtly ambition, and is ready to abandon poverty for policy if he may do so 'with virtue' – since 'men that fall low must die' as surely as those 'cast headlong from the sky'. At the midpoint of the play he and Monsieur find strange mutual reassurance in proffering mirror-images of each other's moral corruption – while physical corruption, as Bussy finally recognises, is all that is in prospect after a life he describes as 'nothing but a courtier's breath'. Yet even here he talks himself into a mood change, from existential nihilism to stoic resignation: 'a Roman statue' supported by his sword.

Bussy's behaviour is no less erratic than his self-estimation. Yet the inconsistency is at one with a play whose world is equipoised between action and narration, melodrama and reflective philosophy, and where language is made to substitute for action as often as to reinforce it. The dramatic focus also shifts, from the relationship between Bussy and Monsieur which is central at the opening, to points at which the King and the Guise seem more instrumental in the shaping of events, to the closing emphasis on the future of Montsurry's marriage to Tamyra – this latter the more disconcerting since the death of Bussy effects a closure which should resist reopening. (Yet reopen it Chapman does, in *The Revenge of Bussy D'Ambois*, which assigns the duty of avenging Bussy's murder to his brother, Clermont – a Hamlet-like intellectual as reluctant to action as Bussy is impulsive, yet arguably just another, posthumous version of Bussy himself, in a stage world where motive shifts shape as readily as selfhood.)

The only still point is the figure of the King, though even he has variously to stoop to participate in the action and to rise above it as a symbolic figurehead and dispenser of justice – inviolable even to Bussy, as in Monsieur's taunting refrain that he will do 'anything, but killing of the King' (III, ii, 356). Ironically, it is such a figure who conventionally conducts the moral mopping-up operation after a tragic climax; but here the King disappears from the action soon after the failure of his 'reconciliatory' feast, as if recognising that he was not, after all, wrapping up a comedy. No vice-regent to God, this – indeed, Bussy's belief that 'Fortune, not Reason, rules the state of things' counts God out of the reckoning at the start, while the Friar, sole representative of the Church, acts less as priest than pander, even in his ineffectual after-life. If Fortune rules over Reason in this play, it is a Fortune – or the operation of chaos theory – guided by momentary impulses in a godless universe. The conclusion is steeped in an experiential despair that was soon to find its echo in *King Lear*: 'Nothing is made of nought, of all things made; / Their abstract being a dream but of a shade.'

The playwright's craft

STRUCTURE The five-act division is Chapman's, not the imposition of later editors, and one would like to think that the musical interludes in the original private theatre staging were appropriate to the events covered by the breaks – respectively, the three-a-side duel, the consummation of Bussy's affair with Tamyra, the ill-advised reconciliatory banquet, and the cliff-hanging pause between the discovery of the adultery and its consequences. The parabola of Bussy's rise and fall is all the smoother for the absence of sub-plots; but this undeviating throughline does make the final debate between Montsurry and Tamyra appear more a trailer for a sequel than integral to the already completed action.

LANGUAGE Chapman's verse is a strange yet sinuous blend of high-flown rhetoric verging on bombast with sharp colloquialisms which undercut pretension. The often complex syntax of what Swinburne called this 'tumid and turbid exuberance of speech' demands close attention, which can be given on the page (if necessary by re-reading) but is demanding in the theatre if it is to convey more than a generalised impression. Yet the verse demands to be spoken, for its energy is dramatic, not reflective – like Chapman's more readily assimilable prose, given free rein during the quizzing of Pero (III, ii, 170–266).

CONVENTIONS The 'Nuncius' was far less familiar in Elizabethan than in classical tragedy (whence his name derives), although those who followed the 'neoclassical' rules would have had violence always reported through such a messenger rather than seen on stage. Here, his intervention would appear partly a matter of avoiding a contest difficult for boy players to portray – but also one of the more obvious ways in which Chapman reminds us, precisely through a stressed convention, that we are, indeed, watching a play. Such might also be his purpose when Monsieur and the Guise enter 'above' (that is, on the balcony over the stage) as choric commentators upon rather than participants in the action, when the climactic focus shifts to the Montsurry–Tamyra–Bussy triangle.

STAGE PRACTICE   As the climax of *Hamlet* testifies, duelling was popular with audiences, but Bussy's pre-eminence is seen only in the encounter with Montsurry – whose presumed ineptitude would have been easier for boy players to emulate than the skills and thrills of the three-a-side duel, which, as discussed above, is merely reported by the 'Nuncius'.

In performance

The play was first performed by the Children of Paul's, probably in 1604, and first printed in 1607. When the Paul's company disbanded, its plays were taken over by the Queen's Revels, who may well have revived *Bussy* with their leading player, Nathan Field, in the title role, along with its sequel at their Whitefriars playhouse in 1610. Now well past boyhood, Field took the play with him when he left the company to join the King's Men in 1616. He died in 1619, but *Bussy* remained in the King's repertoire into the 1630s; and a prologue, probably written for a Court performance in 1634, mentions two further actors in the role. This prologue, together with other substantial additions to the text, appeared in a new edition in 1641. Charles Hart took the title role during the Restoration, and William Mountfort in a version 'improved' by Thomas D'Urfey in 1691. Rare university and 'little' theatre productions apart, the play then disappeared from the stage for the best part of three centuries, until Jonathan Miller directed a production for the Old Vic in 1988. David Threlfall's Bussy, variously likened to Rambo and a sullen football hooligan, was widely felt to be understated, but there was a welcome for Sarah Kestelman's Tamyra, described by Christopher Edwards as a 'beautifully paced portrait of stealthy lust', and for Hugh Ross' Monsieur, which Michael Billington found 'calculating, dry and shifty, as he sends words winging to their targets like poisoned darts.'

Eastward Ho!
Chapman, Jonson and Marston

1605

Source

None known for the main plot, other than as a variation on
the biblical theme of the Prodigal Son. One of Masuccio's prose
tales in *Il Novellino* (1475) perhaps suggested the sub-plot of
Security's hapless assistance in his own cuckolding.

The story

Touchstone, a self-made goldsmith of Cheapside, has two
daughters: the proud and ambitious Gertrude and the modest
and prudent Mildred; and two apprentices, both gentlemen
born: the lazy but cunning Quicksilver and the industrious
Golding. Yearning to be a lady and ride in a coach, Gertrude
plans marriage to the outwardly suave but in truth penniless
Sir Petronel Flash. Gertrude has her mother's blessing, but
Touchstone refuses any dowry beyond a piece of land already
in her name. Quicksilver's drunken behaviour after the wedding
breakfast earns him his dismissal, and Touchstone also releases
Golding from his indentures – with the intention of encouraging a match between the worthy youth and his remaining
daughter. Quicksilver takes refuge with the usurer Security,
who is also bawd to his mistress, Sindefy. The pair plan to
finance Sir Petronel's projected voyage to Virginia in return
for the mortgaging of Gertrude's land, and to have Sindefy
taken on as her lady's maid. The lawyer Bramble witnesses the
deed, and Gertrude sets off into Essex towards her husband's
non-existent castle. Sir Petronel asks for Security's help in a
plot to take Bramble's wife aboard as his mistress. But his true
designs are on Security's own young bride, Winifred – in
whose seduction Security unwittingly assists during a convivial

send-off for the Virginian adventurers. The revellers get too drunk to heed the tavern drawer's warning of an impending storm, and embark in a boat to take them to their ship downriver – closely pursued by Security when he finds that his wife is missing. All the voyagers are wrecked, having got no further than Cuckold's Haven, where a butcher's boy gives a running commentary as one by one they wade ashore. Sir Petronel and Quicksilver – their ship now impounded and all hopes of restoring their fortunes dashed – are committed to jail at Touchstone's behest by none other than Golding, who has risen rapidly from newly liveried goldsmith to deputy alderman. Touchstone ignores all pleas for mercy, even from the sadder but wiser Gertrude, who finds refuge with her charitable sister. Golding is impressed by the jailer's reports of the devout behaviour of Quicksilver and Petronel, and by sending a false report of his own imprisonment gets Touchstone hastening to the jail, where he is able to witness for himself their apparent repentance. Touchstone duly forgives his errant son-in-law and pardons Security – now reconciled with Winifred – on condition that he gives Sindefy a dowry so that she and Quicksilver can be wed.

The authors and their collaboration

For Chapman's life, see under *Bussy D'Ambois*, p. 89; for Jonson's, under *Every Man in His Humour*, p. 57; and for Marston's, under *The Malcontent*, p. 73. While the seamless quality of the three writers' collaboration is remarkable, such multiple authorship in itself was not: of nearly 1,600 known plays of the period, it has thus been calculated that 370 were of anonymous authorship and almost as many again collaborative – and the actual proportion was probably higher, to judge from Henslowe's records of payments. Although collaboration was often a means of getting a topical story dramatised while interest was still strong, many collaborations were creative partnerships rather than journalistic expedients – a reminder that our own concern that a work of art should express its maker's unique sensibility is an inheritance from the romantics, whereas the Elizabethans more often sought to create representative than individual characters and qualities. We may thus view the preoccupation of our play's modern editors with seeking to slice it up between its three authors as misplaced; but for what it's worth the consensus is that Marston wrote most of Act I and II, i; Chapman from II, ii, to IV, i; and Jonson from there to the end – with all the authors interpolating passages into each other's work.

The historical context

The law of primogeniture (the inheritance of an estate by the firstborn son) ensured a steady entrance of younger brothers into professions such as the legal and clerical, while others preferred to take their chance as officers in the army – for which James' peace with Spain now limited the need. Increasingly, such hapless cast-offs of gentility were apprenticed into crafts where they might secure a future by their own efforts: and so both Quicksilver and Golding (unlike the apprentices of *The Shoemakers' Holiday*) are gentlemen born, but destined to join the ranks of the bourgeoisie.

Queen Elizabeth had been parsimonious over distributing honours, and was furious when Essex exercised his commander's right to distribute knighthoods in battle, since this led to ill-feeling among those who felt themselves no less deserving in civil life. James went to the other extreme: to 550 knights at the end of the previous reign, he added over 900 in the first four months of his own, declaring it an obligation that all those worth £40 a year should take a knighthood, mostly in return for ready money. This practice so debased the title that he was forced to invent an hereditary variation, the baronetcy, in 1611. It was the sneer at James' traffic in knighthoods (IV, i, 198–201), along with a reference to the proliferation of Scots (III, iii, 44–52), that landed Chapman and Jonson in prison.

The mixture of greed, adventurousness and credulity motivating Sir Petronel's projected voyage to Virginia was typical of such expeditions. The colony had been named in the Queen's honour by Sir Walter Raleigh in 1585: but its original settlers disappeared without trace, and Raleigh's expedition up the Orinoco in 1595, in which the Queen herself invested, proved fruitless in its quest for Eldorado – an entirely mythical land of gold, not at all unlike Captain Seagull's vision of Virginia (III, iii, 15–50).

The world of the play

Elizabethan comedy largely took place in some variation on Shakespeare's Illyria – an exotic, often timeless foreign land, where English clowns, knights, servants and rustics none the less littered the landscape. Though Shakespeare wrote on well into the Jacobean period, his comedies never strayed closer to home than the Windsor of *The Merry Wives*; but the new reign saw comedies of contemporary London life come into vogue, rooted in an everyday reality far from the never-lands of Virginia – or, for that matter, Essex.

Eastward Ho! sits, in attitude as in time of writing, between Dekker's *The Shoemakers' Holiday*, with its view of a sturdy and mutually supportive citizenry, and Beaumont's *The Knight of the Burning Pestle*, which presents Londoners as dullards whose morals are as dubious as their tastes. For where the worlds of those play are framed by unambiguous authorial views of 'the city', in *Eastward Ho!* the three authors leave their audience in search of an attitude. They present us with both the best and the worst of the city – perceived not only as place but as state of mind: as at once a source of industry and of petty-mindedness; as conducive to entrepreneurial energy but also to ruthless greed. So 'good' characters such as Touchstone and Golding tend to a meanness of spirit induced by the protestant work ethic and by boundaries of propriety which limit imagination as well as ambition; and the 'bad' at least display an openness to life beyond the walls, in an age for which the parable of the Prodigal Son became an exemplary as well as a cautionary tale.

If the characters thus evade easy judgement, their complexity has less to do with 'realism' than with that affectation or rigidity of mind which Jonson called a 'humour'. Touchstone's problem is that Thatcherite tendency common to moralisers who lack empathy: he believes that everybody else should be just like him, and rejects all dealings with those who are not 'one of us', even if they be his own wife and daughter. Security embodies the belief prevalent in Thatcher's heyday, displayed by Caryl Churchill in *Serious Money* (1987), that money can best be made from money itself, free of the risks run daily by the merchant, the farmer and the craftsman (II, ii, 119–41) – while Sir Petronel seeks fool's gold in the New World, and Quicksilver plans to salvage his fortunes by minting his own money (IV, i). This is a world, in short, of debased coinage, actual and moral, in which the self-proclaimed 'Touchstone' can offer only the trickle-down effect of Golding making his marriage feast from leftovers at the spendthrift's table.

It remains arguable how far the boy players in the original production would have heightened its satire by their assumed sophistication, muted it by their innocence, or merely titillated jaded palates by their precocity. But it can be no accident that the least equivocal characters in the play are not only the humblest but also the closest in age to their earliest actors, and so least in need of the disguises by which their comrades, however conventionally, aped their elders. Potkin, the drawer of the tavern, finding his gale warning ignored, sets out to rescue Winifred if not from the waves at least from the ignominy of discovery by her husband in her half-drowned state; while the butcher's boy Slitgut, though less charitable than his fellow menial, delivers a commentary from his vantage point on Cuckold's Haven that is worldly-wise beyond his years.

The title of *Eastward Ho!* was doubly ironic – in part wry acknowledgement of the recent use of *Westward Ho!* by Webster and Dekker; in part recognition that a voyage from London to the New World must set out in the opposite direction, down the Thames. Here, too, lies Essex, where Gertrude learns to be more clear-sighted than Don Quixote, who (also in 1605) reinvented a tavern as a castle from which to defend the honour of damsels in distress. Such knights of old, as Gertrude reflects, 'would help poor ladies; ours make poor ladies'.

If Gertrude learns her lesson, it is questionable whether Sindefy ends up defying sin or defiantly unbothered by its consequences – and even more questionable whether Quicksilver's repentance is more than expedient. Jonson, the presumed author of the last act, usually preferred a climactic feast to a marriage, and here celebrates a very unglamorous alliance – between an adventurer and a whore, with a dowry enforced from a usurer – reminiscent of the sort of punitive marriages meted out so recently by the Duke in *Measure for Measure*. And while Quicksilver is more resigned than Shakespeare's Lucio to 'marrying a punk', the commonsensical Sindefy is as silent as Isabella at the prospect of her own imposed match.

The playwright's craft

FORM Some critics distinguish between 'citizen comedies' such as *The Shoemaker's Holiday*, which celebrate their subject, and 'city comedies' like *The Dutch Courtesan*, which satirise it. As we have seen, *Eastward Ho!* is not so easily categorised, but since its satire is directed against all mental rigidities which lead to excess in behaviour, it may more helpfully be aligned with other 'humours' comedies in the Jonsonian tradition.

LANGUAGE The sudden and temporary shift from prose to verse at III, ii, 224, probably signifies a switch of authorship rather than anything to the play's purpose. Indeed, it is somewhat disruptive to the flow of the prose, which elsewhere tends to smooth out its authors' habitual weaknesses.

STRUCTURE The satire bites because it is carried along by a roistering comedy whose variety of character, incident, language and pace gives, for example, the outrageous *faux* gentility of Gertrude or the garrulous fantasising of Seagull a prominence which outweighs their importance to the plot.

CONVENTIONS   If Quicksilver follows the path of the Prodigal Son, it is worth noting (as Touchstone does at IV, ii, 83–4) that Golding's progress is kin to that of a 'worthy apprentice' whose legend has survived in pantomime form to the present day – that of Dick Whittington, minus the cat.

STAGE PRACTICE   Slitgut enters at the start of Act IV 'discovering Cuckold's Haven above', and then climbs 'this famous tree' in order to hang up the traditional horns. A temporary pole or structural column must thus have enabled the actor to ascend from main stage to balcony, whence he could watch the voyagers wading ashore along his own and the opposite bank. The reference to the 'middle door' in the opening stage direction confirms that the Blackfriars had three doors upstage.

In performance

Eastward Ho! was first staged at the indoor Blackfriars in the summer of 1605, and three early printed texts suggest immediate popularity – probably renewed when the satire against James had been excised, since the play was presented at court before the King in 1614. Nahum Tate adapted it in 1685 as *Cuckold's Haven*, with no greater success than Garrick's revival of the original in 1751, though Charlotte Lennox's reworking of 1775, as *Old City Manners*, was more favourably received. Other than in student revivals, the play then disappeared from the stage until it was given in three versions by the Mermaid Theatre – first in a fit-up staging at the Royal Exchange in 1953; then in the theatre's permanent home at Puddle Dock (close by Blackfriars) in 1962, a production which Kenneth Tynan found 'a model of organised exuberance'; and finally, unsuccessfully, in a musical version in 1981. The RSC revived the play at the Swan in Stratford in 2002, in an admired production by Lucy Pitman-Wallace. Several critics singled out for praise Amanda Drew's Gertrude – in Benedict Nightingale's typical view, 'a bleating, lisping mix of the imperturbably self-delighted and the hilariously fake genteel'.

The Dutch Courtesan
John Marston

1605

Source

The main plot is derived from an inserted story in the French
pastoral romance *Les Bergeries de Juliette* (1585), with philoso-
phical underpinning from two of Montaigne's *Essays* (1581–88,
as translated by John Florio, 1603). The tricks in the sub-plot
were familiar from old farces and the literature of roguery.

The story

The rakish Freevill, planning to marry Beatrice, demure elder
daughter of Sir Hubert Subboys, means to cast off his mistress,
the Dutch courtesan Franceschina. His cold-blooded friend
Malheureux, accompanying him to meet Franceschina, finds
himself enchanted by her wit and charm. The courtesan is
enraged when she learns of Freevill's desertion, and promises
to become Malheureux' mistress if he will kill his friend and,
as token of the deed, bring her a ring given to Freevill by
Beatrice. Malheureux cannot extinguish his desires, but confesses the plan to his friend, and the pair agree to pretend to
quarrel at the celebrations for Freevill's betrothal to Beatrice,
and then to report Freevill as killed in the resulting duel.
Freevill promises to go into hiding, and to reveal himself only
if Malheureux faces prosecution – but in fact he means to cure
him of his infatuation, and, disguising himself as a young
pander, tells Beatrice and Sir Lionel of his own death and of
Malheureux' planned visit to Franceschina. At the courtesan's
lodgings, Malheureux is overheard 'confessing' to Franceschina
and thrown into prison. In the comic sub-plot, Cocledemoy,
a parasitical fantastick, plays a series of practical jokes on the
devious vintner Mulligrub, the last of which lands Mulligrub

in jail. On the morning of both men's execution, Freevill and Cocledemoy reveal their deceptions. Malheureux is shocked out of love for Franceschina, Mulligrub cured of his cheating ways, and the marriage of Beatrice and Freevill proceeds – as does that of her younger sister Crispinella and her suitor Tysefew, whose duels of verbal wit have finally brought them to admit their mutual attraction. Franceschina is packed off to jail.

The author and his work

For Marston's life, see under *The Malcontent*, p. 73. There is some dispute as to whether this play preceded or (as I agree) followed Marston's collaboration with Chapman and Jonson on *Eastward Ho!* but it is certainly a product of the same year.

The historical context

The Dutch Courtesan is full of quotations (over forty, by one scholarly count) from the *Essays* of Montaigne, the French writer who virtually invented the form, and whose English translator, John Florio, invested them with his own fluency and gusto. (Most are from an essay in the third book, 'Upon Some Verses in Virgil'.) With its infusion of personality into philosophy, the essay form almost accidentally became the first to engage in 'psychological' explorations of human experience, through an internal monologue in which the objective reality of the subject and the writer's (perhaps conflicting) feelings about it mesh into a revelation of individuality – as opposed to the typicality which art more usually sought to represent, or the eccentricities which it claimed, through mockery, to cure.

At its best, the dramatic soliloquy – as in the clear and recent example of *Hamlet* – achieved a similar effect; but Marston, more traditionally, employs contrasting characters to dramatise conflicting opinions, and this can lead to debates redolent more of artifice than feeling. In just such a debate at the opening of the play, Freevill appears to be stating an opposing case to Malheureux as much out of delight in disputation as in the sexual freedom he is ostensibly defending. This is very much an argument between young men schooled (as Marston himself had been) in the Inns of Court – the 'third university' of the land, whose location in London made it as much a finishing school where the offspring of the well-to-do might polish their manners and sharpen their wits as an academy for the training of aspirant lawyers. Significantly, 'Give me my fee!' is Freevill's clinching line, to an imagined clientele of grateful whores.

When Malheureux first finds himself falling in love with Franceschina (I, ii, 79–80), he declares: 'Now cold blood defend me! What a proportion afflicts me!' This reflects a continuing belief in the concept of the four 'humours' or bodily fluids – blood, phlegm, yellow bile and black bile – whose balance (or lack of it) was thought to determine human temperament and health. Cold blood suggested a tendency to melancholia and proneness to sudden outbursts of passion – a classical diagnosis of an offence against the classical ideal of the 'golden mean'. Where Aristotle had argued philosophically for this, the coolly modern Montaigne does so from experience. So the historical context for this play is intellectual more than it is social or political – reflecting the tension between old and new ideas, expressed in traditional and innovative forms, which gave such energy to the age.

The world of the play

The Dutch Courtesan deals with strata of society more familiar in later 'comedies of manners', when the focus of action had shifted from the City to the West End, than in other city comedies of its time – not least in the apparent lack of occupation of all but a few minor characters (the vintner Mulligrub being the sole exception – apart, of course, from those whose trade is sex). Nor is there that close specificity of location which distinguished *Eastward Ho!* as it does Jonson's London plays: not even the prison in which Malheureux and Mulligrub are held gets a name; and it is unclear whether Franceschina

has City lodgings or lives across the river, in the 'entertainment district' on Bankside (where customers for the public
playhouses rubbed shoulders with those for the brothels and
animal-baiting arenas). We might, for all the local colour we
get, be in Illyria – or the supposed 'Vienna' of *Measure for
Measure*. Given the lost potential for 'recognition laughs', the
near-anonymity of the setting is surprising.

Least of all does Cocledemoy appear to have a local habi-
tation or a trade, though maybe his ill-assimilated learning
suggests a hanger-on at the Inns of Court – a sort of failed
eternal student scraping acquaintance and sustenance as the
'knavishly witty City companion' he is dubbed. Yet his serial
conning of the Mulligrubs seems no less obsessive than any
obsessions of theirs he may be intending to cure. His eventual
claim that it has all been done simply 'for wit's sake' places
him not so much in the world of 'humours' comedy as in that
of the mischievous Vice figure from the old morality plays, or
of Brighella, the wily servant of the Italian *commedia*.

He and the Mulligrubs interact with the characters of the
main plot only at the very beginning and end of the play.
Echoing Freevill, Cocledemoy gets his own set speech at the
start in defence of prostitution as a worthy profession – deem-
ing it 'most worshipful of the twelve companies' since, unlike
the others, it does not thrive by the loss or suffering of its
customers (I, ii, 30–56); and at the end his 'cure' of Mulligrub
reflects Freevill's of Malheureux. Yet in performance these
similarities are less apparent than the gear-shifts from higher
to lower in each act.

As for Crispinella and Tysefew, they are good exemplars of
the verbally bantering couple who, like Shakespeare's Beatrice
and Benedick in *Much Ado*, sublimate a reluctantly acknowledged affection beneath constant raillery. They seem at times
to be in a play of their own, and though ostensibly part of the
main action they affect it scarcely at all – but then neither does
Marston's complaisant Beatrice, who pales into insipidity beside her sprightly sister (in the 'real' world, Crispinella would
probably have made a more compatible bride for Freevill). As

for Malheureux, so excessively is he a 'man of snow' that when (like Angelo in *Measure*) he does give way to passion, it is un-governable; yet Freevill, who initially argues for sexual free-dom, ends up driving his friend back to chastity. Epony-mously unhappy, Malheureux at the end of the play gains his life but no other consolation. A few months in the arms of Franceschina might have taught him useful lessons about his fellow creatures, not to mention his own sexuality.

The problem with Franceschina is that she is given the humanity of a genuine passion for Freevill which breaks the bounds both of her typology and (to the old bawd Mary Faugh's disgust) of her trade; but she is then shunted back – both by accent and by action – into being an easy hate-figure for the audience. True, a good actress will mute the risibility of her cod-Dutch accent (and Marston makes a better stab at phonetic fluency than Shakespeare in *Henry V*, where Kate's schoolgirl English is almost as naff as the excruciating Irish and Welsh). And given that the role may originally have gone to the prettiest boy in the company, the accent may even have added a tinge of ambiguous eroticism to an 'otherness' that (as with Shylock) can either heighten sympathy or stiffen prejudice. But, like her counterpart Angellica Bianca in Aphra Behn's Restoration comedy *The Rover* (1677), she remains a loose end both morally and dramatically at the close of the play (although she, unlike Angellica, has the title role). There cannot be many who, seeing the other characters' faults for-given, are not disquieted when this victim of her own passions is consigned to 'the extremest whip and jail'. (Does not that other Beatrice, of *Much Ado*, seek proof of love with a very similar injunction: 'Kill Claudio'?) Simply, Marston ducks the issue to which he has earlier given prominence: a comparison between the ethics of capitalism and those of the brothel.

This is, then, a play in which the expectations and con-ventions of comedy constantly rub up against the worries and wounds of 'real life'. It is neither better nor worse for that: Shakespeare's so-called 'problem plays' work in much the same way, and perhaps we should no less allow Marston the privilege of using comedy to make an audience uncomfortable about being presented with an over-comfortable conclusion.

The playwright's craft

FORM Though usually regarded as a city comedy, *The Dutch Courtesan* may, despite its familiar urban setting, also be viewed as more in the mould of tragi-comedy, since it raises issues of tragic import – the consequences of intemperate passion, the nature of trust, the imminence of mortality – but gives all a reconciliatory climactic twist.

LANGUAGE The movements from prose into verse occur more or less according to one's expectations that the more solemn and reflective moment should be poetically elevated – though in practice the verse tends to seem rather dutiful after the swift-paced, inventive and action-driven prose. As so often, Marston is at his richest linguistically with his furthest-out characters: thus Cocledemoy's language is, in one critic's nice description, 'pure skat, real Ella Fitzgerald stuff'. *The Dutch Courtesan* is also one of the most scatological plays of an age which did not shrink from the naming of bodily parts and functions, here as much those of excretion as reproduction.

STRUCTURE Although some critics have seen Cocledemoy as 'a comic version of Freevill', and Mulligrub of Malheureux, in performance such resemblances are submerged in a 'sub-plot' which quickly takes off on its own account and at times threatens to take over the play.

CONVENTIONS Though Freevill anticipates the witty rake of Restoration comedy – the man of strong sexual appetite just waiting to be reformed by a 'good marriage' – the choice he faces between *virgo* and *meretrix*, chaste maiden and cunning courtesan, goes back at least to the the Roman comedies of Plautus. Similarly, some of the descriptions in the 'Dramatis Personae' – of Tysefew as 'a blunt gallant' or Caqueteur as 'a prattling gull' – were to remain familiar into the Restoration period and beyond. As ever, we note the ease with which disguises enable deception – whether Freevill's of his own father and beloved, or Cocledemoy in the multiple versions of himself which infallibly baffle the Mulligrubs.

STAGE PRACTICE   The play begins at night, as the lanterns carried by the three pages would have signified whether in the afternoon light of a public playhouse or in the darkened auditorium of a private theatre. We do not know if the lighting of the indoor stage could have been adjusted so that the lanterns served practically to illuminate it.

In performance

The Dutch Courtesan, like *Eastward Ho!*, was first staged at the indoor Blackfriars playhouse in the summer of 1605 by the boys' company known as the Children of the Revels, whose oldest members would by now be seventeen. A continuing stage life is suggested by the record of two performances at court in 1613 by an adult company, the Lady Elizabeth's Men, who by then evidently owned the play. But for three centuries thereafter it was to be seen only in adapted versions – mainly drawing on the Cocledemoy sub-plot, which even surfaced during the Commonwealth as the brief 'droll', *The Cheater Cheated*. Aphra Behn's *The Revenge* (1680), characteristically more sympathetic to Franceschina, was in turn adapted by Christopher Bullock as *A Woman's Revenge* in 1715, and during the vogue for ballad opera as *Love and Revenge* in 1729. Marston's original was restored to the stage by Joan Littlewood's Theatre Workshop at Stratford East in 1954, and again in 1959; and the play was among the early productions of the National Theatre, playing at Chichester and the Old Vic in 1964 under the direction of William Gaskill. There were later 'fringe' productions at the Man in the Moon Theatre, London, in 1990, with the roles of Franceschina and Beatrice doubled, and at the Orange Tree Theatre, Richmond, in 1992.

A Yorkshire Tragedy
Anonymous

1605

Source

The pamphlet account of *Two Most Unnatural Bloody Murders*, entered for publication in June 1605. Walter Calverley, who refused to plead at his subsequent trial, was pressed to death for the murder of his two children on the following 5 August.

The story

Two servants greet their fellow, Sam, returning after a long absence in London. While there, his master has not only taken a wife who has borne him three children, but consumed his inheritance in riotous living, and now needs his brother at university to stand security for him. The Wife despairs at her husband's behaviour, which threatens to 'consume his credit and his house'; she is even more concerned that his plight has provoked him only to rage and self-pity instead of repentance. Sure enough, when the Husband appears he berates his wife for his own misfortunes, and orders her to sell her dowry to support his indulgence. He spurns the place at court which the Wife persuades her uncle to secure him, ignores the remonstrances of friends, and is only made more furious when he is defeated in a duel provoked when the Husband impugns the Wife's virtue. The Master of his brother's college arrives with news that the brilliant young scholar has been thrown into jail for the Husband's debts. Leaving the Master with the promise of 'a sufficient answer', the Husband, despairing of his situation, severely wounds his wife, kills two of his sons, and sets out to murder the youngest, which is away at nurse. The Master raises a hue and cry which overtakes the Husband, who, begging a last meeting with his Wife and confronted with the bodies of the murdered infants, is at last remorseful, and gains her forgiveness before being hauled off to jail.

The authorship

The play almost certainly reached the stage in the summer of 1605, after Calverley's arraignment but before his trial and execution – described in a later pamphlet, whereas here, as in the source, the murderer's fate remains uncertain. The title-page attribution to Shakespeare in the first printed edition of 1608 led to the play's inclusion in the Third Folio of his works published in 1663 and among the 'apocryphal' plays appended to various later collected editions. This is now thought unlikely, although claims are still made for his authorship of the noticeably more forceful Scene i. Other attributions have been to Thomas Heywood, mainly on grounds of subject matter; George Wilkins – whose The Miseries of Enforced Marriage (c. 1607) can be viewed as a kind of 'prequel' to our play; and, now thought a strong probability on stylistic evidence for Scene i, Thomas Middleton.

The historical context

We are reminded throughout the play that the Husband's behaviour brings not only pain to his wife and children, but dishonour to an ancient family name. Landed gentility did not always signify a lineage such as that of the Calverleys, for it could be bought as well as inherited. Between the Dissolution of the Monasteries in 1539 and the outbreak of the Civil Wars in 1642, of the 960 families in Yorkshire who were regarded as gentry, nearly 400 were thus forced to sell all or part of their estates: yet the total of landed families in the county increased from 557 in 1540 to 679 in 1642. These figures tell their own story of social mobility, with new wealth always ready to buy its way to social status, as old families suffered the indignity of descent into yeomanry or worse. The position of the Calverleys was all the more difficult because as recusants – Catholics who refused even nominal conformity to the rites of the Church of England – they were subject to fines and their lands to forfeiture. When Walter Calverley's father died in 1596 even the guardianship of the son and heir passed out of the family; and by 1602, shortly after Walter's coming of age, the whole estate had been put in trust. No wonder, perhaps, that the original of our 'Husband' felt so alienated and impotently angry; and our own times tell us how readily such men may turn their anger upon the soft and available targets of wife and children. Calverley failed to kill his youngest child only because it was away 'at nurse' – a sign of a residual clinging to social status, for only gentlefolk put out their infants to be breast-fed by others (as, we recall, was Juliet, whose Nurse, like so many, remained a surrogate mother). At his trial, Walter suffered the agonies of being pressed to death because he refused to plead, thus sparing his wife and surviving child the confiscation of his goods which would have followed a formal conviction. In death as in life, the tragedy of this Yorkshire family remained inseparable from the socio-economic realities of its time and place.

The world of the play

The world of *A Yorkshire Tragedy* is one of 'fearful melancholy, ungodly sorrow'. Its ineluctably despairing Husband 'walks heavily as if his soul were earth' – as it might be, upon the heath of *King Lear*, which was probably written in the same year, and whose nihilism is echoed when the Wife declares of the Husband: 'Nothing will please him until all be nothing' (Sc. iii). Early in the play she expresses the belief that he is behaving as if 'some vexed spirit / Had got his form upon him' (Sc. ii) – and at the end the repentant Husband seems to endure the physical casting out of an evil spirit: 'Now glides the Devil from me, / Departs from every joint, heaves up my nails' (Sc. x). So is the author of *A Yorkshire Tragedy* presenting us with a portrait of diabolical possession – of evil so pure that its casting out leaves the Husband able only to compound his sin by despairing (as had Dr Faustus) of divine providence?

Or do we seek for a psychological explanation to fit the known facts of the affair? Did the real Calverley 'simply' suffer from an extreme form of what the Jacobeans knew as melancholy and we call depression? Or do we diagnose him across the void of time as a paranoid schizophrenic – bearing in mind, with Freud, that since Sophocles' *Oedipus* the drama has portrayed such conditions long before they were given medical labels? In such a state of mind, to murder one's own children to spare them continuing so tainted a family line might carry a perverted kind of logic. And we can never know whether the baggage of hearsay brought to the play by the original audience and actors would have lent subtextual continuity to the mention in Scene i of Calverley's earlier mistress 'still puling for his love'. Though she is never mentioned again in the play, this first love is prominent alike in the ballad and in the later *Miseries of Enforced Marriage* (where the abandoned woman commits suicide); and the Husband's repeated references to his wife as a whore and his children as bastards may thus be turning upon them his own guilt for a troth plighted and broken – which would have made his marriage adulterous in the eyes of the church.

If we assume the audience to have been well versed in the scandal, we have to stretch the boundaries of the play-world to include such external factors, irrelevant though these would be to the consideration of most plays; and they inevitably increase the inaccessibility of *A Yorkshire Tragedy* over time. Should we therefore simply dismiss it as a piece of proto-tabloid shock-horror? Though the haste with which it was written and rushed to the stage may suggest journalistic sensationalism, the play does somehow transcend such ephemeral origins, not least in the author's decision to depict only the final catastrophe, which gives the action a tightness of focus and a concision rare in Jacobean drama. A formal precedent has been sought in the early Tudor 'interludes' (not least because the impersonal nomenclature of 'Husband' and 'Wife' suggests a striving for typicality going back to *Everyman* and *Mankind*); but in my own view *A Yorkshire Tragedy* comes closer to more recent one-act plays which turn on single events, or even the definition of a mood, rather than developing an action with all its causes and consequences. Notably, the foreshortening of events and of language, and the lack of nuances in favour of emotions and attitudes simply and starkly presented, are reminiscent of the expressionist dramas of the period around the First World War – and so too is the subject matter, of a strident yet embattled male sexuality.

While the Husband behaves without sympathy for or even recognition of the feelings of others, every kind of humiliation is also inflicted upon him: the physical beating he suffers at the hands of the Gentleman, the verbal assault of the Master, the spiritual suffering he at last admits at the sight of his dead children. As in Strindberg's pre-expressionistic *The Father* (1887), at the end we do not know whether he will live or die. Again like *The Father*, this is an uncomfortable play in that we are denied the satisfaction of either tragic catharsis or readily attributable blame. As I write, today's tabloids are mixing gushing sympathy for the families of two children murdered in a Cambridgeshire tragedy with hysterical repugnance for their presumed murderers. In this Yorkshire tragedy of two children murdered long ago, is the Wife's belief in her husband's remorse the loving folly of a 'battered woman' succumbing to blandishments which would readily turn to renewed violence? Or proper Christian forgiveness of those who know not what they do? The play is none the worse for raising more questions than it answers.

The playwright's craft

FORM   The play is usually regarded as a 'domestic tragedy' in the concern it shares with *Arden of Faversham* (c. 1590) and *A Woman Killed with Kindness* (1603) with the affairs of middle-class folk rather than those which touched the nobility or state – though the issues it raises are of more than private import.

Like *Arden*, it has to do with murder, yet it also explores, as does *A Woman Killed*, the nature of the marital relationship which is at its core.

STRUCTURE Unless we share the belief, which I believe mistaken, that the play is an inexplicably separated fifth act to Wilkins' *Miseries of Enforced Marriage* (which ends with a premature reconciliation), we are left with a work of an hour or so in length – common enough for interludes of the early Tudor period and later with the advent of curtain-raisers and afterpieces, but unusual in an age when an audience's expectations were of at least the 'two hours' traffic of our stage'. The title-page description of *A Yorkshire Tragedy* as 'one of the four plays in one' raises the intriguing possibility of a double or even quadruple bill: if so, it is possible that Scene i, almost certainly by a different hand, was added later to contextualise the play in the absence of its companion pieces, which remained unpublished and are now for ever lost.

In performance

We rely upon the title-page claim in the first quarto text of 1608 for the information that the play was first presented by Shakespeare's company, the King's Men, at the Globe, and beyond this nothing is known of its early staging. During the eighteenth century two adaptations – Joseph Mitchell's *The Fatal Extravagance* and F. G. Waldron's *The Prodigal* – were based on *A Yorkshire Tragedy*, but the original was not seen again until given as a benefit performance at the Federal Street Theatre, Boston, in 1847. A Russian translation reached the St Petersburg stage in 1895. When the play at last returned to England, it was appropriately in provincial productions – at Birmingham Rep in 1958; at the Theatre Royal, York, in 1972; and in an adaptation touring out of Doncaster in 1979, which stressed the problem of violence against women in present-day Yorkshire. London productions followed at the Old Half Moon Theatre in 1982 and at the Grove Theatre in 1991.

Volpone
Ben Jonson

1606

Source

Legacy-hunting is a recurrent classical theme, and satirising
humankind through the medium of a bestiary also goes back to
Aesop, while there are echoes of the late-medieval morality
tradition in Jonson's personification of vices and virtues; but he
assimilates all these elements into an entirely original work.

The story

The wealthy Venetian aristocrat Volpone, assisted by his wily
servant Mosca, feigns mortal illness to feed the hopes of a
succession of dupes, who bring him lavish gifts in hopes of
being made his heir. The lawyer Voltore presents him with a
piece of gold plate; the merchant Corvino arrives with a rich
pearl and a diamond; and the deaf and senile Corbaccio not
only offers a purse of gold coins, but promises to disinherit
his own son, Bonario. Mosca encourages all their hopes, and
when he tells his master of the beauty of Corvino's young wife,
Celia, Volpone is determined to see her. Close by Corvino's
house, an English visitor, Sir Politic Would-be, is discussing
his eccentric interests with a young fellow-countryman, Peregrine, when Mosca and Nano, Volpone's dwarf, arrive, disguised as zanies, to set up a stall for their master, who appears
in the guise of a renowned mountebank. His sales pitch draws
Celia to watch from her window, until a furious Corvino arrives
to disperse the crowd and scold his wife. But Volpone, charmed
by Celia, sends Mosca to tell Corvino that the mountebank's
oils have revived him, and that his physicians now prescribe a
young woman, 'lusty and full of juice, to sleep by him'. Assured
by Mosca that Volpone is impotent, Corvino duly offers up

his wife to the 'invalid'. After shaking off the attentions of the talkative Lady Would-be, Volpone, left alone with Celia, fails to overcome her virtue, and finally attempts rape; but he is thwarted by Bonario, who has concealed himself to learn the truth about his disinheritance. When the case is brought before the magistrates Mosca succeeds in making the youth appear an ingrate plotting to murder his father, and Voltore persuades the court that Celia and Bonario are the guilty parties. Sir Politic discourses with Peregrine about his projects and purchases, but Peregrine is accused by Lady Would-be of being a courtesan in disguise, and humbles the knight by persuading him to conceal himself in a tortoise-shell while a search of his house reveals all his 'intelligence' to be culled from playbooks. Volpone, who has had Mosca put it about that he is dead and that Mosca is his heir, watches gleefully while Mosca taunts the legacy-hunters, and disguises himself in order to join in their humiliation. But the trio confess their own misdeeds to the magistrates to wreak their revenge on Mosca – who assists in his own downfall by trying to spring his 'fox trap' on his master. In falling out, the pair reveal each other's duplicity, and the magistrates mete out punishment to the fraudsters and victims alike.

The author and his work

For a general outline of Jonson's life, see *Every Man in His Humour*, p. 57. Shortly after the staging of that play in 1598 he had converted to Catholicism during his imprisonment for duelling, and when he tried his hand for the first time at tragedy, with *Sejanus* in 1603, by his own account he was called before the Privy Council for its supposed papist leanings. In 1605 he was again briefly in jail for his part in *Eastward Ho!* and was soon to come under renewed suspicion for his closeness to Catesby, a chief conspirator in the Gunpowder Plot. Despite this, and perhaps because *Sejanus* found no greater favour with audiences than with the authorities, he turned to writing masques and other courtly entertainments, which was his main activity and source of livelihood until 1609. During this time *Volpone* – said to have been written in just five weeks – was Jonson's only new comedy for the public stage.

The historical context

When we refer to this period as the 'golden age' of English drama, we are using a term which had much more precise connotations at the time. Elizabethans and Jacobeans, so far from believing they lived in a golden age, looked back further even than the 'golden age' of Latin literature to the Golden Age of ancient myth, when Cronus ruled over a tranquil time of eternal spring in which men lived without labour in harmony with the brute creation. In this world, paradoxically, there was no need of gold as a form of currency – so Volpone's famous opening speech refers rather to the present 'age of gold', in which the precious metal is a measure of material wealth which can all too easily become, as it has for Volpone, an object of veneration or virtual worship. Such an obsession offended against the Aristotelian ideal of the 'golden mean', a middle way between renunciation of the world and excessive indulgence in its pleasures. And the alchemical quest to distil gold from base metals (the theme of Jonson's next play) continued, as did the plundering of South America for gold both real and (as in the quest for Eldorado) imaginary. That Jonson chose to set his play in Venice was in this context entirely appropriate: this Italian city state, at the hub of the trade routes of the early modern world, was not only a centre of mercantile capitalism and the usury needed to support it (the subject of Shakespeare's *The Merchant of Venice*), but of the magnificence of urban adornment this enabled and sustained.

The world of the play

Volpone sets two worlds in ironic tension: the teeming, exuberant world of the Renaissance, exulting in its own energy and enjoyment of material wealth; and the world of spiritual poverty which was its underbelly, in which exploitation of one's fellows supplanted older values of kinship and hospitality. Volpone's opening speech thus translates belief in God into worship of gold: indeed, Jonson is more realistically 'for all time' than Shakespeare in recognising that economic imperatives are now more significant than spiritual ones in driving people's lives. The greed thus validated encourages willing self-deception – as soft-sold by Volpone or, in our terms, during the 'dotcom' stock-market frenzy.

As audience, we have a bifocal vision of Volpone, seeing his simulated illness at once as a symptom of a pervasive moral decline and as a brilliant impersonation, a delightful comic performance. Volpone shares this delight. He is indeed a voluptuary: not of the sexual desires which deflect him nor even of the riches which provide self-affirmation, but in 'the cunning purchase of my wealth' – the brilliance of the acting by which he demonstrates his power of manipulative control over his inferiors. So long as he lets the victims believe it is they who are in control, all is well: but the whole crazy construct collapses when Volpone's endgame results in their humiliation.

Volpone needs applause – indeed, the one glimpse we are allowed of his past self is during the wooing of Celia, when he recalls the ladies' approval of his performances as a child actor (III, vii, 159–64). He portrays Celia as every kind of creature but herself, and attempts her seduction by promising delight through role-play – the taking of 'modern forms' and 'many shapes' which he imagines she will desire both to share and applaud. Thwarted of this hope, he throws off his final disguise and so invites punishment not just because he has been betrayed by Mosca but because this betrayal has lost him his only audience. He covets attention as much as he covets gold.

Mosca, while he also exults in his powers of dissembling and outdoes Volpone in manipulative skills, never loses sight of his own materialistic ends; and only a single flawed assumption – that his master would prefer poverty to punishment – prevents him achieving these. As for the *avocatori*, or magistrates, they are shown to be little better than those they judge, whether competing for the supposedly wealthy Mosca as son-in-law or distributing punishments as much concerned with class distinctions as with crimes.

In this sense *Volpone* is a deeply serious play, which holds up a mirror to the unnatural man that the acquisitive society breeds. But it is also, of course, one of the most continuously and ingeniously comic plays in our national repertoire – or, perhaps more accurately, a rapid succession of interlocking situation comedies, each intrinsically funny, but each also in danger of bursting like a bubble if and when it touches another. As in farce, it is Mosca's task to provoke yet further laughter by improvising expedients 'on the fly', to keep all these little bubbles of self-deception floating safely apart.

Sir Politic observes other such worlds as a tourist in Venice, and infallibly misreads them. He provides excellent if incidental mirth, with a delight in irrelevance and insignificance refreshingly different from the other characters' calculation of their every word and action. Yet beneath it all his own self-obsession, if less dangerous, is no less absolute, and he has so persuaded himself that he is an astute practitioner of statecraft that he is readily fooled by Peregrine's warning that he is suspected of spying. And in the end his own protective bubble of a tortoise-shell – surely as surreal as it is symbolic – proves no less impregnable than any other.

In a play by Shakespeare, Bonario and Celia would have been (as Coleridge wished them) young lovers, or become so; and their marriage would have brought some harmony even to this fractured state. Yet Jonson denies them more dramatic energy than is absolutely necessary, and even qualifies their virtue with hints of self-righteousness. In the end, he bestows only a premature inheritance on Bonario and a tripled dowry on Celia – before packing her off to her father, who presumably fixed up the original mismatch with Corvino. The lonely futures of the only two innocents in a play which condemns acquisitive greed are to be cushioned by . . . cash in hand.

So Jonson wants us at once to delight in the multiplicity of comic incident in his play, and also to think about his refusal, as here, to observe the conventions: in this way, he confronts us with the spiritual emptiness of a society in which, it seems, there is no moral order to be climactically restored. This a crueller and less accessible play than Jonson's later master-pieces, *The Alchemist* and *Bartholomew Fair* – not least because of its very complex mix of the verbal alchemy of Volpone and Mosca with a fairground, carnivalesque inversion of expected moral values. The play leaves us as dizzy as the *avocatori*, but it also demands that we, not they, make the final judgements.

The playwright's craft

FORM   In his prefatory 'Epistle', Jonson acknowledges that some may question whether he has met the true requirements of a comedy; and he appeals to ancient precedent to show that the form has as much claim to 'imitate justice and instruct' as to 'stir up gentle affection'. In our less generically prescriptive age we might consider *Volpone* an early example of a 'black' or 'dark' comedy, self-consistent on its own terms, and meeting the simple expectation that a comedy should make us laugh.

STRUCTURE   The great 'set-pieces' of the play are purpose-fully varied in their structure. The bedroom sequence of the first act presents us with a series of separate comic 'routines' between Volpone, Mosca, and the succession of gulls; the mountebank episode in the second act is essentially a comic solo, allowing Volpone to burst forth from his invalid coughs and grunts with sustained oratorical bravura; while the court-room encounters bring together those who have so carefully been kept apart – the first permitting Mosca's quick wit to triumph over the truth, the second leading to the conver-gence of all the intrigues and their implosion in Volpone's gesture of defiance and self-defeat.

LANGUAGE   The doggerel incursions of Volpone's 'family' and his own spiel as a mountebank apart, this is Jonson's first play entirely in blank verse, and its variety is astonishing, from

Volpone's lavish sensualities to Would-be's splendid inanities. The love of lists – whether of Volpone's possessions, Androgyno's invented ancestry, the sensuous luxuries promised to Celia, or the minutiae of Sir Politic's daily round – is only the most explicit deployment of Jonson's essentially accumulative verbal technique: down-to-earth even at its most allusively metaphorical, connecting with our daily lives rather than our dreams. Volpone, whether poet of possessions, mountebank or would-be lover, remains self-aware, showing off even to himself. Mosca veers from the need to meet his clients' whims and whinges (and to show a calculated complicity with his master) to an impish solipsism which reaches an extreme of self-delight in his soliloquy at III, i.

CONVENTIONS *Volpone* is peopled by human beings, however corrupt, not by the bestiary whence Jonson draws his characters' names. Fables – ever since Aesop's in the sixth century BC, and including the medieval 'Fox Who Feigned Death', often cited as a model for this play – set out to show people behaving like animals, not animals like people. While it can be entertaining to dress up Volpone as a fox, Mosca as a fly, Corbaccio as a crow, or Sir Pol as a parrot, this is not really to Jonson's point: and to universalise the play into folklore is to dull the edge of its satire. The names hint neither more nor less at the characters' propensities than such contemporary 'charactonyms' as Aguecheek, Overdone, Malevole and Littlewit, or the Fainalls and Dolittles of later times.

STAGE PRACTICE A tester (or canopied four-poster) bed would almost certainly have been among the properties of the King's Men, perhaps on castors to enable its trundling out as required for the first and third acts. The play makes no unusual demands on expected resources, though it does require elaborate costuming – perhaps (as in the Italian *commedia*, to which there are several allusions) suggestive of the species of its nominal bestiary. Volpone himself would need numerous costume changes for his switches between personae.

In performance

Volpone was first played at the Globe by the King's Men in 1606, with Richard Burbage presumably taking the title role, and also, as the dedication attests, at the Universities of Oxford and Cambridge. Its immediate popularity continued into the Caroline period, and from the Restoration well into the eighteenth century, during the earlier part of which James Quin evidently made the role of Volpone very much his own, as did Robert Wilks that of Mosca. In 1771 a version pruned by George Colman supplanted the original, and after 1785 the play disappeared from the stage altogether for well over a century, until the experimental Phoenix Society revived it for two performances in 1921. Since then it has become one of the most frequently revived non-Shakespearean plays of its time, with over fifty productions before the end of the century, and a wide variety of interpretations. Both Wilfrid Lawson at the Malvern Festival of 1936 and Donald Wolfit at the Westminster Theatre in 1938 played Volpone as a man in the prime of life, devouring experience with gusto, while Ralph Richardson, in George Devine's Stratford production of 1952, was a magnifico verging on decrepitude. The photographically real Venice of this production was followed in 1955 by a modern-dress version from Joan Littlewood's Theatre Workshop, with Mosca as a spiv arriving on a bike and Sir Pol carrying a snorkel – while a version in Stratford, Ontario, directed by David William in 1971 set the play in a *fin de siècle* Venice with the Would-bes brash Texan tourists. Of two productions for the National Theatre, Tyrone Guthrie's in 1968 was a veritable aviary, its birds of prey replete with beaks and talons, while Peter Hall's in 1977 restored a sense of the Renaissance, with an aloof Paul Scofield as Volpone and John Gielgud as a Bertie Woosterish Sir Pol. The first RSC revival followed in 1983, directed by Bill Alexander in the intimate Other Place. Here, Richard Griffiths' bulky Volpone loomed very large indeed, but set a slow pace which was sustained by some ponderous verse speaking.

The Revenger's Tragedy
Cyril Tourneur?

1606

Source

The Lussurioso–Castiza plot strand may derive, via Painter's
Palace of Pleasure (1566–67), from one of the tales in Margaret
of Navarre's *Heptameron* (1559), or the real-life assassination
of a Medici on which it was based; while Lussurioso's surprising of his parents has been traced to a 1587 translation of the
Aethiopica of Heliodorus. But the treatments are distinctive
and integrated into an action which, while full of allusions to
other contemporary works, is otherwise original.

The story

Vindice seeks to avenge the death of his betrothed, Gloriana,
poisoned by the lecherous but now ageing Duke when she
spurned his advances. Vindice's brother Hippolito, in the service of the Duke's son Lussurioso, persuades his master to
engage Vindice, disguised as the malcontent Piato, to pursue
his lustful designs – upon their own sister, Castiza. As Piato,
Vindice tests the virtue of Castiza, who remains resolute in
her honour; but to his distress he is able to persuade their
mother Gratiana to plead Lussurioso's cause. Meanwhile, the
Duke's youngest stepson (known only as Junior Brother) goes
on trial for raping the courtier Antonio's wife, who has killed
herself rather than suffer the dishonour. The brazenly guilty
prince is given a stay of sentence by the Duke at the pleading
of his mother – who is herself enamoured of the Duke's bastard
son, Spurio. Hoping to divert Lussurioso from visiting Castiza,
Vindice as Piato tells him of this affair. However, Lussurioso
surprises not the guilty couple as he expects, but his own
father – who assumes that he himself is the object of his son's

murderous intentions and packs him off to prison. Secretly happy at the prospect of their stepbrother's execution, the Duchess' elder sons, Supervacuo and Ambitioso, persuade the Duke to give them a signet ring as authority to proceed – but the Duke's guilty conscience prompts him to send a reprieve, and the ring is assumed to authorise the death of the Junior Brother. As Piato, Vindice has been hired by the still lustful Duke to procure the favours of a 'country lady', and he arranges the meeting to coincide with an assignation between the Duchess and Spurio, after applying poison to the lips of Gloriana's garishly adorned skull. This the Duke is deceived into kissing, and he dies in agony after being forced to watch his wife's embraces. Lussurioso determines to rid himself of Piato, accusing him to Hippolito and Vindice (now presented in his own person) of seeking to corrupt their sister. The brothers bring their mother to repent her earlier laxity, and Gratiana and Castiza are reconciled. Lussurioso, as the new Duke, banishes the Duchess, but he is murdered by Vindice and Hippolito during a celebratory masque – then Ambitioso, Supervacuo and Spurio are killed disputing who is to succeed him. It is Antonio who is now elevated, and Vindice and Hippolito, expecting his gratitude, confess to the old Duke's murder; but Antonio, fearful of their future intentions, orders their immediate execution.

The authorship

The Revenger's Tragedy was first published anonymously in 1607, but *The Atheist's Tragedy*, the only other play attributed to Cyril Tourneur, appeared with his name on the title-page four years later. The similarity of titles may have led to the attribution of the earlier work to Tourneur first made in a play-list of 1656, and generally accepted until claims began to be made on Thomas Middleton's behalf towards the end of the nineteenth century. The pendulum of preference continues to swing, at present towards Middleton, but there is no external evidence either way. Of Tourneur we know little – not even a date or place of birth or education, or anything of his family circumstances. The single other play likely to have been wholly his, the tragi-comedy *The Nobleman* (1612), is lost, and his few other prose and verse writings were largely occasional and undistinguished. He appears to have relied largely on the patronage of the Vere and Cecil families, and died in 1626 of an illness contracted while accompanying Sir Edward Cecil on the Cadiz expedition of the previous year. I leave his name attached to *The Revenger's Tragedy* largely as a gesture of disbelief that the play was in any sense typical of Middleton at this stage of his career. As with *A Yorkshire Tragedy*, expending too much energy over the authorship distracts from an appreciation of the distinctive qualities of a play which speaks for its moment in time more recognisably than it does with any known individual's voice.

The historical context

Only during the eighteenth century did the term 'character' come to denote a role in a play, and although the Jacobeans were already writing 'characters' of real individuals – often to praise some likely patron or to mourn his passing – they still used the word chiefly to suggest a satirical portrait of a particular type: 'An Elder Brother', 'A Pedant', 'A Shopkeeper', and so on. This was the mode of the 'character writers' who, following the precedent of the ancient Greek philosopher Theophrastus, would assemble a number of such 'character' sketches into book form. As Sir Thomas Overbury explained, introducing his own collection: 'To square out a character by our English level, it is a picture . . . quaintly drawn in various colours, all of them heightened by one shadowing.' Thus, when Vindice, watching the Duke and his family pass over the stage at the start of *The Revenger's Tragedy*, talks of these 'four excellent characters', he is not casting an ironic reflection on their moral probity but declaring them perfect of their *types* – the ageing adulterer, the lecherous heir, the calculating stepmother and the bastard. Their names are so glossed in Florio's dictionary *A World of Words* (1598), as are most others used in the play: thus, Castiza is 'chaste' and Supervacuo 'vain' or 'superfluous'. Even such minor figures as Dondolo the 'gull' or 'fool' and Nencio the 'idiot' are given names of unequivocal significance – while Vindice *means* 'revenger of wrongs' and his *alter ego* Piato is, appropriately, 'squat, cowered down, hidden'. Despite the greater individuality with which Shakespeare endows many of his characters, even he did not expect bastards to behave other than as, well, bastards (as in *Much Ado* or *King Lear*); and Tourneur's audience would readily have accepted that the 'excellent characters' of this play were neither more nor less than their typology implied.

The world of the play

'When the bad bleeds, then is the tragedy good' (III, v, 205) is the thrust of a play rooted in Vindice's contempt for a corrupt and incestuous court, hell-bent on the hedonism enabled by power. This is not a world much tinctured by virtue, never by mercy; and Vindice is cool, even impishly calculating, in his revenge, never agonised by the self-doubt of a Hamlet. When he employs his dead mistress' skull, it is not (as in *Hamlet*) to reflect on mortality following an accidental unearthing by a comic gravedigger, but as an instrument – cherished through nine years of decay – of a horribly ironic (and iconic) revenge. And so far from suffering fortune's slings and arrows at every turn, in his wry commentary upon the action Vindice becomes the shadow-author of a play in which God's role is perceived to be that of cosmic stage manager, producing thunder on cue. Though the conceit is not unfamiliar, here it is the metaphor which gives flesh to the characters, not the characters to the metaphor, as Vindice conducts his grotesque puppet theatre – not unlike that of the modern Polish auteur Tadeusz Kantor, who peopled his works with the living dead and bustled about the stage in person, arranging them to his satisfaction.

Although Vindice is the most closely-drawn character in the play, any 'real' self remains elusive. Like Hamlet, he conceals

his character of revenger beneath the assumed character of a
malcontent, first as Piato, later as an alternative version of himself. Finally he takes on a further role in the fatal masque – by
which time he has dressed up the murdered Duke in Piato's
clothes, and so 'killed' his alter ego, as he has been ordered.
His motives remain as ambiguous as his identity. There is no
ghost here calling for vengeance: so is it the long-ago poisoning of Gloriana that spurs Vindice into action – or the death
of his father, who died 'of discontent, the nobleman's consumption', having suffered the Duke's 'depletion' of his estates?
Lussurioso duly affirms that 'discontent and want / Is the best
clay to mould a villain' (IV, i, 47–8) – but what credence should
we give to the judgement of this well-born sensualist, who is
far more villainous than Vindice?

Eliot saw in Tourneur 'the loathing and horror of life
itself' of 'a highly sensitive adolescent with a gift for words'.
Yet it is not 'life itself' which horrifies Tourneur, but the arbitrary casualness of evil. Thus, incest (as it would have been
perceived) here hinges not on self-doubts and deceptions, as
in *Women Beware Women*, or on affirming a love that is none
the less true for being forbidden, as in *'Tis Pity She's a Whore*,
but on almost offhand sexual opportunism. The atmosphere
is a blend of the late-medieval pessimism of an Hieronymus
Bosch with the proto-existential angst of a Baudelaire.

To this, of course, the setting of an Italianate court makes
its contribution; yet while the chauvinistic prejudices of an
English audience are duly satisfied, one suspects also a covert
disgust at the excesses of all courtly behaviour – not least the
English. In 1606, the likely year of the play's composition, the
visit of James' brother-in-law from Denmark had thus occas-
ioned notoriously debauched celebrations – which contrasted
with nostalgically tinged recollections of the sober court ruled
by that other virginal Gloriana, England's own late Queen.

In this court there are no cardinals such as lurk, however
hypocritically, around the Italianate tragedies of Webster or
Middleton; nor, for that matter, does any character but Vindice
show a sense of purpose beyond the immediate gratification

of desires. Vindice does not succumb to the temptations of the society he despises, but he often has to creep into its dark corners to turn lust and greed to his own purposes. In testing Castiza's virtue, and in allowing his mother to make light of prostitution in the service of 'our betters' (II, i, 153), he is drawing her down the same path that has led to the death of his own mistress and of Antonio's wife; and in poisoning the lips of Gloriana's skull he is permitting the Duke a perverse consummation of an old and thwarted passion.

The play is full of such *peripeteia*, or ironic reversals – one critic has counted twenty-two, from the lecherous Duke's condemning of his son for lechery to Vindice's execution not for his crimes but out of Antonio's fear that he might be their next victim – though one might feel this to be less an irony than the punch-line of a black joke. Some scenes build up not so much to reversals as comic double-takes – as when Lussurioso, very much alive, greets the stepbrothers who have just been taunting his supposedly severed head, to their consequent confusion and chagrin (III, vi, 73). 'Horrid laughter' is never far from the surface in this play.

Double standards, too, are ironically juxtaposed. Gloriana escaped the Duke's *droit de seigneur* in the same way as Antonio's wife now redeems her honour – by death. Against Antonio's unseemly 'joy' in his wife's suicide (I, iv, 74) is set Gratiana's contempt for virginity, reconstructed as a commodity for purchase by 'our betters' (II, i, 153). Lussurioso is almost proud to be 'past my depth in lust' (I, iii, 88), yet furiously intent on preventing the Duchess from sating her own desires.

The Revenger's Tragedy is thus much more than a morality play with added sex and violence or a *memento mori* from an emblem book brought to dramatic life – though its original audience may well have been reminded of both. Such associations, and all the 'sententiae' and the verbal echoes, are stirred into a mix which, while utterly distinctive in the means and modes it deploys, is both very modern in portraying the banality of evil and very much of its time in its quest for the cause and its despair of curing its author's sense of spiritual malaise.

The playwright's craft

FORM   *The Revenger's Tragedy* anticipates its self-aware theatricality by proclaiming its sub-genre in its very title. 'Tragical
satire' probably better sums up the modern critical view of its
generic quality – its characters perceived as morality-type
figures who lack the fine shading required for 'true' tragedy.
Less prescriptively, we might suggest 'social tragedy' as a label
for the play, since Vindice is seeking revenge on the whole
court and the values by which it survives.

STRUCTURE   With unobtrusive craft, the play alternates episodes of action or fast-moving intrigue with scenes of reflection
on death, sexuality, and evil which provide their philosophic
underpinning. The play is unusual of its kind in that the killing of the ostensible target for revenge, the Duke, has been
accomplished as early as III, iv.

LANGUAGE   The practical language of revenge is chirpily
down-to-earth, as when Vindice, having killed the old Duke,
comments of his potential successors, 'As fast as they keep up
let's cut 'em down' (as they do). The play also has a large
quota of 'sententiae' – moral commonplaces, often proverbial
and often signalled by rhyming couplets – whose simplistic
sentiments contrast strongly with the originality of metaphor
elsewhere in the play, which typically employs quite precise
and literal terms in images of startling concision – as when
Gloriana is said to have made 'a usurer's son / Melt all his pat-
rimony in a kiss' (I, i. 26–7), or committing a capital crime is
likened to putting one's 'life between the judge's lips' (III, v,
76). The imagery is insistently of food or other forms of consumption, often related to sexuality – as throughout the soliloquy in which Spurio reflects that 'some stirring dish / Was
my first father' (I, ii, 180–204).

STAGE PRACTICE   The procession 'passing over' the stage,
at the play's opening is a requirement in a number of plays of

the period, though whether this actually involved mounting stairs up to and down from the stage (and possibly entrances and exits through the auditorium) is not known. Here and elsewhere in the play, costume plays an important part on signifying status. In addition to the property skull needed for Gloriana, the play requires a more recently severed head for Junior Brother at III, vi (four 'Turks' heads' are listed among Henslowe's stage props). As in the recent *King Lear*, storm effects are also called for.

In performance

We have no information regarding the Jacobean staging of the play beyond the claim on the title-page of the first edition of 1607 that it had been 'sundry times acted by the King's Majesty's Servants' – presumably at the Globe on Bankside. Two revivals by the Marlowe Society, in 1937 and 1959, and three amateur productions were followed by the first modern professional revival, by Brian Shelton at the Pitlochry Festival Theatre in July 1965. Then, a year later, came Trevor Nunn's revelatory Stratford production for the RSC. Ian Richardson in the title role modulated between grim anticipation, fawning deception and vengeful triumphs leading compulsively to his own destruction; while the court exuded the nastiness of bored and brutal adolescence, as much in Patience Collier's mutton-to-lamb Duchess and David Waller's prim but prurient Duke as in Alan Howard's prissy, preening Lussurioso. An explosion of regional and fringe productions – five in the 1970s, eight in the 1980s, seven in the 1990s – has since made this one of the most frequently revived of non-Shakespearean plays. A second RSC production, by Di Trevis, was staged at the Swan Theatre in 1987 in an eerily lit setting by Michael Levine redolent of corruption and decay. Antony Sher as Vindice gave, in Carole Woddis' words, a 'restrained yet passionately intelligent' performance, 'turning from ragged outsider to scheming avenger', looking 'with his vivid red-crested wig and full-bodied beard like some demonic garden gnome.'

Francis Beaumont
The Knight of the Burning Pestle

1607

Source

The play is essentially original, though Cervantes' novel about
the 'Knight of the Doleful Visage', *Don Quixote* – the first part
of which was published in Spain in 1605, but not translated
into English until 1612 – shares its mock-chivalric theme.

The story

The Prologue to a play called *The London Merchant* is interrupted by a Citizen and his Wife from the audience, who
clamber on stage and demand that that their apprentice Rafe
be given the role of a 'grocer errant', the Knight of the Burning Pestle. Accordingly, the plot of the intended play – in
which the prodigal Jasper and the dull but worthy Humphrey
are rivals for the hand of Luce, daughter of the merchant
Venturewell – merges with the mock-chivalric adventures of
Rafe (with two fellow apprentices playing his squire and his
dwarf), which the Citizen and his Wife invent and adapt at
their whim. In a sub-plot, Jasper's parents, the Merrythoughts,
fall out over old Merrythought's cheerful improvidence, and
Mistress Merrythought and her younger son Michael join
Luce and her lovers in their adventuring round the northern
suburbs of London. The grocer-knight confuses matters with
his would-be gallantry, mistakes the Bell Inn for a hospitable
castle, and 'frees' the patients of a local barber-surgeon. Luce's
planned elopement with Jasper is thwarted by her father, who
forces her back home – but Jasper, with the help of old
Merrythought, pretends his own death and wins his bride by
gaining entrance in his coffin. All being reconciled, the Citizen and his Wife demand a climax in which Rafe honours the

City as Lord of the May Day Revels, before meeting a tragic end and delivering a funeral oration upon his own heroic life.

The author and his work

Francis Beaumont was born around 1584, the son of a well-to-do Leicestershire lawyer. Following his father's death he left Oxford without a degree to become a member of the Inner Temple, but preferred the literary life, and published a long Ovidian epic, *Salmacis and Hermaphroditus*, in 1602. His seven-year association with John Fletcher began in 1606 with the Jonsonian comedy *The Woman Hater*, and thereafter it is difficult to disentangle which of the fifty-odd plays attributed to them were indeed collaborations, which singly authored, and which written with or by others. The profusion of attributions – falsely canonised by the folio collections of 1647 and 1679 – suggests how saleable their brand of romantic tragi-comedy had become; but modern scholarship limits to around a dozen the plays in which Beaumont truly had a share. Of these, *Philaster* (1609), *The Maid's Tragedy* (1610), and *A King and No King* (1611) are generally considered the best, with Beaumont's probably the guiding hand. We shall never know the truth of the gossipy John Aubrey's anecdote that the two friends also 'lay together' and 'had one wench in the house between them' – but the collaboration did come to an abrupt end with Beaumont's marriage to an heiress in 1613. He died three years later, and was buried in Westminster Abbey. *The Knight of the Burning Pestle* was possibly his only non-collaborative play, though a masque presented by the Inns of Court to celebrate the marriage of the Princess Elizabeth in 1613 was also his sole work – and probably his last.

The historical context

Though Shelton's translation of Cervantes' *Don Quixote* may have been circulating in manuscript, it is thought unlikely that *The Knight of the Burning Pestle* owes a direct debt to the novel: simply, the citizens of London were no less in thrall to the vogue for chivalric romance than those of Barcelona or Madrid (*Palmerin de Oliva*, from which Rafe reads in Act I, was also in Don Quixote's library). But, like Beaumont's play, Cervantes' novel has outlived the target of its satire – and to miss its irony, as does the modern musical version, is to make 'Dream the Impossible Dream' a desirable instead of a delusive objective. Indeed, the chivalry that Rafe, like Quixote, is trying to emulate had always been an 'impossible dream', having more to do with aristocratic play-acting (perpetuated in the tournaments loved both by Elizabeth and by James' heir, the young Prince Henry) than the rough pragmatism of medieval conduct – while 'courtly love', still idealised in the writings of Sidney and Spenser, was encoded in the songs of troubadours rather than the behaviour of courtiers.

As his 'audition piece', Rafe offers a slightly misquoted version of Hotspur's speech on honour from *Henry IV, Part One*. But, as we saw in discussing *Bussy D'Ambois*, Hotspur's perception of 'honour' has more to do with self-assertive machismo than the service of others, while Prince Hal believes he can acquire Hotspur's honour simply by killing him. No wonder Falstaff curtly dismisses the whole concept as 'a word', and that in our play Rafe and the Citizen's Wife observe that modern knights are renowned chiefly for their profligacy and foul language (I, 241–50). Plays such as Heywood's *Four Prentices of London* and Day and Wilkins' *The Travels of the Three English Brothers* encouraged citizen audiences to believe that their own class could set a better example of true nobility; and it was just such aspirations above their station that laid them open to the mockery of their 'betters' – as, for the past seven years, in the satires of the private theatres, which Beaumont's grocer and his wife intend no longer to endure. Before censuring their tastes or questioning their wisdom in venturing into a private playhouse, when they would feel more at their ease in a public one, we should remind ourselves that it was to audiences containing a goodly proportion of Georges, Nells and Rafes that Shakespeare owed his fame.

The world of the play

The multiple worlds in *The Knight of the Burning Pestle* are of contested and overlapping boundaries. A grocer (George) and his wife (Nell) are watching a citizen comedy, *The London Merchant*, in the same theatre and in the same 'real time' as the actual audience. Upon this are superimposed the chivalric adventures of Rafe, into whose more protracted time-scale they also enter – as when the Wife asks Rafe, after a night passes between the second and third acts, 'How hast thou slept tonight?' or when George insists on paying Rafe's tavern reckoning. The mollified innkeeper then transforms the local barber-surgeon into the giant Barbaroso for Rafe to slay, so that he may set free his captives – who in truth (whatever that may be) are patients being treated for venereal disease (and so suffering the 'burning pizzle' of the crudely punning title).

By this time we are wanderers in a surreal, *Alice in Wonderland* world where illusion and reality elide with the intensity of a childhood dream – or within the ever-shortening attention spans of the citizens (as George has succinctly put it at II, 268, 'Plot me no plots'). Rafe is whisked off to Moldavia for a platonic encounter with the Princess Pompiona and restored to the City to celebrate May Day. Then he drills the levy at Mile End before appearing with an arrow through his head to read his own obituary. All this the apprentice takes in his stride, the burlesque working in part through the familiar means of bathos, as hyperbolic flights descend into absurdity, and in part by counterpoint, with the genuine vitality of Rafe's more colloquial manner in comic tension with his would-be chivalric blunderings.

All these worlds are bounded by the walls of the playhouse in which Nell makes her final appeal for applause – at once as an actor, as a member of the audience, and as hostess of a spur-of-the-moment party for sharing 'a pottle of wine and a pipe of tobacco'. The play anticipates Pirandello in its complex metatheatricality, and even verges upon the postmodern in its embrace of the audience's reception. Evidently, its 'privy mark of irony' (as the dedication has it) was too much for the original audience. And yet, essentially, it is all great fun – and, more surprisingly, good-natured fun. For while ostensibly satirising middle-class values, Beaumont comes closer to celebrating them – if perhaps a touch complacently, from a position of social superiority. He allows no surrogate on stage either for himself or for those young wits in the audience who would be more than ready to ridicule George and Nell for their lack of education and ignorance of theatricality. And while the grocer and his wife are often obtuse, sometimes even downright silly, they are never shown as other than a generous and well-matched couple. In their workaday relationship the husband is clearly an equal rather than a dominant partner – but never to the extent that Nell becomes the conventional nagging shrew. At the end of Act III she gets the better of the argument over the rights and wrongs of the Merrythoughts' behaviour, but is readily reconciled when her husband goes in search of beer – which she proceeds to share with the actors before tipping the boy who has danced during the interlude.

Beaumont's refusal to dehumanise the citizenry, though it perhaps disappointed an audience anticipating class warfare, makes his play the more accessible today. And, after all, the critique of the citizen comedy *The London Merchant* comes from the citizens themselves, whose hold on reality collapses the fabric of conventions which hold it flimsily together, and from Rafe, who turns its action topsy-turvy with his interventions. But even the inner play, if by intention absurd, exudes optimism – and there is not a villain to be found among its characters. Venturewell comes closest, but only as a stern patriarchal merchant conforming to type, and there is no 'bad apprentice' to contrast with the 'good' – for Humphrey is a harmless buffoon, while the 'prodigal' of the play, Jasper, sins only in daring to love his master's daughter. And Luce's deception of her father's preferred suitor is of course allowable since it is in the interest of finding her own true love.

Distinctly the oddest character in the play (or plays) is the compulsively cheerful Merrythought, forever bursting into snatches from the three-dozen or so ballads in his repertoire and refusing to be miserable in the face of imminent poverty and starvation. Far from being ridiculed or corrected for his humour, he is presented as an incorrigible (and eventually justified) believer in the power of serendipity who (as one of the play's modern editors, Sheldon Zitner, puts it) 'manages to unite the Epicurean with the Stoic'. Although only a minor character, he bestrides the action in the manner of a Falstaff or of Ursula in Jonson's *Bartholomew Fair* – a Lord of Misrule, infusing the play with a spirit of the carnivalesque. And while Merrythought subverts the play's values from within by refusing to take anything seriously, Rafe does so from without by taking everything very seriously indeed.

It is a 'privy mark of irony' indeed that *The Knight of the Burning Pestle* continues to live on the stage while the later tragi-comedies of the Beaumont and Fletcher partnership, which rarely see the light, strike us as in need of creative input from George and Nell. Sadly, fashionable success deterred Beaumont from returning to that looking-glass world of self-aware theatricality in which the characters of *The Knight* act and see themselves reflected.

The playwright's craft

FORM   Although earlier plays had included episodes of burlesque, such as the mock tragedy of 'Pyramus and Thisbe' in *A Midsummer Night's Dream*, or parodic characters, such as Ancient Pistol, *The Knight of the Burning Pestle* is the first sustained dramatic burlesque in English. Later examples – from Buckingham's *The Rehearsal* (updated by Sheridan as *The Critic*) and Fielding's *Tom Thumb* to Tom Stoppard's *The Real Inspector Hound* – are relatively scarce, perhaps because good burlesque helps to laugh the objects of its parody out of existence.

STRUCTURE   The five-act structure usual in plays for the private (or indoor) theatres is here stressed by the citizens' comments on the interval music and dancing – with the effect that the action seems more continuous for their eliding presence. One of the play's editors, identifying 31 'units of action' in the play, observes that a mere eleven of these are devoted to *The London Merchant*, while the citizens and Rafe are dominant in the remainder (and of course intervene throughout). All the disconnected incidents and disruptions can, of course, be justified (if justification be needed) as Beaumont's satire upon the arbitrary and episodic plotting of chivalric romances. Beyond that, the action has the kind of unity achieved by a music-hall bill or a television comedy – a unity unknown to Aristotle but as familiar to a modern audience as *Monty Python*.

LANGUAGE   Rafe adapts his idiom to its occasions, lapsing from mock-romantic flights into the workaday, and indulging in a fine flourish of antique 'fourteeners' in his role as master of the May Day Revels. Humphrey speaks in couplets whose sense is nonchalantly subordinated to their need to rhyme, while he good-naturedly allows his listeners to choose what meaning or metaphor suits them best. The play's linguistic styles range as widely as its action, and along the way there are even some proto-Malapropisms – such as George's loyal retitling of Heywood's play as *Rafe and Lucrece*.

CONVENTIONS   Although Nell expresses cooing adulation for several of the boy players, she never comments on the (presumably) prettiest boy taking the role of Luce; so the cross-dressing convention remains impregnable here, although over at the Globe (and probably in the same year) Shakespeare's Egyptian queen was intensifying rather than shattering illusion when 'she' foresaw 'some squeaking Cleopatra boy my greatness'. This is another 'prodigal' play in which, as with Quicksilver in *Eastward Ho!*, the prodigal is treated with some sympathy – while, true to the play's spirit, Jasper stands the parable on its head by returning home richer than he left (and in so doing inverts another parable, that of the talents, when he contemptuously casts down his ten-shilling portion only to find Mrs Merrythought's casket of jewels in its place). His 'love test' of Luce is an extreme example of the convention we first encountered in Lacy's testing of Margaret in *Friar Bacon and Friar Bungay*; and when (to George's disgust) Jasper gets his girl in the end, it is by means of the 'coffin trick' to be found in a number of contemporary comedies.

STAGE PRACTICE   The presence of spectators seated on the stage, as are the citizens here, was permitted (one suspects with some reluctance) only in the private houses.

In performance

The dedicatory epistle to the first printed edition of 1613 notes that publication had rescued the play from oblivion, so 'utterly rejected' was its first performance – probably by the Children of the Chapel, then playing as the Children of Black-friars after their own indoor theatre. Nor is there any record of further performances until 1635, when it was being played at the Cockpit in Drury Lane, and was even called for at Court in the following year. It enjoyed greater success in the first two decades after the Restoration, with a new Prologue written by Nell Gwyn, but after 1682 disappeared from the stage until it was revived by the Mermaid Society at the Royalty Theatre in 1904, with Nigel Playfair as Rafe. Since then it has become one of the most frequently revived Jacobean comedies, with numerous amateur and student stagings in addition to profes-sional productions directed by Ben Iden Payne at the Gaiety Theatre, Manchester, in 1908; by Frank Benson at Stratford-upon-Avon in 1910; by Nigel Playfair at the Birmingham Rep in 1919; at Leeds Playhouse in 1933; in a touring production by George Devine in 1951; at the Marlowe, Canterbury, in 1966; at the Greenwich Theatre, London, in 1975; and in a touring production by the Bubble company in 1979. Michael Bogdanov, in an RSC production at the Aldwych in 1981, added yet another layer to the action, with the citizens as taxpayers outraged by subsidies for highbrow plays, and Rafe, played by Timothy Spall, aspiring to be a hero out of Barbara Cartland.

The Roaring Girl
Middleton and Dekker

c. 1608

Source

The plot, despite its deep roots in the comic conventions of
young love triumphing over paternal disapproval, is original,
though the character of Moll Cutpurse is a romanticised version of a notorious contemporary cross-dresser, Mary Frith.

The story

Sebastian, son of Sir Alexander Wengrave, feigns a betrothal
to the notorious 'roaring girl' Moll Cutpurse, hoping that the
prospect of such an alliance will soften his father's opposition
to his real love, Mary Fitzallard. Sir Alexander sets his servant
Trapdoor to spy on Moll and seek cause for her arrest. Moll
herself is meanwhile browsing at the stalls of three city shopkeepers, whose wives' affections are being besieged by fashionable gallants: the impecunious Laxton is wooing the wife of
the apothecary Gallipot, while the gambler Jack Dapper has
set his sights on Mistress Tiltyard, the featherer's wife, and
Goshawk is raising false suspicions of her husband's fidelity to
win over Mistress Openwork, the seamstress. Laxton, taking
Moll to be a common whore, arranges an assignation – which
Moll keeps, only to humiliate Laxton in a duel. She also gets
the better of Trapdoor, but good-naturedly takes him into her
service. Gallipot is persuaded by his wife that she had a prior
betrothal to Laxton, and he agrees to buy off the claim. Moll
and Trapdoor arrive just in time to rescue Jack Dapper, whose
own father had wanted to teach him a lesson by having him
arrested for debt. Moll, in male attire, springs none of the
traps set by Sir Alexander and Trapdoor to prove her a thief,
but takes on Mary, disguised as a page, to enable the lovers to

meet when they wish. Openwork exposes Goshawk as a liar and would-be adulterer, while Laxton, failing to prise more money from the wily apothecary, claims that his intentions had only been to test Mistress Gallipot's virtue; the reconciled gallants and citizens depart to dine together. Moll unmasks Trapdoor's disguise as a discharged soldier, and the pair show off the canting language of thieves for Dapper and some fellow roisterers. Sir Alexander, hearing rumours that Moll and his son are already married, readily agrees to an offer from Mary's father, Sir Guy Fitzallard, to give up his estate if he cannot prevent the match – provided that, if he succeeds, Sir Alexander will make over half his own fortune to his son. At last Mary appears as Sebastian's true bride and Sir Alexander repents all his actions – even being reconciled with Moll, recognising that he has been swayed by the 'common voice', in ignorance of her noble nature.

The authors and their collaboration

For Dekker's life, see under *The Shoemakers' Holiday*, p. 65, and for Middleton's under *Women Beware Women*, p. 202. The two had previously collaborated with three others on the lost tragedy *Caesar's Fall* (*c.* 1602) and together on *The First Part of the Honest Whore* (*c.* 1604). But Dekker's benevolent optimism and Middleton's sharply satiric outlook may not have made for an easy partnership: Dekker wrote *The Second Part of the Honest Whore* alone, and the two did not work together again after *The Roaring Girl* (though some date this as late as 1611).

The historical context

In his mock-dedicatory preface, Middleton notes that 'the time of the great crop-doublet' – that beak-like extrusion around the male belly which reached its most tumescent in the early 1590s – coincided with a period of 'huge bombasted plays'. However we judge his claim that the present 'time of spruceness' in fashion was also reflected in the drama, apparel was evidently much on Middleton's mind – just a few years after the repeal of the sumptuary laws, which had attempted to regulate the mode of one's dress according to one's social status. Theatrical companies had never been subject to such restrictions: given the absence of scenery, the status of characters had to be signified by their costumes, and the inheritance of a noble patron's cast-offs was often a main source of supply for the wardrobe. There appears to have been no statutory sanction against cross-dressing – of which, again, the theatres were leading exponents, through the requirement (unique to England) for boys or men to take female roles. One scholarly inventory lists almost eighty plays between 1570 and 1642 in which 'heroines' assume male disguise – though against theorising as to the homo-erotic or transsexual implications of this practice must be set the pragmatic utility of boys being better able to disguise themselves as boys than as girls (albeit at one remove). For a woman character to wear male costume and take on male attributes such as smoking and 'roistering' while remaining (at least for most of the play) undisguisedly female was a rarer theatrical event, as was that of a male character taking on female disguise – an issue to which we shall return in discussing Jonson's *Epicoene, or The Silent Woman* (p. 146). Stir into a mix which thus blurred social as well as sexual boundaries the bisexuality of the King, who favoured pretty male courtiers, and we may be dealing with freedoms whose exercise caused anxieties unknown under a strict dress code and a Virgin Queen. Intriguingly, the real-life Mary Frith gave some sort of one-wo/man show on the stage of the Fortune in the spring of 1611, in male attire.

The world of the play

The Roaring Girl has until recently been among the most unjustly neglected of Jacobean plays, since its frank exploration of transgressive sexuality offended long-sacred taboos, while its style of comedy confused generic expectations, whether of the romantic or citizen mode. Unlike such cross-dressing plays as

As You Like It and *Twelfth Night*, the setting is not some far-away forest or Illyrian never-land, but the ebb and flow of city life at the very doors of the theatre. And while there is a conventional romantic heroine named Mary who adopts her male disguise out of necessity in the cause of true love, there is also an unromantic heroine named Moll who is determined to stay single, and who dresses like a man while never denying her womanhood – at her first appearance (II, i, 174) she is wearing both male and female garments. The landed gentry, idle town gallants and hard-working tradespeople are set expectedly at odds – but reconciled by a central character from beyond all their worlds, a woman who tramples the boundaries of social class as she does those of gendered behaviour.

If Mary and Moll represent opposite extremes of Jacobean womanhood – for the quiescent Mary wants nothing better than the marriage and male domination Moll despises – the shopkeepers' wives bustle interestingly in between. It would be unhistorical to expect them to push harder against the restrictions of marriage, but they are humanly tempted, resist the temptation, and in the end are reconciled to dull but useful husbands, whom they keep companionably at heel without becoming the shrews of orthodox typology. The citizen husbands and wives, like Moll (on whose assistance they have no need to call), spark an individuality which their 'betters' lack.

It is not only a modern audience, open to sexual diversity, that finds Moll an attractive figure: Middleton and Dekker clearly intended her as such, and in overlooking the less respectable features of her real-life original they have given us a kind of Robin Hood in drag – an outsider whose sense of natural justice is respected even by the criminal fraternity who despise the 'official' justice represented by Sir Alexander and Sir Davy. We know from the casual briskness of Moll's injunction to return a stolen purse (V, i, 303-6) that it will be acted on without question. Ironically, the one thing she is not very good at is disguise: her attempt to pass herself off as a musician does not even fool Sir Alexander – though it helpfully deflects attention from Mary, in attendance as her 'page'.

When Sebastian kisses Mary in this guise, and Moll comments wryly, 'How strange this shows, one man to kiss another', there's a hint of a relished attraction towards such boyishness in his response: 'Methinks a woman's lip tastes well in a doublet' (IV, i, 45, 47). But as to whether Moll herself is 'straight, gay, or bi', we are given no clue – for even her (as usual) jocular admission that she loves 'to lie o' both sides of the bed' may be no more than a rejection of any limitation on her independence. So is she 'simply' the uncomplicated tomboy the title suggests? Or is her sexuality ideological – and, if so, does it embody proto-feminism or a hermaphroditic idealism that goes back to Plato?

There is no 'real' Moll to make such questions answerable from the text, but of course they occur to the reader constructing her character from the page just as they have to be addressed by an actress on the stage – not least because Moll transcends the boundaries usually set by Jacobean typology, and is one of the few characters in the drama of the time for whom taking part in a play seems almost incidental to a life being lived beyond its fictions. She thus recognises the complexities of her own desires in an almost incidental confession of the strange sexual fantasies of her dreams (IV, i, 102–8, and 113–23). Yet while 'being awake, I keep my legs together', she has to keep them apart to play her favoured instrument, the viol – and it is such offences against 'ladylike' norms that lead most of the characters of the play to regard her as a whore. But playing the viol, smoking and on occasion joining in the bawdy talk no more makes her a prostitute than knowledge of the canting tongue makes her a thief.

The play cannot usefully be split into 'main' and 'sub' plots, for Moll is, strictly, a mere accomplice in the former – while her defeat of Laxton (in other respects a minor character) is at the very core of the play, both in terms of the flow of events and in the extended statement it prompts from Moll as to the wrongs inflicted upon women (III, i, 71–113). In a play which largely avoids the dangers of sentimentality in Dekker's benevolence while drawing the crueller stings of

Middleton's satire, mutual forgiveness is pervasive – the citizens and gallants even going off to supper together – so it is all the more notable that it is Laxton, believing that Moll's womanhood is for sale, who is singled out for humiliation.

To be bested by a woman bearing the symbolic penis-extension of a sword makes the humiliation all the worse for a man with such a name. That he is thought to 'lack stones' (testicles) is underlined by Sir Alexander's clearly deliberate Freudian slip at I, ii, 55–6 – just one of a proliferation of double (or single) sexual *entendres* in a play whose almost every speech, from high and low characters alike, contains ill-concealed references to sexual or excretory functions. This running subtext reflects the very obsessions which Moll well recognises, but refuses to allow to govern her own free soul.

Often the sexual innuendo connects with the matters of dress and dress-making which also form recurrent motifs. In the opening scene Neatfoot thus sets the tone when he nudgingly refers to Mary, disguised as a seamstress, as his master's 'needlewoman', with its slang meaning of 'whore'. And the tradesmen we meet all deal in items of dress – the exception being the tobacconist, who enables Moll to trespass upon another supposedly male preserve. For most of the characters dress signifies both sex and class – but classless Moll Cutpurse, dressing as she chooses and and mannish when the mood takes her, strolls with composure through the play, chirpily refusing to signify anything but her own independence of spirit.

The playwright's craft

STRUCTURE   The act-divisions are not present in the original, whose eleven scenes are conventionally indicated by clearances of the stage. The structure accommodates all kinds of diversionary incident, and may be thought irregular in its arousal of expectations of a conventional thwarted-love plot in the first two scenes, from which Moll is absent – as indeed she is well into the third, though her presence is then pervasive in seven of the remaining nine, and she effectively takes over the play.

LANGUAGE   The language of the play switches easily between prose and loose blank verse, often though not always in accordance with the social status (or import of speech) of the characters. As already noted, sexual innuendo is pervasive. The scene in which Moll, Trapdoor and Tearcat converse in the obscure cant of the underworld draws on the materials Dekker also employed in prose works such as *The Bellman of London* (1608) and *The Gull's Hornbook* (1609).

CONVENTIONS   Though metatheatricality is not stressed in the play, we note how Sir Alexander's description of his galleried chamber would have applied equally to the square enclosing structure of the Fortune theatre (I, ii, 13–32).

STAGE PRACTICE   The three shop-counters may suggest the use of openings in the back (tiring-house) wall, though two are more usually assumed, and an 'open-plan' arrangement, as later required for the booths in Jonson's *Bartholomew Fair*, may have been employed.

In performance

We know of no performance of *The Roaring Girl* between its staging at the Fortune by Prince Henry's Men and its revival in 1970 by the Dundee Repertory Company, directed by Keith Darvill. This was followed by several student versions, and in 1983 by an RSC production played in tandem with *The Taming of the Shrew* in Stratford and at the Barbican. In a production by Barry Kyle which evoked, in Michael Billington's judgement, 'the teeming variety' of city life, Milton Shulman liked Helen Mirren's performance as Moll – 'full of eloquence, bravado and a splendid shiny-faced swagger', and John Barber found this 'sexless, loveable cove', with her 'tousled curls, gypsy sunburn, round-shouldered slouch and Cockney vowels' quite unlike 'any other character in English drama'. The Steam Industry brought the play to the Finborough Theatre in 2000.

Epicoene, or The Silent Woman
Ben Jonson

1609

Source

Morose's hatred of noise derives from an oratorical declam-
ation by the Ancient Greek rhetorician Libanius (translated
into Latin as *Morosus*), and the device of the boy-bride from *Il
marescalco* (1533), a play by the Italian satirist Pietro Aretino.

The story

Truewit, conversing with his friend Clerimont at his toilet,
laments the misfortunes of their fellow-gallant Dauphine,
whose uncle Morose is obsessively fearful of noise – and now,
as Dauphine arrives to tell them, is planning to marry a 'silent
woman' found for him by his barber Cutbeard, and disinherit
Dauphine by begetting an heir. The foppish Sir Amorous La
Foole appears with an invitation for all to dine at Captain
Otter's, where they will be able to meet not only the 'silent
woman', Mistress Epicoene, but the members of the so-called
'college' of ladies, 'an order between courtiers and country
madams', whose Amazonian façade is belied by their readiness
to bend before every fashionable opinion. At his lodgings,
Morose is instructing his servant in the arts of silence when
Truewit bursts in to proclaim as noisily as he can the dis-
advantages of marriage. Dauphine is meanwhile enjoying the
spectacle of the would-be scholar Sir John Daw garrulously
proclaiming the virtues of silence to Epicoene: but his amuse-
ment turns to consternation when Truewit enters to boast of
his stratagem – for, as Dauphine now informs his friends,
Epicoene has assured him of a slice of his uncle's fortune once
they are married. However, Cutbeard arrives with news that
Morose believes Dauphine to have been behind Truewit's dis-

suasions, and is now more intent than ever upon matrimony. Introduced to Epicoene in person, Morose is charmed by her modesty – but once the marriage ceremony is over, he finds that his bride has, after all, a sharp tongue and a far from submissive nature. His dismay is compounded by the arrival of all the gallants, gulls and ladies, determined on a riotous celebration of the nuptials. While the collegiate ladies take Epicoene to their bosoms, the young men plot to deceive Daw and La Foole – first to rivalry, and then to panic at the prospect of having to fight a duel, which they avoid only to their mutual dishonour and discomfort. Meanwhile, Cutbeard and Otter have disguised themselves as lawyers, and discourse loudly to Morose on every possible ground for the divorce he now heartily desires. Despite Morose's false confession of his impotence, and a no less false confession from Daw and La Foole that they have both lain with Epicoene, no solution can be found – until Dauphine offers to release his uncle from his torment in return for an annual income and the assurance of becoming his heir. When Morose agrees to this, Dauphine pulls off Epicoene's wig to reveal that 'she' is a boy.

The author and his work

For an outline of Jonson's life, see *Every Man in His Humour*, p. 57. For most of 1609 the London theatres were closed by the plague, but it was none the less a busy year for Jonson, now at the meridian of his fortunes. In February his *Masque of Queens* was chosen to open the new Banqueting House at Whitehall, and in the following month he contributed what we would now call a 'site-specific' entertainment, *Britain's Burse* (only recently rediscovered), for the opening of the New Exchange, a covered shopping precinct near Charing Cross. During the following months, he was combining work on *Epicoene* with a commission to write *Speeches at Prince Henry's Barriers* – part of the ceremonial jousting planned for the investiture of the young heir as Prince of Wales (a title he was to enjoy for only two years before his death in 1612). The success of the entertainment, held early in the New Year of 1610, must have helped to console Jonson for the suppression of *Epicoene* a month or so later, following a complaint from the king's cousin, Lady Arbella Stuart, that it connected her name with that of the Prince of Moldavia – an impostor who had once claimed an engagement to Lady Arbella herself.

The historical context

Cross-dressing was not confined to plays. Among the other exploits of the Prince of Moldavia was a daring escape from a Turkish prison disguised as a woman, while in 1610 Lady Arbella herself, being confined in the Tower, made a successful albeit short-lived escape – disguised as a boy. Nor were plots to thwart inconvenient marriages merely the stuff of drama – for just as Dauphine in our play needs to protect his inheritance by preventing his uncle from fathering a child, Lady Arbella was incarcerated because James feared that her marriage would pose a threat to the succession of his line. He himself was bisexual only so far as was needful to beget heirs, and otherwise neglected his wife for his successive favourites, Somerset and Buckingham. The boy company which staged *Epicoene* had even lost its royal patronage three years earlier on account of John Day's *The Isle of Gulls*, which not only included among its characters a man disguised as a woman but also, more contentiously, a king who preferred handsome young men to his wife. Misogynist writers generally regarded the garrulousness supposedly endemic among women (and so hated by Morose) as less reprehensible than the use of the cosmetics which Truewit eccentrically defends in *Epicoene*. For, like a love of fine clothes, 'painting' was a likely symptom of the sins of pride or lechery – or both.

The world of the play

The cold, cruel world of *Epicoene* is remarkable for a complete absence of love interest. Nothing more is heard of Clerimont's

'mistress abroad' – mentioned by Truewit in the opening scene
in the same breath as his 'ingle at home', the boy whose homosexual favours Clerimont is off-handedly assumed to enjoy.
And Dauphine is apparently more embarrassed than flattered
when Truewit persuades the collegiate ladies to turn their
sexual attentions towards him. Not only is the male fellowship between Dauphine, Truewit and Clerimont untroubled by
women, but the female collegiates (about whom we quickly
learn that they 'live from their husbands') also preserve intact
a collective identity which is described as 'most masculine or
rather hermaphroditical'. And even that 'precious manikin'
Sir Amorous is said to be inseparable from Sir John Daw. The
only husband among them is Otter – who married for money,
and is under the thumb of a spouse who 'takes herself asunder'
every night 'into some twenty boxes' and next day 'is put together again, like a great German clock' (IV, ii). Attitudes to
women in this play are in varying proportions contemptuous,
camp or cowed: but they are never touched by affection.

Nor is male companionship more than superficially close.
Daw and La Foole would resort to duelling if they dared, while
Dauphine, Truewit and Clerimont are constantly critical of
one another. Truewit, shocked that Dauphine seems ready to
accept Jack Daw's offer to sacrifice his left arm if it will spare
him fighting a duel, thus chides: 'How! Maim a man forever
for a jest? What a conscience hast thou!' 'As good maim his
body as his reputation,' grumbles Dauphine – but although
he contents himself with giving him six good kicks instead
(IV, i), Truewit has later to restrain him from tweaking off La
Foole's nose. It is not necessary to interpret these pranks (as
do some) as symbolic castrations: they are actual physical
cruelties, and it is Dauphine who enjoys inflicting them, just
as he derives as much sadistic satisfaction as economic benefit
from humiliating his uncle.

Truewit is rather the voyeur, delivering his own caustic
running commentary on events, and engineering sub-plots to
observe their workings rather than to profit from them. And
Clerimont's taste is for mental cruelty: he it is who tempts the

two gulls into boasting they have both lain with Epicoene – a claim they are reluctant to repeat before Morose, apparently out of genuine concern for his feelings. Self-glorifying liars they may be, but they are not unkind. 'Is this gentleman-like, sir?', as Daw asks Clerimont. It is not: and these callous young men do not even have the excuse of the failed celibates of *Love's Labour's Lost*, whose mockery of their inferiors is in a vain attempt to impress the ladies. Here there are no ladies to impress, and the younger males, so far from perpetuating the species (an interest proper to comedy, with its origin in fertility rituals), are anxious to thwart the only character who does wish to do so, the despised Morose. That he is even humbled into a 'confession' of impotence – a false confession, since his earlier intention to beget an heir is expressed in the privileged honesty of a soliloquy (II, i) – is a symbolic castration indeed.

The most sexually alert characters in a play intended for performance by young boys are . . . young boys. At the very start, Clerimont's page is described as being thrown on the bed by his master's mistress, as he evidently is by his master besides: and at the very end, Epicoene is declared by Truewit to be 'almost of years, and will make a good visitant within this twelvemonth'. True, the sexual ambivalence of Dauphine, Truewit and Clerimont is less up-front than that of the Amazonian ladies, less dysfunctional than that of the unhappy Otters, and lacks the high camp relish of the foppish knights; but so far from representing an ideal of civilised behaviour (as some critics have claimed), these callow youths form a 'college' no less united by sexual and social unease – ostensibly despising the fashionable world, but in reality feeding upon its gossip, egotism and greed.

So one's sense of unease at the end of the play is not really on Morose's account: rather, we are *embarrassed* on Dauphine's behalf, at the bad taste and strength of hatred he displays. This is truly a breach of decorum, whether in the twenty-first or the seventeenth-century sense – for here Jonson, that most conscious of dramatic craftsmen, was, I suspect, uncharacteristically revealing something of his own psyche. Deprived of love by his stepfather, and fated to write his tenderest poetry just four years earlier in an epitaph on the death of his only son, Jonson drew in Morose a man whose real sin is less that he has denied his nephew money than that he has denied him love. Indeed, so far from becoming a surrogate father to his sister's child, Morose twice over insists that he has never even wished to be a godfather. Yet, ironically, it is following his own father's advice, 'that I should look to what things were necessary to the carriage of my life, and what not, embracing the one and eschewing the other' (V, iii, 50–1) that has led him into the self-absorbed neglect of kin of which his hatred of 'all discourses but mine own' (II, i, 3–4) is merely a symptom.

Jonson felt such denials of love too deeply to offer us a neat comic reconciliation. There is no forgiveness for the crushed Morose, tricked out of his heir as well as his money, from a nephew who bitingly hopes only to hear of his funeral. Nor is there any marriage in prospect for the emotionally crippled Dauphine, to give him a son and heir of his own. Morose has killed something in Dauphine – who is, indeed, in many ways closer to his uncle than to his friends: for though he afflicts Morose with the noise of others, he makes remarkably little himself. Even at the close of the play, he leaves it to Truewit to expatiate (at his usual length) on all the consequences of a plot which, until a few moments ago, he has – with psychological truth as well as from dramatic necessity – kept entirely to himself. For Dauphine, as for his uncle, Truewit's chatter drowns out all reflection, and the rest is (the last word of the play, before the final appeal for the audience's applause) silence.

The playwright's craft

FORM In the limited social range of its character types, the control exercised by cynical gallants and choice of a mechanistic rather than inclusive climax, *Epicoene* anticipates the Restoration 'comedy of manners' – lacking the generous spirit of

Jonson's 'humours' comedies, whether in the corrective mode of *Volpone* or the acceptive manner of *Bartholomew Fair*.

STRUCTURE   Jonson follows his usual practice of denoting 'scenes' by changes in the composition of major characters; but on stage the action is fast-flowing and keeps its 'unity of time' in pace with the 'real time' of its staging. However, the action breaks out of such neoclassical confines, with the antics of the collegiate women and the Otters, as also the gulling of Daw and La Foole, semi-detached from the main plot, and appearing almost to supplant it for much of the fourth and fifth acts. Of course, Jonson, having appeared to achieve his 'reversal' in the discovery that Epicoene is far from silent, is keeping in reserve the revelation that she is also far from being a woman.

LANGUAGE   Between two blank-verse comedies – *Volpone* and *The Alchemist* – Jonson chooses prose as his vehicle for *Epicoene*. Given that the characters in the sandwiching plays are almost all dependent upon weaving (or willingly submitting to) fantasies which achieve a perversely poetic quality, prose is clearly more appropriate for the world of *Epicoene*, which is in every sense . . . well, prosaic – full of dialogue which, however comic, is little more than noise. Morose, ironically, is alone in perceiving this: yet irresistibly he also contributes to it.

CONVENTIONS   As so often in Jonson, the choice of names sums up character. Most of the resulting 'charactonyms' are self-revealing, but it's worth noting that the Otters are so called because of the then-prevalent belief that the species was hermaphroditic. While most of the character types are familiar, the sexual *braggadocio* as embodied by Daw and La Foole was newly emergent, and destined to reach its blowsy full bloom in Restoration comedy. The 'exposure' of Epicoene as a boy has been said to call in question the very convention on which it depended: and since the arrival of actresses in 1660, the issue of whether to assign the role to a male or female performer has been central to the play's staging.

STAGE PRACTICE Entrances from the gallery 'above' are required when Morose descends from his attic retreat and the collegiate ladies observe the cowardice of Daw and La Foole.

In performance

According to its original title-page, *Epicoene* was 'acted in the year 1609 by the Children of His Majesty's Revels' – presumably in December, at the Whitefriars playhouse, where the boy company had just taken up residence. By February, the play had been suppressed, and we have no details of further performances in the regular theatres for half a century. But records of two revivals at court during the 1630s suggest that the play had been restored to the repertoire, and it was among the first to be staged after the Restoration in 1660, with Edward Kynaston taking the title role – though it soon became traditional for an actress to play the part. For almost a century the piece remained highly popular, but it evidently proved less of an attraction in Garrick's revival of 1752, and in 1776 he commissioned George Colman to provide an expurgated version – also restoring an actor to the role of Epicoene. After a Covent Garden production in 1784, the next revivals in London were by the Mermaid Society at the Kingsway Theatre in 1905 and the Phoenix Society at the Regent in 1924 – when, according to James Agate, a young Godfrey Winn 'looked well' as Epicoene. There were revivals in the regions at the Birmingham Rep in 1947, at the Bristol Old Vic in 1959, and at the Oxford Playhouse in 1968. Male actors took the role of Epicoene both in the revival at the York Theatre Royal in 1984, directed by Michael Winter, and when Danny Boyle directed the play for the RSC at the Swan Theatre, Stratford, in 1989. In this latter production there were notable performances from David Bradley, whose Morose achieved a quiet dignity despite himself, and Richard McCabe, a truly Jonsonian grotesque whose feats of hapless verbosity as Truewit seemed scarcely able to keep pace with his teeming imagination.

The Fair Maid of the West
Thomas Heywood

c. 1610

Source

None known.

The story

Bess Bridges, a serving girl at a tavern in Plymouth, is in love
with Captain Spencer, who is about to embark on an expedition to the Azores led by the Earl of Essex. After killing a man
in a duel to defend Bess' good name, Spencer is forced to set
sail prematurely, but he entrusts her with the keeping of his
wealth and of a tavern he owns, the Windmill at Foy, before
departing for the islands. Installed at the Windmill, Bess employs Clem as her drawer, and quickly tames the swaggering
bully Roughman. Meanwhile Spencer, newly arrived in the
Azores, is thought to have been mortally wounded trying to
separate two fellow captains during an affray. He dispatches his
friend, Captain Goodlack, back to Foy where, after testing her
honesty, Goodlack confers Spencer's legacy on Bess. The grief-
stricken girl decides to use her inheritance to buy and fit out
a ship to sail to the Azores and bring back the body of her
lover. Dressed as a man, she becomes leader of a crew which
includes Goodlack, the reformed Roughman and Clem, and
lands at Fayal where Spencer supposedly died. There she is
given a false report that Spencer's body has been dug up and
burned as a heretic. In fact, the merchant ship on which the
recovered Spencer was returning to England has been captured by a Spanish galleon, and Bess and her crew defeat the
Spaniards in a sea battle to free their compatriots. When Bess
comes face to face with Spencer she takes him for a ghost,
Spencer fails to recognise the 'young man' being taken below

in a faint, and the ships go their separate ways. Bess becomes the scourge of the Spanish Main until a storm leads to the loss of Goodlack overboard and the shipwreck of Bess, Roughman and Clem. Bess survives only to be captured by bandits, but she is saved by the intervention of the Moroccan Bashaw Joffer, who takes her to his master, Mullicheg, King of Fez. Preserving her chastity against the blandishments of the King, Bess eventually contacts Clem and Goodlack who have both survived, and all are reunited on the day Bess sits beside the King in judgement of felons. To her amazement she is also confronted by Spencer. A tearful reunion follows, and Mullicheg gives his blessing to their marriage.

The author and his work

For Heywood's earlier life, see *A Woman Killed with Kindness* (p. 81). Though the dating of this play is uncertain, its references to Essex's seafaring exploits would have been untactful – following his disgrace, almost treacherous – much before 1610. Heywood at this time was still writing for Queen Anne's Men, playing at a converted innyard theatre, the Red Bull in Clerkenwell, and had started work on his sequence of episodic plays on classical myth and legend with *The Golden Age*. *The Silver Age*, *The Brazen Age* (both *c.* 1611) and *The Iron Age* (1612) followed, and he also wrote a major treatise, *An Apology for Actors* (1612), defending his profession from puritan attack. Although Heywood remained with the Queen's following their move in 1617 to the indoor Cockpit in Drury Lane, he wrote little further for the stage until 1624, when he joined Queen Henrietta's, a new company formed by Christopher Beeston at the Cockpit, for whom his work included the romantic comedies *The Captives* (1624) and *A Maidenhead Well Lost* (c. 1625), the tragi-comedy *The English Traveller* (1625) and *The Fair Maid of the West, Part Two*, which was played at court together with the first part in 1630–31. After the company was wound up in 1634, Heywood worked briefly with the King's Men, including collaborations with Brome on a topical piece,

The Late Lancashire Witches, and a comedy, *The Apprentice's Prize*. Between 1631 and 1639 he also wrote seven out of nine annual Lord Mayor's Day pageants for the City of London. Although *Challenge for Beauty* (1635) is his last known regular play, his output of polemical, biographical and other prose works remained prolific until his death in harness in 1641.

The historical context

The romance of Elizabethan seafaring lends a false gloss to the appalling conditions endured by sailors on any long voyage – and the fact that few citizens travelled further than walking distance beyond the boundaries of their own city or parish. The notion of 'abroad' held by the average playgoer would be formed precisely by such plays as this – which in turn shaped the perceptions of other untravelled playwrights (including Shakespeare, who chose ostensibly 'foreign' settings for most of his plays – sometimes emblematically, as in *The Merchant of Venice*; sometimes nonsensically, as in the case of landlocked Bohemia being given a sea coast in *The Winter's Tale*). Prejudice on religious grounds was of course endemic, and historic enmities swayed attitudes to certain races, notably the French and Spanish; but a black person (often randomly a 'Moor' or 'Ethiope') was likely to be viewed rather with curiosity, as an exotic species or embodying the savage nobility of an Othello. Heywood here shows the English casting particular scorn on the Italians for their obsession with vengeance, and links 'the rich Spaniard and the barbarous Turk' as prime targets for plunder (ironically, since Spain's full independence from the Ottoman Empire had been gained only a century earlier). In 1596 the Earl of Essex led a raid on Cadiz, in which a landing to loot the town had allowed the Spanish fleet to slip from harbour; so in the following year he and Raleigh planned to attack and destroy the fleet, now anchored at Ferrol, to clear their way for an attack on treasure ships returning from the Indies (plundering the plunderers, as it were). The gathering of seafarers at the beginning of our play is for this voyage to

the Azores, which was beset by tensions between its leaders –
and also by bad weather, which dispersed the Spanish fleet as
it sailed out of Ferrol bound for an attack on Falmouth.
English seafaring luck held, it seemed, even when English
judgement failed, and so the voyage became part of the popular mythology of the times. Heywood, always nostalgic for
the days of Good Queen Bess, could not actually send her off
on the high seas: instead, he created in her namesake Bess
Bridges a sort of Raleigh in petticoats.

The world of the play

Heywood's typical stage world is poised midway between
Dekker's and Shakespeare's: his chief interest, like Dekker's, is
in the deeds of ordinary folk, who invariably turn out more
virtuous than their social superiors; but, like Shakespeare, he
takes journeys of the imagination into foreign climes or the
further reaches of history and myth. It's a combination which
invited the kind of ridicule heaped by Beaumont in *The Knight
of the Burning Pestle*; but here the adventuring through time
and space is managed with disarming energy – and only between the fourth and fifth acts does it require the kind of choric,
narrative link used by Shakespeare to pace out *Henry V*.

So *The Fair Maid of the West* makes a sort of domestic complement to the *Ages* plays, dramatising the myths of Ancient
Greece, on which Heywood was then starting work. It's not
just that Bess is embarking on her own voyage of Odyssean
quests, obstacles and discoveries, but that, as in Homeric epic,
the tight-knit plot and sequential 'development' expected in
more regular drama give way before the picaresque 'and then,
and then' structure of discursive storytelling. Moreover, as in
Brechtian epic, the episodes are to an extent self-sufficient,
making dramatic points on their own account – the tavern
scenes of the first act, for example, not only full of local
colour but of economic insight. When Spencer kills Carrol
after he has insulted Bess, the drawers' immediate reaction is,
'How! A man killed, say'st thou? Is all paid?' (I, iv) – and the

short scene which follows reassures us that all is paid indeed. This is superfluous to the 'plot', but not to our wry awareness of the priorities of Elizabethan innkeeping. Additionally, as in Defoe's novels a century later, apparent irrelevance has the effect of reinforcing an otherwise tenuous verisimilitude.

Ironically, one of the reasons that Heywood is dismissed as a journeyman playwright, not only beside such figures as Shakespeare and Jonson but in comparison with the likes of Webster and Middleton, is that whereas they give dramatic expression to the tensions between the lost certainties of the past and the emergent capitalism of their own age, Heywood seems more comfortable with a 'mixed economy' of values – not unthinkingly so, but in relation to the concerns of ordinary, acceptive people rather than exceptional, resistant heroes or villains. Thus, *A Woman Killed with Kindness* refutes tragic expectations in its title, and *The Fair Maid* is a comedy which fits neither the romantic nor the satiric mould: for all its globe-trotting, its qualities are, essentially, domestic.

Where Heywood does challenge the conventional wisdom, it is from the perspective of one living in the present rather than hankering for the past. Spencer's test of Bess' virtue and Goodlack's attempts to prove it flawed spring from assumptions about the fickleness and inherent inferiority of women which Heywood certainly did not share (as his *Gunaikeon* of 1624 bears compendious testimony). So he shows Bess as displaying selfless nobility in the service of others, while Spencer, obsessed with keeping ill-advised oaths, conceives honour as the preservation of self-image. But it is through action rather than argument that the prejudice is questioned.

Not only is honour in this play embodied by a woman, but by a woman from the lower orders. This joint celebration of feminine and proletarian virtues may be no less romanticised than in later melodrama, but it gives the play an interestingly 'transgressive' subtext. Like Moll in *The Roaring Girl*, Bess is assumed to be a whore on account of her outward appearance: but she refutes such a lazy 'characterisation' of tavern wenches, just as she resists any ready-made dramatic typology –

while other characters who appear better to fit traditional moulds also break out of them. Spencer, as we have seen, is at once a brave seafarer destined to win Bess after five acts of misadventure – and a self-regarding misogynist. Goodlack, despite his name, turns from devious opportunist into faithful friend; Roughman, apparently a 'braggart soldier', is soon cured of being a braggart (and becomes a sailor instead); and poor Clem is all and none of the classical cunning servant, the Tudor clown and the honest apprentice. Beneath its deceptively simple surface, *The Fair Maid* offers its audience not only vicarious thrills and spills but its author's gently optimistic yet properly complex view of late-renaissance hopes and failings.

The sequel

It was perhaps twenty years later that Heywood wrote *Part Two* of *The Fair Maid*, in which Mullicheg and his rejected Queen, Tota, cast lustful eyes on Bess and Spencer, and are thwarted by a 'bed trick' (as used in *Measure for Measure*) which puts King and Queen into each other's arms instead of those they hoped to seduce. Bess and her friends escape, but Spencer is recaptured, and saved only by the honourable action of Joffer, who is himself rescued from Mullicheg's revenge by the escaping English. So impressed is the King with their nobility and constancy that he releases them, loading their home-bound ship with gold. The piece lacks the energy and disrupts the self-containment of its progenitor: and while the shift from action to introspection may have better suited the temper of a Caroline audience, it does not play to Heywood's strengths.

The playwright's craft

FORM   A comedy insofar as it has a happy ending, the play is rather, as discussed, an adventure in the narrative, 'storytelling' mode. Designed (as Heywood put it in the *Apology for Actors*) to 'moderate the cares and heaviness of the mind', its tradition stretches from Homeric epic to humble chapbook tale.

LANGUAGE Lamb described Heywood as 'a sort of prose Shakespeare'. In this play, his blank verse certainly works best when reined in most perfunctorily by its beat.

STAGE PRACTICE The Moroccan scenes would have been elaborately costumed, and the 'act long' or 'hautboys long' specified before them were intended to allow time for dressing the stage with exotic properties. Given the existing scenes on shipboard, it seems likely that the purpose of the chorus at the close of IV, iv, was also as much to allow time for setting the stage as to apologise for not showing more of Bess in action.

In performance

We know nothing of performances of *The Fair Maid* until it was published along with its sequel in 1631, following a performance of both parts at court by Queen Henrietta's Men. There is a passing diary reference to a revival in 1662, and a 'novelisation' published in the same year described the play as 'often acted with general applause' – but the only surviving record for over two centuries is of an adaptation by Stephen Kemble at the Haymarket in 1791. The Phoenix Society staged the first modern revival at the Lyric, Hammersmith, in 1920, and Barry Jackson mounted a production for the Malvern Festival of 1932. Apart from a musical version by Jack Emery at the Northcott, Exeter, in 1971, the single revival in the second half of the last century was a condensed adaptation of both parts at the RSC's Swan in Stratford and at the Mermaid in London in 1986–87, directed by Trevor Nunn – 'substantially as a jape, the Elizabethan equivalent of a *Carry On* film', in the view of Giles Gordon. Imelda Staunton as Bess – 'the Pearl White of the Spanish main', according to Martin Hoyle – was 'fiery, bucolic, passionate and . . . heart-rendingly serious in moments of grief', while Andrew Rissik commended Pete Postlethwaite for turning Roughman from a 'potentially tedious stereotype' into 'a lewdly comic charlatan from whom life always demands fresh resources of guile'.

The Maid's Tragedy
Beaumont and Fletcher

1610

Source

The plot is original, though specific incidents have parallels
in Sidney's *Arcadia* (1590) and Bandello's *Novelle* (1554) – both
sources the authors drew on elsewhere.

The story

The King of Rhodes has ordered a young courtier, Amintor, to
break off his engagement to Aspatia, daughter of his trusted
but tetchy counsellor Calianax, and instead marry Evadne,
sister to Melantius, Amintor's dearest friend. Newly returned
from the wars, Melantius increases the distress of the abandoned Aspatia by assuming she is the bride in the nuptial
celebrations now being prepared. After these reach their climax
in an elaborate masque, Amintor retires with Evadne to their
bedchamber: but Evadne refuses to consummate the match,
revealing that the King has arranged it as a cover for their
illicit affair. Amintor feels unable to take revenge upon his
own sovereign, and on the following morning plays the role
of newly-wed husband so well that the King at first believes
the couple have really made love. But Melantius realises that
all is not well, and eventually wrings the truth from his friend.
Confronting his sister with her dishonour, he brings her to
repentance, and then urges his old enemy Calianax to surren-
der the fort in his charge, from which to pursue vengeance
against the King. Calianax begs for time to consider, but
betrays the plan to the King – who is persuaded by Melantius
that Calianax is suffering from senile delusions. Disgusted at
serving so credulous a monarch (besides wanting to be on the
winning side), Calianax decides to give up the fort. Evadne,

having tied up the sleeping King in pretended love-play, stabs him to death, and Melantius proclaims their wrongs from the walls of the fort – so persuasively that the King's brother, Lysippus, promises him pardon. The despairing Aspatia now disguises herself as her soldier brother and seeks out Amintor, ostensibly to avenge her honour – but in fact hoping to receive a fatal wound in the duel she provokes. When Evadne arrives to confess to the King's murder, Amintor refuses to condone regicide, and she kills herself – as does Amintor, when Aspatia reveals her identity before she dies. Melantius discovers the dying Amintor, and Lysippus, now King, vows that he will 'rule with temper', taking example from these events.

The authors and their collaboration

For Beaumont's life, see *The Knight of the Burning Pestle*, p. 132. John Fletcher was born in Rye, Sussex, in 1579, son of a clergyman who became Bishop of London. He began his prolific playwriting career with the children's companies, writing *The Faithful Shepherdess* for the Queen's Revels Children in 1608. Another early independent work, for the King's Men, *The Woman's Prize; or, The Tamer Tamed* (1611), was a proto-feminist sequel to *The Taming of the Shrew*, following which Fletcher probably worked with the semi-retired Shakespeare on *Henry VIII*, *The Two Noble Kinsmen* and the lost *Cardenio*. Later, as 'house dramatist' for the King's, his most frequent collaborator was Massinger, their joint output including *The Custom of the Country* (1619), *The Beggar's Bush* (1622) and *The Spanish Curate* (1622). Other plays of his sole authorship included *The Chances* (1617), *The Island Princess* (1621), *The Wild-Goose Chase* (1621) and *Rule a Wife and Have a Wife* (1624). He died in 1625. His quite brief partnership with Beaumont (from around 1606 to 1613) had its 'brand name' attached to some four dozen plays, but their actual collaboration probably produced no more than ten, the best remembered being *The Maid's Tragedy*, *Philaster* (1609) and *A King and No King* (1611). While tradition has it that Fletcher was the 'ideas man' of the team, and Beaumont the one who tended to give these ideas shape, it is rather a matter of shared sensibility that makes their output distinctive – a sensibility well adjusted to the 'sophisticated' taste of Blackfriars audiences for romantic plays on intricately plotted, aristocratic themes, which raised issues of serious import but offered a reconciliatory and not too morally contentious outcome.

The historical context

The nuptial masque in the first act of *The Maid's Tragedy* at first seems superfluous to the plot – especially at that stage of the play, which we expect to be concerned with initiating action and getting across necessary exposition. But in its way the masque here does both, by creating an equivalence between the play's ostensible setting in some timeless 'Rhodes' and the immediacy of the Court of King James. Here, the uneasily harnessed team of Ben Jonson as writer and Inigo Jones as designer were transforming the masque from an archaic, even rustic entertainment – such as 'The Masque of the Nine Worthies', invented by Shakespeare for *Love's Labour's Lost* around 1594 – into an urbane, elaborately staged compliment to the ruling monarch which was also an explicit or implicit affirmation of his divine right.

Although often assumed to be medieval in origin, the concept of a divine right of kings emerged in England only in the late fifteenth century. Soon it lent useful support to the 'Tudor Myth', bestowing retrospective legitimacy upon the dynasty as saviours of the nation from the centuries of conflict caused by the usurpation and murder of Richard II – a process dramatised from first to last in Shakespeare's history plays. As the first reigning monarch of the House of Stuart, acknowledged only on her deathbed by Elizabeth as her heir, James had a practical as well as an intellectual interest in asserting his divine right; but he had to tread cautiously, since he needed the money that only Parliament could vote. The issue was a very live one in 1610, when *The Maid's Tragedy* was written, with its authors having Lysippus declare to Melantius that 'The breath of kings is like the breath of gods!' (I, i, 16) around the time that Parliament was ordering a book espousing the same sentiments to be burned and its author declared a traitor. Soon after, Parliament was dissolved by James, complaining that it had 'encroached upon many of my privileges'.

Beaumont and Fletcher prudently sidestep politics by making their King a libertine – which stretches Amintor's belief in his 'divinity' to the limits, but also allows Lysippus to predict 'sudden deaths' for all such 'lustful kings' (V, ii, 295–6). In the event, ironically, it was the chaste if politically inept Charles I who was to fall to the executioner, while his famously lustful son survived to reign unscathed and father numerous illegitimate offspring – though his Queen proved unable to produce an heir. Primogeniture – the inheritance of a title by the eldest son – sustained the operation of the sexual 'double standard' by making fathers obsessively concerned with the legitimacy of their sons – and the virginity of their brides. Hence the shock value of Evadne's sneer when Amintor attributes her reluctance to maidenly modesty: 'A maidenhead, Amintor! / At my years!' (II, i, 190–1).

The world of the play

The courtly world of *The Maid's Tragedy* is far from those of the Italianate or Iberian courts, redolent of intrigue, in which revenge tragedies are more typically played out: it is, precisely, closer to the Court of King James in its blend of shady sensuality and self-absorption. That the King's liaison with Evadne needs to be concealed is crucial to the plot, and the play is full of allusions to and anticipation of sexual activity; yet the inescapable impression is of chronic *coitus interruptus*, alike of overt and sublimated sexual acts. Aspatia's laments bemoan her loss of sexual as well as romantic fulfilment, while Amintor's sexual frustration on his wedding night is compounded by the denial of its alternative outlet through violence, since the naming of the King 'wipes away / All thoughts

revengeful' (II, i, 304–5). There follow multiple swords un-
sheathed only to be returned impotent to their scabbards –
and the crucial reversal of the play follows just such an un-
sheathing, when Melantius taxes Evadne with her dishonour
(IV, i, 97). The death she inflicts on the King, bound helpless
to his own bedpost, is scarcely an honourable one; while the
play's second victim, Aspatia, simply by being a woman, drains
all honour from the one actual duel that is fought – and both
Evadne and Amintor commit suicide. A final thwarted un-
sheathing occurs when Melantius makes to stab himself – and
the audience must decide whether he will, as he vows, seek
death by other means or (as his earlier pragmatism suggests)
become a creature of influence in the new regime.

Melantius is, indeed, close kin to Fortinbras, a man expert in
picking up the pieces of enemies' misfortunes; and other characters, too, seem at times to have wandered in from *Hamlet* –
notably the cantankerous Calianax, an after-image of Polonius,
the despair of whose spurned daughter resembles Ophelia's.
But although eponymously this is Aspatia's tragedy, she is
absent from the middle part of the action – only to re-emerge
not as Ophelia, but a tragic version of Viola, a woman fighting a duel in male guise. These echoes remind us how dependent the play is on self-aware theatricality and an audience's
willing acceptance of the conventions of revenge tragedy –
notably, the need for delay and byplay to draw out the action,
all the more needful in the absence of a comic sub-plot. While
the delays serve a necessary dramatic purpose, they also provide an opportunity for feelings to be dwelt on, explored and
luxuriated in; and this brooding upon characters' sensibilities
evidently appealed to Blackfriars audiences, and was a main
cause of Beaumont and Fletcher's popularity.

The action is duly fleshed out by the masque in the first act;
by the King's doubts over Evadne's faithfulness and by Melantius' cross-examination of Amintor about his secret woe in
the third; and, in IV, ii, by the business between Melantius
and Calianax over the fort, resulting in the wily younger
man's shaming of the counsellor before the King. In this res-

pect, it may seem surprising that the matter of regicide is not the subject of further agonised and time-consuming debate, but it would have been incautious for the authors to venture far into such dangerous territory. Evadne's murder of the King is thus presented as a crime of passion, not a political act.

The King at first assumes a quite different sort of passion – that his mistress is trying out the 'pretty new device' of a bondage game (V, i, 47), and Evadne describes her stabs as 'love tricks' (V, i, 103). This is not the only occasion when titillation impinges upon tragedy: in II, i, Evadne's ceremonial undressing by her ladies goes as far towards strip-tease as decorum (or the young boy playing the role) would allow, and is accompanied by the aphrodisiac urgings of Dula – her song at II, i, 79–84 a celebration of promiscuity. Evadne's refusal of conjugal rights to Amintor is thus conducted, almost tauntingly, *en déshabillé*. Yet the play carries little erotic charge: and the intended irony of both Amintor and the King suffering sexual disappointment at a moment of high arousal is dispersed by a negative energy which suffuses the whole play.

Thus, Amintor does *not* marry Aspatia. He does *not* sleep with Evadne. He does *not* kill the King. Evadne retreats from a selfish, bitchy individuality into becoming a receptor for her brother's ideas. Aspatia simply retreats, consummating only her morbid desire *not* to live. Her father is chronically in retreat – like Lysippus, following the impulse of the coward *not* to be on the losing side. Melantius is a control freak, whether in directing the affairs of his sister and friend or in the little power game he plays with Calianax and the King. And in the end he does *not* succeed in committing suicide.

It's not just that we cannot imagine these characters living lives before the play begins. The same might be said of the characters of Webster or Middleton: but there we have a compensatory sense that their natures are being existentially determined by their actions. In *The Maid's Tragedy* there is no such determination, just a dramatic plot being ingeniously but lifelessly worked through by characters who have function but very little force in a play which has brilliance but lacks depth.

The playwright's craft

FORM   The play, while sharing many characteristics of the tragi-comic romances which were the authors' stock in trade, is transformed by its final act into an example of what we might call 'romantic tragedy'. It is not so much Aspatia's grief as Evadne's sin which makes a reversal towards comedy (such as occurs in *The Malcontent*) impossible: in *A Woman Killed with Kindness* the loss of a woman's chastity is similarly irredeemable (as its false assumption is the crux of *The Winter's Tale*).

STRUCTURE   Although Dryden referred to its 'labyrinth of design', the play is, despite its twists and turns, quite simple to follow on stage. The five act-divisions are probably original, following the practice of the indoor, 'private' theatres.

LANGUAGE   The only apparent relevance of the choice of Rhodes as a setting is that it is an island, lending some consistency to recurring reflections on the ebb and flow of tides and fortunes, on rocks battered by waves, on the treacheries of quicksand, and on seas that can turn within the hour from calm to stormy billows. Predicating such imagery are scenes often structured as two-way debates between contrasting or opposing characters, the arguments following their own logic rather than a rhetorical pattern. Prose (in the absence of 'low' characters) is rare, though the fluent if unmemorable blank verse is varied when Evadne and Dula banter in rhyming couplets in II, i, until Aspatia joins in and darkens the mood.

CONVENTIONS   The use of a masque to state a theme (albeit ironically) rather than to provide a cover for climactic bloodletting (as more often in revenge tragedy) is distinctive.

STAGE PRACTICE   An upper level is utilised for the walls of the fort from which Melantius speaks in V, ii. A four-poster bed (as in V, i) was a not unknown requirement in plays of the time, as in *Volpone* and, later, *'Tis Pity She's a Whore*.

In performance

The early quarto editions of *The Maid's Tragedy* describe it as
'acted at the Blackfriars', where it would have been among
the earliest of the plays presented by the King's Men in their
new indoor playhouse, probably with Richard Burbage in the
role of Melantius. It would have remained in the repertoire
when the company returned to the Globe for the summer
months, and was also performed at Court in 1612–13. That
the Calianax thread survived as a 'droll' during the Commonwealth suggests a continuing theatrical popularity, and it was
among the earliest plays to be revived by the reconstituted
King's company after the theatres reopened in 1660. Over the
next few decades Charles Hart established himself in the role
of Amintor, opposite the Melantius of Michael Mohun, their
successors including Robert Wilks and Thomas Betterton –
Melantius the latter's last role before his death in 1713. The
play's popularity lasted into the 1720s, but apart from a few
revivals in the 1740s it was then lost to the London stage until
the twentieth century, with revivals at the Royalty in 1904 and
the Court in 1908. In 1921 a young Sybil Thorndike played
Evadne in a Phoenix Society production at the Lyric, Hammersmith, and four years later the role was taken by Edith
Evans, opposite Ion Swinley's Amintor, for the Renaissance
Society at the Scala. Bernard Miles omitted the masque from
his Mermaid production of 1964, and Philip Prowse omitted a
good deal else from his adaptation at the Glasgow Citizens' in
1979. At the RSC's intimate Other Place in Stratford in 1980
Barry Kyle's modern-dress production achieved, in Michael
Billington's words, a decisive shift 'from classical Rhodes to
contemporary Harold Robbins country', capturing 'the play's
tone of kinky perversity' at the expense, however, of its 'political dimension'. Irving Wardle noted the 'emphasis on male
attachment' in the 'great ruling passion between Amintor and
Melantius', played by Rob Edwards and Tom Wilkinson, while
Benedict Nightingale praised the 'serene sexual contempt' of
Sinead Cusack's Evadne.

The Alchemist
Ben Jonson

1610

Source

Jonson was widely read and, being well (though sceptically)
acquainted with alchemical literature, he uses its terminology
accurately. He would also have known the Roman dramatist
Plautus' *Mostellaria*, prototypical of many farcical comedies
about wily servants who abuse an absent master's trust.

The story

Lovewit having fled London on account of the plague, his butler Jeremy, under the alias of Face, has teamed up with a con-
man, Subtle, and a whore, Dol Common, to part the gullible
from their money by pretending to be alchemists. Once they
have resolved the rowdy dispute which opens the play, the trio
resume their operations, with Subtle using arcane jargon to
deceive a succession of gulls: Abel Drugger, a tobacconist seeking guidance in laying out his premises to secure the best profit
(and later in winning the hand of the wealthy widow Dame
Pliant); the lawyer's clerk Dapper, hoping to become a successful gambler; the country cousin Kastril, who wants to behave
like a quarrelsome town gallant; the puritans Ananias and
Tribulation Wholesome, intent on multiplying the funds of
their sect; and Sir Epicure Mammon, with his extravagant fantasies of a sensuous lifestyle. Despite the growing suspicions
of Sir Epicure's companion Surly, these dupes are fleeced as
ingeniously as they are kept apart; but a halt is called by the
return of Lovewit, to face the complaints of his neighbours
and the outrage of the gulls. Face, now once more Jeremy the
butler, is forced to confess all; but although Subtle and Dol
are sent packing and the gulls (with the exception of Dapper)

undeceived, Face wins a reprieve by stage-managing a marriage between Lovewit and the well-endowed Dame Pliant.

The author and his work

For a general outline of Jonson's life see *Every Man in His Humour*, p. 57, and for the context of his more recent work *Volpone*, p. 116, and *Epicoene*, p. 147. *The Alchemist* was evidently written either in the winter between the plague closures of 1609 and 1610 or during the later of these, which began in July. I am persuaded by those who (from references in the text) give 1 November 1610 as the first London performance.

The historical context

Strictly, alchemy is the pursuit of the 'philosopher's stone' for the transmutation of base metals into gold – itself the subject of my contextual introduction to *Volpone* (p. 117). It also embraced the quest for a universal solvent, and for the 'panacea', or remedy to cure all ills. Jonson's knowledge of the jargon and methods of alchemy is accurate enough, but since Subtle and Face are using it exclusively for the mystification of their clients audiences may safely remain mystified too. It is useful to bear in mind, though, that just as no hard-and-fast distinction can be drawn between the studies of astrology and astronomy during our period (even mathematical signs being viewed with caution, as perhaps concealing magical formulae), so alchemy was still inseparable from what we would dignify as 'scientific' chemistry. Even the downmarket equivalents of alchemists – those 'cunning men' (said to be as numerous as the clergy) who performed folk magic to cure the ills, restore the fortunes and tell the futures of country folk – were more often tolerated than persecuted. And did not the King himself encourage the belief that his touch would cure scrofula, the King's Evil? Respected alchemists included John Dee – for some years an adviser to the old Queen – who while at Cambridge had staged Aristophanes' *Peace* with flying effects evidently well ahead of their times, and the avid theatregoer Simon Forman, who left us rare eye-witness accounts of performances at the Globe. The connection between theatricality and confidence-trickery, both dependent on the skills of the performer to woo an audience, is not accidental, as Jonson's 'Argument' to the play makes strikingly clear.

The world of the play

The action of *The Alchemist* occurs on 1 November 1610 'in the Friars', the fashionable area around the old monastery, where the Blackfriars playhouse was itself situated. Since this was also a time when wary Londoners like Lovewit were venturing back home after the plague, it does seem that Jonson intended his play to be as contiguous as possible in time, place and circumstance to its first audience. So how has such an apparently topical play on so arcane a subject come to be regarded as one of the comic masterpieces of the British theatre? For that matter, how can a play so beautiful manage not to have a single beautiful person in it?

Every age has had its preferred solution to the riddle of existence, but in essence the alchemists' belief that all matter derives from a common source doesn't differ that much from our acceptance of a universe exploding outwards from a singularity. More mundanely, the temptations of alchemy are different in kind but not at all in intention from those by which the unwary continue to be parted from their money. Before we scoff at Jonson's victims of mock-alchemy, we should pause to consider whether Abel Drugger's desire to arrange his shop more lucratively is any different from trusting in *feng shui* to achieve the same end. And how many Dappers of today devise 'infallible' systems of gambling – or persist in the even more distant hope of scooping the Lottery jackpot? Religious and quasi-religious sects continue to equate salvation with donations, and 'lifestyle' magazines and 'reality' TV shows tempt the likes of Kastril into emulating petty celebrity – while the fantasies of latter-day Sir Epicures are variously catered for by internet pornographers, gourmet chefs, and the manufacturers of luxury bathrooms. With a global superpower declaring the 'pursuit of happiness' a constitutional right, alchemy has been displaced by more varied options for arousing but never quite fulfilling our desires. The world of *The Alchemist* is very close to our own.

Above and beyond this, *The Alchemist* is simply one of the most rip-roaringly *energetic* plays ever written, bursting at the seams not just with activity but with the sheer perverse drive of its characters in the varieties of their gullibility and greed. Much of its sheer speed derives from the need to prevent people from bumping into each another, the pace quickening as the success of the scams enthuses the victims to pursue their promised fortunes. Volpone, of course, had a similar succession of visitors to be kept from coinciding, but his were intent on the shared objective of becoming his heir, whereas the customers of Face and Subtle seek an eccentric variety of ends – their original ambitions worked on by the con-men to keep them entrapped. Drugger's ambitions are thus enhanced from increasing his trade to marrying his wealthy neighbour; Dapper's from a wish to win at dice into a belief that his aunt, the Queen of Faery, will make him her heir; and Ananias from embezzling the property of widows and orphans for conversion into gold to the conviction that minting coinage, forged but protestant, will empower the Anabaptists to rival the Holy Roman Empire. While richly comic in their wrenching reconciliation of the material and the spiritual, Ananias and his sidekick Tribulation seem downright evil in their perverted religiosity; but Jonson's view of humanity was now maturing into tolerance, and most of the other ambitions here on display are closer to follies than crimes, whether kept within Drugger's shopkeeperly limits or boundless in the imaginings of Sir Epicure – who (albeit for his own greater glory) would even wish to do humanity some good.

So we are invited to share Lovewit's amused tolerance of his butler's deception, though recognising the comic necessity – which Lovewit's intervention determines – that all the schemes should ultimately fail. This is not least because Subtle and Face are deceiving not only their dupes but themselves. Hence the importance of the hilarious slanging-match which opens the play *in medias res*, and of the final act in which it decisively shifts both in direction and location, moving out of doors as we finally meet the neighbours Dol was anxious should not overhear the quarrel. Clustering round the door of this house of dreams, they enter into comic competition to feed Lovewit their little gobbets of scandal. Although unnamed, even these tiny cameo roles are individualised – Sixth Neighbour, for example, all a-flurry with anxiety to chip in, usually too late and unheard, and only getting noticed (after a double-take) with the implicit admission that he is clearly as put-upon indoors as out. 'About,' he says – rounding off somebody else's verse line with his tentative interjection – 'About / Some three weeks since I heard a doleful cry / As I sat up a-mending my wife's stockings' (V, i, 32–4).

Some see Face, Doll and Subtle as embodying respectively the world, the flesh and the Devil, and so kin to the vices of the old moral interludes. But these seducers are from a more sophisticated world, beyond the simple verities of the homiletic tradition but very aware of their clients' need for what the critic Stephen Greenblatt has elaborated with brilliance as 'Renaissance self-fashioning' – the shaping of one's identity into a kind of idealised and theatricalised image of itself. Kastril is the extreme example, desiring to excel in dispute and duelling, careless of the cause so long as the image is right. And Sir Epicure is already well practised in self-imaging, like the Marlovian overreachers whose comic counterpart he is, his hyperbole already fleshing out his fantasies to his own satisfaction as they delight audiences with their confident plunges from extravagance into bathos. Even Surly, who sees though the deceptions, is self-deceiving in his belief that he is out for moral justice: what he really seeks is to boost his own self-image.

Subtle, Face and Dol have a remarkable flair for collective improvisation, intuitively recognising and playing off each other's strengths, whether overcoming crises of convergence or seizing a chance to increase their booty. And amidst the almost continuous frenzy, the sheer comic panache of certain episodes almost transcends their hilarity. Most notable, perhaps, is the turning of the tables upon the suspicious Surly, as he stands imprisoned in his disguise of a Spanish grandee unable to speak English, and so is impotent to act as insult after insult is heaped upon his dignity. No less momentous is the final emergence of Dapper from the privy, forgotten until he has nibbled away his gingerbread gag, but at last to be granted an audience with his Aunt of Faery. And briefly but stunningly memorable is Ananias' return at the moment of maximum tumult, declaring with all the dignity he can muster, 'Peace to the household' (IV, vii, 42).

In a less imaginative play-world, Surly would have been not a truculent gamester but a presentable gallant, successful in his scheme to outsmart wrongdoing and to capture the heart of an heiress, thereby simultaneously mending his fortunes while saving her from betrothal to some roguish old lecher. Here, it is the roguish old lecher who snatches the heiress, and scoops the jackpot of treasure stashed away by Face and Subtle in the cellar. With a quiet authority that charms or outflanks opposition, Lovewit accomplishes this almost casually in the last act – no doubt also ensuring that Jeremy's allegiance to him will be constant, since he is clearly Subtle's superior in guile. The pair share the Epilogue between them, good-naturedly apologising for or explaining away the breaches in dramatic decorum, and leaving us cheerfully ignorant of Jonson's views on the rights and wrongs of it all.

The playwright's craft

FORM Although clearly a 'comedy of humours' by Jonson's own definition, in that each of the gulls has a predominant passion which corrupts his judgement, we might more helpfully think of *The Alchemist* as a farce of the finest vintage, in that the pace builds out of the need to keep contingent characters apart, and then accelerates until going off the tracks becomes an inevitable comic catharsis.

STRUCTURE Jonson juggles with no fewer than seven comic plots in continuous time, and as in *Volpone* allows the victims to take centre stage one at a time, with Subtle, Face and Dol as masters of ceremony holding it all precariously together (the scene-divisions reflecting these 'units of action' rather than clearances of the stage). The main action has been played almost as far as it can go when Surly's Spanish impersonation permits a new comic twist, as of course does the arrival of Lovewit to give a fresh impetus to the final act – as Richard Cave has nicely expressed it, 'like a musical coda: a surprising finale . . . achieved by a magnificent flourish of all the foregoing themes'.

LANGUAGE We note both the sheer variety in style and tempo of the blank verse – from a singular pentameter of curses shared between six speakers (I, i, 107) to the extended sybaritic elegies in which Mammon wafts away on clouds of his own hyperbole. Each of the characters has his or her own expressive idiom, designed to conceal motive behind jargon or circumlocution, until Lovewit arrives to cut through it all with concision, clarity and a ruthless will.

CONVENTIONS Apart from observing the convention that disguise is always impenetrable, and (one assumes) the movement of the action downstage to signify 'outside' in the last act, the play depends on remarkably little beyond Jonson's verbal wit and the physical dexterity of the actors.

STAGE PRACTICE Modern productions which fill the stage with alchemical clutter miss the point that Subtle's workshop remains unseen – might not need to exist, had it not eventually to explode. In modern terms, he is seeing his patients in his consulting room, or as it might be on the analyst's couch. Hence the play would have been no less readily performable on the bare stage of the Globe than at the Blackfriars. The wardrobe, however, would have been kept busy in both playhouses, supplying the constant changes of costume required for the disguises of the three tricksters.

In performance

Although *The Alchemist* was performed in September 1610 in Oxford, during a tour necessitated by plague closure, it was almost certainly intended for a first staging by the King's Men at their new winter quarters, the Blackfriars; and the date on which the action takes place, 1 November 1610, may well also have been that of the first London performance. The play's popularity during Jonson's lifetime continued into the Restoration and (though increasingly in censored versions) into the eighteenth century, when David Garrick made Drugger one of his favourite and most regularly revived roles. William Poel rescued the play from Victorian obscurity and restored its textual fidelity in a production for his Elizabethan Stage Society, first seen in 1899 and twice revived, with a young Lewis Casson playing one of the neighbours. Other productions by 'little' theatres followed, and in 1932 a revival by the Birmingham Rep was taken to the Malvern Festival. Tyrone Guthrie directed the play for the Old Vic Company, in wartime exile at the Liverpool Playhouse, in 1944. Together with a later Old Vic revival, by John Burrell at the New Theatre in 1947, this restored active theatrical interest in the play. Notable later productions included Joan Littlewood's, for Theatre Workshop at Stratford East, in 1953; a new version by Guthrie for the Old Vic in 1962, played in modern dress; an adaptation by Peter Barnes for the RSC, directed by Trevor Nunn at The Other Place in Stratford and subsequently at the Aldwych, in 1977; a production by Griff Rhys Jones at the Lyric, Hammersmith, in 1985; and a co-production by the National Theatre and Birmingham Rep in 1996, directed by Bill Alexander.

The White Devil
John Webster

1612

Source

The play is based on the notorious love affair in Italy between
an actual Vittoria and Duke Bracciano from their meeting in
1581 to his death and her murder in 1585. Of the numerous
manuscript versions of this affair which soon began to circu-
late, it is thought most likely that *The White Devil* is based on a
German account in a newsletter written for the Fugger bank-
ing house and a *Letter Lately Written from Rome*, translated in
1585. Although the real Bracciano died a natural death, most
of the play derives, albeit loosely, from historical events.

The story

Flamineo, in the service of the Duke Bracciano, learns from
Camillo, husband of his sister Vittoria, that she is being urged
by the Duke to become his mistress. Sure enough, Vittoria is
ready to exchange the 'jewel' of her chastity for the jewel she
is given by the Duke. Alone with her brother, she tells him of
a dream, which Flamineo interprets as incitement to murder
Camillo and Bracciano's wife, Isabella. Isabella confides to
her own brother, the Duke Francisco de Medici, and the
Cardinal Monticelso, Camillo's uncle, her fears that Bracciano
is unfaithful. The Duke is angered alike by their admonitions
and by the doting humility of his wife, and swears on oath
that he has divorced her. He is then shown in dumb-show by
a conjuror that Isabella has been poisoned and Camillo killed
in a pretended accident. Vittoria is brought to trial for her
husband's death, and her arraignment rapidly develops into a
duel of words between herself and Monticelso. Cutting short
her dignified but devious responses, the Cardinal sentences

her, along with her black maidservant Zanche, to confinement in a house for reformed prostitutes. News of Isabella's death is brought by her son Giovanni, and Flamineo pretends madness to avoid close questioning. Francisco, planning to avenge the death of Isabella, secures the help of Lodovico, her former admirer recently returned from exile. Bracciano and Vittoria plan to escape to Padua, there to marry under cover of the confusion caused by the death of the Pope. But Monticelso is chosen as new Pope, and excommunicates Vittoria, while secretly approving the plans of Francisco and Lodovico for revenge upon Bracciano. Disguised as a valiant Moor, Francisco is made welcome at Bracciano's court, with Lodovico and Gasparo in his company. Flamineo, quarrelling with his brother Marcello, kills him in the presence of their mother Cornelia. Lodovico and Gasparo sprinkle poison into the helmet which Bracciano is to wear for a coming tournament, and as he lies dying in torment taunt him with their true identities before strangling him. Flamineo, banished by the new young Duke Giovanni, learns that his mother has been driven mad by the death of Marcello, and finds a 'strange thing . . . compassion' stirring in him. He claims to have vowed to Bracciano that neither he nor Vittoria should outlive the Duke, but is persuaded by Vittoria and Zanche to avoid the sin of self-murder by letting them shoot him, before taking each other's lives. Instead they trample upon Flamineo's supposed corpse, whereupon he rises to reveal that the pistols were not loaded. Lodovico and Gasparo then arrive and stab all three, who die lingeringly – Vittoria with a defiance which reconciles brother and sister. Lodovico implicates Francisco in the conspiracy before being taken to his death. Giovanni vows: 'All that have hands in this, shall taste our justice.'

The author and his work

John Webster was born around 1580 into a prosperous middle-class family, his father a coachbuilder and wagonmaker with premises in Smithfield, north-west of the City of London.

The business was continued by his brother, perhaps helping to support Webster's career in the theatre – for, by contrast with most professional dramatists, his output was scarcely sufficient to provide a living. His law studies in the Middle Temple evidently incomplete, he is first heard of in the theatre from payments made to Dekker, Middleton and himself by the manager Philip Henslowe in 1602, and two years later was entrusted with the 'additions' to Marston's *The Malcontent* (see p. 74). Two 'citizen comedies' – *Westward Ho!* (1604) and *Northward Ho!* (1605) – followed, in collaboration with Dekker, and in 1607 a history play, *Sir Thomas Wyatt*. Around 1612–13 he wrote in quick succession the two great tragedies which have sustained his reputation; but whereas *The White Devil* had its first performance at the Red Bull, an open-air theatre of low repute, *The Duchess of Malfi* (see p. 193) was performed by the King's Men at the indoor Blackfriars. Apart from *The Devil's Law Case* (1617) Webster's later dramatic output was largely collaborative, with civic celebrations and occasional verse completing a modest canon. Beyond these bare facts we know little of his life – or even the exact date of his death, though his fellow playwright Thomas Heywood refers to him as dead by 1634.

The historical context

As the birthplace of the Renaissance, but also cradle and focal point of Catholic authority, Italy aroused mixed feelings of admiration, loathing and horrified fascination in the average Englishman; and as early as 1570 Roger Ascham had singled out the traveller to Italy as most liable to be tainted by foreign parts. Its multiplicity of kingdoms and city states came under the competing sways of French, Spanish and German invaders; while the intrigues of such ruling families as the Medicis and the Borgias – as recorded in Guicciardini's *History of Italy* (first translated into English in 1579) – were inextricably linked in the popular mind with the supposedly amoral and atheistic teachings of Machiavelli. Thomas Nashe addressed the nation as if it were itself a character of particular viciousness: 'O Italy, the academy of manslaughter, the sporting place of murder, the apothecary-shop of poison for all nations: how many kind of weapons hast thou invented for malice?' Jacobean tragedy thrived on and contributed to this view: not only did it make for a convenient kind of dramatic shorthand, but permitted, at least on occasion, an obliquely critical attitude towards domestic concerns. Vices not conspicuously absent from the court of King James could be more safely castigated abroad, while comment upon religion, otherwise taboo, could be scarlet-cloaked in the sayings and deeds of scandalous papist cardinals – such as Webster's Monticelso in this play, and his even less scrupulous Cardinal in *The Duchess of Malfi*.

The world of the play

Although the arraignment of Vittoria and the murder of Bracciano are Webster's inventions, most of what appear to be improbabilities in this play are factually derived: the real-life Bracciano did murder Isabella; Flamineo did act as his sister's pander and arrange her first husband's murder; Monticelso was indeed elevated to the papacy in the midst of the crisis; and brother and sister did meet cruel deaths at the instigation of Lodovico. But Webster draws his action into a sharper, tighter focus, giving us characters who behave not in response to the slow happenstance of years but to a surge of action impelled by their own needs and desires.

He appears to shape that action according to the conventions of 'revenge tragedy', but in truth reshapes these for his own ironic purposes. The most enigmatic of his characters, Flamineo, is like Hamlet in assuming the guise of the malcontent; yet so far from being also a revenger, his involvement in the murders of Isabella and Camillo – intended to *prevent* the revenge of the wronged wife and husband vividly anticipated in Vittoria's dream (I, ii, 229–55) – only precipitates the need for the brooding Francisco and the austere Monticelso to assume the revengers' role. Even death is presented as a sequence of ironic contrasts. The dumb-shows evoked by the Conjuror (II, ii) serve to distance us intellectually from the murders of Isabella and Camillo, and so to shift our attention to the response of Bracciano. The first, pretended death of Flamineo (V, vi, 100–44) actually parodies the kind of dying speeches to which revenge heroes were prone (and, played with style, may aptly become quite comic, since an audience can scarcely take seriously such lines as 'My liver's parboiled like Scotch holy-bread'). Easing tension, the mock-death leaves us less inclined to laugh at the sheer extent of the ensuing slaughter – but readier to question the nature of the 'reality' of the dying rhetoric that has so recently been burlesqued.

In the *Poetics*, Aristotle, arguing for the pre-eminence in a play of action over character, declared that a man's happiness or otherwise is decided by the choices he makes – especially 'when those are not obvious'. And this comes close both to Webster's Jacobean view of 'character' and to what we would today call 'existential' choice, by asserting that our individuality is shaped not (as in 'realist' drama) through the deterministic effects of heredity and environment but, as with the characters here, through the sum of our own actions and the choices determining them: truly, existence preceding essence. Throughout the play, then, Flamineo and Vittoria act not through such 'essential' selfhood as Shakespeare's characters bode forth, but in response to events.

There is also a strong economic imperative to Flamineo's actions (unlike, say, those of Iago, the Shakespearean character most ambiguous in his 'essence'). This is clear from our first glimpse of this impoverished hanger-on at court, and is made acrimoniously explicit in the argument with his mother over his lack of an inheritance (I, ii, 308–45). Vittoria's marriage to Camillo has also been dictated by her family's financial plight. She is wooed not with professions of love but promises of reward – from a jewel in exchange for the 'jewel' of her chastity to the ultimate reward of becoming Bracciano's duchess.

For a play which gives an irresistible impression of a world in moral disorder, *The White Devil* is much concerned with matters of justice – punishment for sin, rewards for services rendered. In one of those 'short syllables / That stand for periods' so characteristic of the play, Lodovico's curt exclamation in the opening scene, 'Courtly reward! / And Punishment!' (I, i, 3–4), has been taken by some critics as a statement of its theme (Muriel Bradbrook well summed up Webster's characteristic verbal style as 'small packets of energy' which are 'implosive rather than explosive'). Even the election of the Pope is hedged about with hints of corruption (IV, iii, 24–32), while Lodovico believes Monticelso capable of secret bribery – 'the modest form of greatness!' (IV, iii, 143). And the final act is bursting with references to rewards – and, of course, punishments, as when Flamineo, claiming from his sister a 'Reward, for my long service' (V, vi, 8), is instead cursed with the lot of Cain for the murder of his brother.

The 'Arraignment of Vittoria' is in this respect exemplary of Webster's dialectical technique, as our already ambivalent feelings about the 'white devil' herself shift strangely in her favour when she fiercely parries Monticelso's vituperation. Our attitude to all the main characters is kept in a similar state of flux, their deaths thus becoming the resolution not only of the play but of our own (perhaps unconscious) debate about their natures – as Kenneth Tynan put it, 'hypnotised by their own reflection in the eyes of death'.

Although some critics have seen in the play an orthodox admonition that judgement must be left to God, Flamineo, at least, expects neither grace nor damnation, his death merely 'i' th' way to study a long silence' (V, vi, 203). While reasons or 'motives' can be found for his actions, it is probably more helpful to understand him through his behaviour and his attempts at a kind of self-definition: he *becomes* what he does. A profession of a faith in self rather than in God is summed up in Lodovico's cry as he is dragged off to the rack and the gallows: 'I do glory yet, / That I can call this act mine own' (V, vi, 293–4). Vittoria and Flamineo, at least, share this sense of unyielding responsibility for their own actions.

The playwright's craft

FORM Webster's highly personal 'take' on revenge tragedy has been discussed above. In this respect it's also worth mentioning that in his prefatory note, 'To the Reader', he stresses that he has consciously ignored such classical requirements of tragedy as 'height of style, and gravity of person'. Nor, we might add, has he included any sub-plots or scenes of comic counterpoint. This is, distinctively, 'Websterian' tragedy.

STRUCTURE There are no act- or scene-divisions in the original text, with the exception of the unusual designation of 'The Arraignment of Vittoria' as a set-piece. This, combined with the absence of sub-plotting, gives an urgency and 'flow' to the action appropriate to a play in which characters have constantly to adjust and react to the onrush of events.

LANGUAGE With its abrupt metrical variations and passages of disjointed thought, Webster's blank verse often traces what we would today call a character's 'stream of consciousness'. He can also accommodate readily both a highly formal style – as in Monticelso's 'Shall I expound whore to you?' speech (III, ii, 78–101) or the proto-naturalism which follows, with its cut-and-thrust of argument between Vittoria and her accuser and interjections from Francisco and the ambassadors (101–24). Even in this short episode the effects are many and various: two or three characters may share the same metric line (104, 109–10), or the addition of an extra syllable (a 'feminine ending') may assist the continuity of sense into the next line (108) or give added emphasis (121). We note also how the alternation of short, sharp sentences, colloquial rather than grammatical, with more formal speech effectively sharpens the attention we pay to both (110–18).

STAGE PRACTICE Strands of verbal imagery frequently get a visual complement – the pervasive imagery of corruption thus vividly brought to life when the ghost of Bracciano produces a skull from beneath lily flowers (V, iv, 124–41); while the motif of painting is 'displayed' in the dumb-show murder of Isabella. Vittoria's arraignment (III, ii) offers a more formal spectacle, as do the ceremonies surrounding the election of the Pope (IV, iii) and the preparations for the tournament intended to celebrate Bracciano's marriage (V, ii–iii).

In performance

Despite its poorly received first staging at the open-air Red Bull, Clerkenwell, in 1612, *The White Devil* became sufficiently popular in Webster's lifetime for a second edition to be called for in 1631, which referred to the play as having been 'divers times acted' by the Queen's Men at the indoor Phoenix. It was among the earliest of the old plays to be revived after the Restoration, but was neglected from the turn of the eighteenth until the twentieth century, when James Agate, writing of a production at the Scala in 1925, compared Vittoria to the 'vamp' of silent films. A further 'little theatre' production followed in 1935 at the St Martin's. Kenneth Tynan found the first post-war production, at the Duchess in 1947, 'infinitely terrifying', and although the play then became popular with amateur and student groups, and had regional productions in Oxford, Edinburgh and Liverpool, it was not seen again in London until it joined the National Theatre's repertoire in 1969. Glenda Jackson played Vittoria at the Old Vic in 1976, Philip Prowse directed a heavily cut version dominated by its own set for Glasgow Citizens' Theatre, in 1984, but restored most of the text for his subsequent revival for the National Theatre in 1991, in which Josette Simon played Vittoria – 'fine, proud and wonderfully defiant', in Benedict Nightingale's judgement. Gale Edwards directed the play as 'full-blooded melodrama', according to Charles Spencer, for her RSC production at the Swan in 1996 and in the Barbican's Pit in 1997; while Rhoda Koenig described Philip Franks' production at the Lyric, Hammersmith, in 2000 as transplanting the play to 'the post-war Rome of *La Dolce Vita*'.

Bartholomew Fair
Ben Jonson

1614

Source

Aside from the fairground setting (see 'The Historical Context', below), the play is entirely Jonson's invention.

The story

After an Induction in which the Stage-Keeper proposes terms for the audience's reception of the play, the first act sees the arrival of a succession of visitors to the house of the aptly named Littlewit and his pregnant wife Win: the young gallants Winwife and Quarlous, and the puritan zealot Zeal-of-the-Land Busy, all three in contention for the hand of Dame Purecraft, Win's widowed mother; the bad-tempered Wasp and his foolish pupil Cokes, who is to be betrothed against her wishes to Grace Wellborn; and Cokes' sister, the wife of Justice Overdo – who, besides being magistrate of the court set up to oversee the Fair, is Grace Wellborn's guardian. Despite the misgivings of Wasp and Busy, all are persuaded to join in a visit to the Fair to indulge Win's craving for roast pork. The second act takes us into the Fair itself, first introducing us to Justice Overdo as he delivers a self-righteous soliloquy on the theme of justice, which he intends to uphold by investigating the corruptions of the fair disguised as a madman. The group of visitors then plunges headlong into the pleasures and temptations on offer, encountering such fairground denizens as fat Ursula, who sells roast pork and ale; the horse-dealer Knockem; the gingerbread-seller Joan Trash; the hobby-horse dealer Leatherhead; the bawd Captain Whit; the opportunist cutpurse Edgeworth and his ballad-singing accomplice Nightingale; and a genuine madman, Trouble-All, obsessed with obtaining Justice Overdo's warrant for everything he does. The ensuing action sees the disintegration of the group of visitors and their more or less hapless enfolding into the fabric of fairground activity, legitimate and otherwise, during which all the authority figures – the disguised Overdo, Busy and Wasp – manage to end up alongside one another in the stocks. In various states of transformation or humiliation, the visitors eventually reassemble for Leatherhead's puppet play. Wasp is downcast at his shaming in front of Cokes, Busy is bested in a dispute with a puppet he has denounced as a heathen idol – and Overdo, intending a truly magisterial entrance in his own person to denounce the proceedings, is discountenanced by the discovery of his wife, being sick amidst Whit's company of whores. Quarlous takes control, announcing his intention of marrying Dame Purecraft, and that Grace Wellborn's marriage licence has been made over to his friend Winwife. Overdo, resigned to making the best of the situation, invites the whole company home to supper.

The author and his work

For a general outline of Jonson's life see *Every Man in His Humour*, p. 57; and for the context of his more recent work *Volpone*, p. 116; *Epicoene*, p. 147; and *The Alchemist*, p. 170. Since that last play Jonson had suffered a blow with the death in 1612 of his patron and protégé Prince Henry, heir to the throne, at the age of eighteen; but despite this, and the failure of his second attempt at tragedy, *Catiline*, a year earlier, commissions for courtly masques continued, and *Bartholomew Fair* was his first new comedy for the public stage for four years.

The historical context

Fairs probably had their origin as gatherings for worship in sacred places, soon also attracting itinerant traders and entertainers, and providing opportunities for the sale of goods and livestock, and the hiring of workers. Bartholomew Fair was one of the great fairs of the Middle Ages, authorised by a charter granted in 1133 by Henry I to his former jester Rahere for the upkeep of the priory and hospital of St Bartholomew, which Rahere had founded in Smithfield, north-west of the City of London. St Bartholomew's Hospital (better known as Barts) survives to this day in Smithfield, but the fair had fallen into disrepute by the nineteenth century, and was last held in 1855. By Jonson's time, its occasion – on the three days following St Bartholomew's Eve, 23 August – was the only relic of saintly association, and it had become largely a place of buying, selling, eating, drinking and all kinds of entertainment. When disputes arose, a special court was convened to dispense instant justice – the Court of Piepowders, its name supposedly a corruption of the French *pieds poudreux*, suggesting the 'dusty feet' characteristic of itinerant tradesmen who went on their way too soon to await regular justice. It is this court, the very humblest in the land, over which Justice Overdo is so proud to preside.

Fairs have provided other writers and artists with a setting for their works – usually, as in the case of Bunyan's 'Vanity Fair' in *Pilgrim's Progress*, to suggest allegorically the trivial nature of human ambitions. Bunyan, as a puritan (deeply sincere in his beliefs, unlike Jonson's Zeal-of-the-Land Busy), was among those who distinguished on moral grounds between leisure and the serious, workaday business of earning a living. This 'protestant work ethic' was markedly different from the medieval conception of work and play as complementary aspects of the seasonal round, with plentiful holidays (holy days) to alleviate toil. Whether those festivities which celebrated the spirit of carnival, as did Bartholomew Fair, were occasions of real subversion or allowed release merely of a licensed and temporary kind has been the subject of much debate. For Jonson, instinctively closer to the medieval tradition, the conflict between its relaxed view of the fair and the censorious puritan attitude would still have been a very 'live' issue; and it is an underlying tension of the play, as it was of Jacobean society itself.

The world of the play

By the time he came to write *Bartholomew Fair*, Jonson had discarded the didactic trappings of his earlier plays, allowing free rein to the impulse to show life as it is – in all its frequent absurdity and with a few ragged edges. And so he gives us a stage world of unobtrusively orchestrated anarchy, peopled by eccentric yet knowable characters in kaleidoscopic combinations. The sheer richness of the bustling life on stage is not unlike that of a painting by Brueghel, such as 'Flemish Fair', or an engraving by Hogarth, who took 'Southwark Fair' as one of his subjects, or a novel by Dickens (whose Miss Flite in *Bleak House* shared the obsessions of Trouble-All). Of specific character types, Walt Disney's Donald Duck is surely in line of descent from Humphrey Wasp, while *The Goon Show* of the 1950s included just such an ingenuous zany as Cokes in Peter Sellers' Bluebottle and a surreal logician the likes of Trouble-All in Spike Milligan's Eccles.

While there are comparisons to be made with more 'legitimate' drama – Jonson, for example, recognised before Harold Pinter that most people do not actually listen to what is being said to them, so driven are they by their own thoughts and desires – it's important to recognise that in *Bartholomew Fair* the comedy is closer to stand-up than to any conventional theatrical kind. For a start, the play is full of *jokes* – visual as well as verbal, and depending on double-takes, overlaps, and even catch-phrases (such as Wasp's 'turd in your teeth') – and such pauses as the furious pace of the action allows are needful for the laughter to die down. So for clues to staging one needs to look not so much at units of action which develop a mood or for moments of emotional crisis between characters as at the techniques of a working comedian – building up to a laugh, then allowing (or sometimes overriding) a subsequent relaxation before preparing the way for the next. Between performers the priority is to achieve not so much psychological as *functional* interplay, such as that displayed by a good comic double-act or well-tuned 'sitcom' team.

The text is therefore much concerned with giving actors clues to the physicalisation of their roles. Sometimes this is by way of a clear stage direction, as when the smell of roast pork causes Busy to 'scent after it like a hound' (III, ii, 79). Sometimes comic 'business' is implicit in the situation, as when Wasp somehow manages to substitute his hand for his foot in the stocks (IV, vi, 102–4), or in the performance of that cony-catching trick of stealing Wasp's precious box from under his nose. And Jonson carefully uses comic incidents to conceal his structuring – for example, by disguising many of his climaxes as anti-climaxes: Win wanting to pee, the watch finding the stocks empty, Busy confounded by a puppet lifting its skirts, Overdo missing his big moment not through any elaborately plotted opposition to his plans, but because his wife chooses that moment to be sick.

Justices of the Peace such as Overdo and puritan zealots like Busy were among those Jacobean figures most intent on confining others within a straitjacket of state or doctrinal authority, as is Overdo in his other role of Grace's guardian – while Wasp, overseeing poor Cokes' every move, embodies that humbler but no less feared disciplinarian, the schoolmaster. In this play it is such control freaks who suffer the worst humiliations – while Littlewit and Cokes, who have least pretension to tell others what to do, accordingly suffer least.

So behind the surface appearance of muddle is a very carefully constructed work, both in terms of its anti-authoritarian 'message' and its formal development. Thus, each act begins with just a few characters on stage (who are given time to 'present' themselves if it is their first appearance), but rises to a hectic climax of overlapping exits and entrances. And so, as each of the fairgoers arrives in the first act, he or she is given a comic 'turn', until the stage is almost overflowing with Littlewit's visitors – who then depart, to permit a more intimate, family scene, in which the household argues itself into joining the expedition to Smithfield. The second act introduces us to the fairground folk and illustrates the interaction between them, and ends with the arrival of the visitors to the fair; while the third is largely concerned with the meeting and merging of the two groups, and is brought to a climax with the arrest of Busy for disruption. This leads to the virtually complete breakdown of the original groups of visitors in the fourth act, and their absorption into the world of the fair. The groups are reunited in the final act, which ends on the reconciliatory note of Overdo's general invitation to supper.

In this play, virtually everybody works for a living – or, like Quarlous and Winwife, is in active search of a rich wife to avoid such a necessity. This may not appear very remarkable, until one compares the situation in Shakespearean comedy, where very few people (and those the lowliest) have to work at all – just as marriage is inseparable from love and romance, whereas here it is largely a matter of money (significantly, it is of more moment to Cokes to lose his purse than his intended wife). Professional men, as Littlewit likes to think himself, may not want to discuss such sordid matters as fees, but Wasp in his forthright way prefers to pay cash for his services, and even works out what he owes in company (I, iv, 14–24).

Jonson himself, however ironically, puts a price on human judgement in his Induction, accepting that the more money a spectator has paid for admission, the greater his due share 'of censure, to like or dislike at their own charge'. Few dramatists before Brecht have been as frank as Jonson in acknowledging that in a materialist society everything and everybody tends to have a price, not least in the market economy of the Fair, while at the same time both despising that materialism and repudiating the idea that any form of 'warrant' is needed to authorise one's humanity.

The playwright's craft

STRUCTURE The puppet play opens the last of what the critic Jacqueline Latham has described as the set of 'Chinese boxes' of which the play is made up. Thus, the 'real' actors of the Induction first take on roles as characters in the workaday world – in which one of them happens to have aspirations as a playwright. They then enter the 'play' area of the fair – inside which is the even more diminutive world of Leatherhead's puppets. Overdo thinks he has been stage-managing his own play, only to find his puppets less tractable than he expects. And, says Cokes, 'we'll ha' the rest o' the play at home'. He, like Jonson at this climactic moment, knows that the play-acting does not end when we step outside the theatre.

LANGUAGE   This is a comedy written exclusively in prose, at a time when the conventional dramatic mode was still blank verse. *The Alchemist*, though full of acceptably prosaic 'low' characters, is nonetheless in verse: but that play is about men's dreams, desires and ambitions – however trivial their limited imaginations may make them – whereas *Bartholomew Fair* is about how people survive in the immediacy of their needs to eat, drink, make money, and make water. Not that the exclusive use of prose imposes any uniformity upon the play's language, for each of the main characters has a highly individualised style, and often an individual range of vocabulary as well. We notice at once the way in which Littlewit and his wife use each other's names, 'Win' and 'John', with a tender frequency and an almost erotic charge, and we may compare the way in which Quarlous seizes every idea and shakes it verbally by the scruff of its neck with his friend Winwife's brusque edicts and retorts. Busy either elaborates a simple idea to absurdity or repeats the same thing over and over again with slight variations of stress or cadence, while Overdo employs the devices of rhetoric and litters his speech with sententious quotations. And Wasp's elevation of sarcasm to a form of high art contrasts with Cokes' spontaneous exclamations of simple pleasure or dismay, as his grasshopper mind jumps from one subject to the next.

CONVENTIONS   The Induction contains much overt comment on the theatre of Jonson's time. The Stage-Keeper's taste for either basic realism or no less basic bawdy (Ind., 10–26) is derided by the Book-Keeper, who casts satirical slights (107–13) both at such old-fashioned blood-and-guts plays as *The Spanish Tragedy* and the newer-fangled improbabilities of Shakespeare's late romances (128–32).

STAGE PRACTICE The Hope, where *Bartholomew Fair* was first performed in 1614, was a multi-purpose venue, and it is tantalising to conjecture that its stage might have been dismantled and the play performed around booths set up in the arena, perhaps with a few trusted groundlings as fairgoing extras for what was in any case an exceptionally large cast.

In performance

In the Induction (161–2), Jonson reminds us that the Hope was 'as dirty as Smithfield, and as stinking every whit'. Presumably the actors cleaned up to present the play next day at court, but no further performances are recorded until the Restoration, when revivals included another performance at court in 1673. The play remained popular through the first quarter of the eighteenth century, but then dropped out of the live repertoire until the Phoenix Society's staging at the New Oxford Theatre in 1921. George Devine's Old Vic revival of 1950 was conceived for the thrust stage of the Assembly Rooms during the Edinburgh Festival, with, according to Audrey Williamson, a very young Dorothy Tutin 'piquant, brown-eyed, and ecstatic' as Win. The National Youth Theatre brought the play to the Royal Court in 1966, and an RSC revival by Terry Hands followed at the Aldwych in 1969. A Young Vic production by Michael Bogdanov ran simultaneously in 1978 with a revival at the Roundhouse by Peter Barnes, who restaged his version for the Open Air Theatre, Regent's Park, in 1987. Richard Eyre directed a first National Theatre production in 1988, and in 1997 Laurence Boswell's updated version for the RSC's Swan, seen two years later at the Young Vic, ranged, in John Peter's judgement, 'from mock-genteel through working-class butch to high punk'.

The Duchess of Malfi
John Webster

1614

Source

The real-life Duchess of Amalfi was widowed at the age of
nineteen in 1498. She then married the major-domo of her
household, had a child by him in secret, fled from her brothers
upon their discovering the truth, and later met an unknown
end. Webster's immediate source among the many published
accounts of this affair was probably the version in William
Painter's *Palace of Pleasure* (1567), itself based on the twenty-
sixth tale in Bandello's *Novelle* (1554).

The story

Antonio, newly returned from France, is full of praise for the
French king's wise government of his court – in contrast to
the corruption of the court of Amalfi under the sway of its
widowed Duchess' twin, Ferdinand, and their elder brother,
the Cardinal. Bosola, a malcontented hanger-on of the Cardinal's, is aggrieved that his master has failed to reward him
for a murder committed at his behest, and at first refuses
Ferdinand's bribe to inform on the Duchess should she plan
to remarry; but he eventually agrees to serve (and observe) her
as provisor of the horse. The Duchess woos and weds her
steward Antonio, but because of his ignoble status keeps the
marriage secret – even when she falls pregnant and is prematurely delivered of a baby son. Bosola discovers the child's
existence, but the identity of the father is known only to
Antonio's friend and confidant, Delio. In Rome, the Cardinal
banters with his mistress Julia, wife of the elderly Amalfi
courtier Castruchio, while Ferdinand has been driven mad by
Bosola's letter telling him of the birth of the Duchess' son.

Amidst rumours and suspicions at Amalfi, two more children are born to the Duchess before Ferdinand, having spent years in seclusion, returns to court. After a bedchamber confrontation between the siblings, the Duchess tells Antonio to flee to Ancona. To cover his departure he stages a dispute over the household accounts – but confesses the truth to an outwardly sympathetic Bosola, who carries news of his discovery to Rome. In consequence, the Pope seizes the Duchy of Amalfi, and the Duchess flees to join Antonio in Ancona – only to be separated again when Antonio is banished, and has to leave with their firstborn for Milan. Bosola pleads in vain with Ferdinand to be merciful to the Duchess and, refusing to torture her further in his own person, disguises himself as a tombmaker, and regales her with a consort of madmen; but she confronts her executioners with a stoic dignity which contrasts with her maidservant Cariola's terror and despair. By the final act Ferdinand has retreated into lycanthropic madness, while the Cardinal, tiring of Julia but fearing she will reveal his own complicity in the Duchess' death, forces her to kiss a poisoned book. Before she dies, Julia reveals the secret to Bosola, and he resolves to assist Antonio, only to kill him in mistake for Ferdinand – 'Such a mistake as I have often seen / In a play.' He confronts the Cardinal with the body, but while attacking him is interrupted by Ferdinand, who stabs them both before the dying Bosola inflicts a fatal wound. Delio intends to establish Antonio's firstborn 'in's mother's right'.

The author and his work

For an outline of Webster's life, see *The White Devil*, p. 178.

The historical context

Ferdinand, condemning his twin sister for her marriage to a social inferior, declares that love should only be looked for ''mongst unambitious shepherds, / Where dowries were not talked of' (III, ii, 128–9). The extent to which 'affectionate' marriages had begun to displace arranged marriages among the middle classes has been touched on in the 'Historical Context' section to *A Woman Killed with Kindness* (p. 82); but so far as the nobility was concerned no match which cast a shadow over the family tree could be countenanced. The need for new financial blood allowed the wealthier middle classes some upward mobility, but great lords simply did not marry their servants – as various of Elizabeth's courtiers had discovered to their cost, and as the poet Donne found in 1601, when he was imprisoned for marrying the niece of his employer, the Lord Keeper. But for a woman like Elizabeth, exercising power in her own right, the need to continue the line had to be balanced against keeping the reins in her own hands. With the example of her sister Mary's marriage to Philip of Spain a reminder of the dangers of an alliance between equals when one of the 'equals' was a woman, she dangled the prospect of marriage as a diplomatic carrot but died as she had lived, a calculatedly Virgin Queen. Our Duchess has, more typically, been displaced politically by her brothers; but she is no less a victim of the emotional politics of her socially unequal second marriage.

The world of the play

There's a clue as to the relative importance of the characters in *The Duchess of Malfi* in the eyes of their first performers in that Burbage, the leading player of the King's Men, took the role of Ferdinand – though in the cast list which prefaced the first printed text of the play his name follows that of Bosola, despite the social precedence more usually observed. And yet Bosola only finds himself in the Duchess' household because her brothers are intent on thwarting *any* remarriage – the Cardinal in order to preserve his power over the Duchy, and Ferdinand on account of his unspoken incestuous love for his sister. So just as Hamlet's horror at his mother's incest was inseparable from its disruption of his succession to his father's throne, so the brothers' motives also blend the lusts of sexuality and power. Incest was to be a more overt theme in *Women Beware Women* and *'Tis Pity She's a Whore*, but is no less compelling for its shallow burial in the subconscious of this play.

Ferdinand's repressed desires would have made his descent into lycanthropy (believing himself to be a wolf) psychologically truthful for a Jacobean audience, both being forms of bestiality – the only difference being, as the Doctor reports Ferdinand's words, that 'a wolf's skin was hairy on the outside, / His on the inside (V, ii, 17–18). Other striking images drawn from the bestiary haunt the play: Bosola describes 'a lady in France, that having had the smallpox, flayed the skin off her face, to make it more level; and whereas before she looked like a nutmeg-grater, after she resembled an abortive hedgehog' (II, i, 28–31); the Cardinal has a premonition of his fate when he sees 'a thing arm'd with a rake / That seems to strike at me' reflected in his fishponds (V, v, 4–5); and the dying Ferdinand compares the world to 'a dog-kennel', before achieving the momentary self-awareness of his dying words: 'My sister, oh! my sister, there's the cause on't' (V, v, 70).

Although the Duchess is one of the most intensely human characters of the Jacobean drama, hers is not an easy character, nor arguably even a consistent one: there is a strange innocence in her bawdy jesting in the privacy of her scenes with Antonio and with Cariola, and she is susceptible to Bosola's false sympathies – but she is alert and incisive in the scenes with her brothers, evading their warnings about remarriage with a joke. If her twin brother is driven by forbidden desires, she too transgresses the boundaries supposed to delimit gender roles, becoming the wooer in her courtship of Antonio and remaining the active partner in their marriage from its proposal to its ending in flight. Though Antonio has been faithful and loving in this subordinate role, once he has to act on his own account all he can do is vainly seek reconciliation with the brothers; and, ignoring the warning echoes of his own words (V, iii), he is denied even the dignity of a tragic death, murdered by mistake for another.

Bosola describes his accidental killing of Antonio as happening 'in a mist' (V, vi, 93), and the echo sequence is but one of the occasions in the play when its characters seem to be wandering through mists of their own imaginings – or of nightmares conceived by others, as in Bosola's haunting of the Duchess with simulacra of the dead and a masque of the living mad, which makes doubly ironic her account of the world as 'a tedious theatre', in which 'I do play a part . . . against my will' (IV, i, 83–4). The moral of the fable of the Salmon and the Dog-fish, recounted by the Duchess to Bosola upon her capture, seems to be that only in death may a measure of one's life be taken (III, vi, 122–43). Yet if the mists clear only at the moment of death, the clarity extinguishes into 'a little point, a kind of nothing', and leads only into 'vaulted graves / That, ruin'd yields no echo' (V, v, 78, 96–7).

While Flamineo in *The White Devil* is a malcontent in consequence of his family's poverty, and uses his character-type to some extent as a disguise, Bosola is as capable as Iago of motivating his discontent – but no more satisfactorily so. He is the pathological malcontent, taking pleasure in manipulation ('control' in the current idiom) for its own sake. He has been a hired assassin, yet relishes the grotesque preliminaries to the Duchess' death more than its execution, which he leaves to others. In telling her the merciful lie that Antonio is safely reconciled with the brothers when she stirs briefly back to life (IV, ii, 343–7), he even shows contrition. Yet his attempts to 'do good' descend in the last act into existential absurdity, his confrontation with the Cardinal only ensuring Julia's death, and his revenge upon Ferdinand wrought upon the very man he is intending to help.

Neither the Duchess nor the most devious character of the play, the Cardinal, is ever given a name: both are defined by their status, as if to keep before us the way in which both are inseparable from their roles. Yes, the Duchess gives tender instructions for her children's care as she confronts her own death, yet in a phrase famous for its resonant simplicity – 'I am Duchess of Malfi still' (IV, ii, 139) – she affirms neither motherhood nor selfhood, but social status. The Cardinal, iron-willed and barely concealing his contempt for his brother, is yet reliant upon the outward trappings of office, and so transforms himself in the dumb-show at the Shrine of Loreto from churchman into soldier with a great ceremony of divestment and investment (III, iv, 7, sd). The change of guise makes the banishment of the Duchess and Antonio, which immediately follows, all the more clearly an exercise of political rather than spiritual authority.

The Cardinal is, then, a cold fish, concerned only with outward show, and he even takes Julia as his mistress more to be fashionable than from desire. Julia's role, though small, serves as an ironic foil to the Duchess – the one a faithful wife to an 'unsuitable' husband, the other married within her own courtly circle, yet taking any man she chooses as her lover – including Delio, who still fancies her and even pursues her to Rome, losing the little dignity Webster had allowed him as a true friend to Antonio. And Cariola, the faithful maidservant to the Duchess, is reduced to panic as she faces death. No one in this play is left with much dignity, the deaths being either calculated and cruel or incidental and ignominious.

Whose tragedy is this? Eponymously, it is the Duchess', yet she is dead before the final act; Bandello, in the novella which was Webster's source, presented it as Antonio's; modern critics, focused upon Ferdinand's otherness, often write as if it were his; and what of Bosola, whose vacillations and self-doubt permeate its action, and who is instrumental in all the deaths until his own? Perhaps this is, more truly, the tragedy of a decaying social order – in which the relationship between church and state is fraught with ambiguities; in which a court and its hangers-on exist in an ethical void; in which socio-economic tensions simmer between the nobility and the lower orders. Usually, despite these dysfunctions, a kind of inertial equilibrium is none the less maintained – but the hypergamous marriage of a Duchess and the incestuous jealousy of her brother open up the cracks, and precipitate chaos.

The playwright's craft

FORM   Tragedy does not here spring from any simple or single cause in *hubris* or the need for revenge, and no single character (but arguably every character) suffers a 'tragic flaw'. As I suggest above, Webster shares the Euripidean perception that tragedy is as much rooted in the nature of society as in the failings of individuals. Leo Salingar describes the play as 'the last . . . for many years to connect private and public morality in anything approaching an inclusive tragic vision.'

STRUCTURE   Unlike *The White Devil*, *The Duchess of Malfi* is shaped into the five-act structure employed in the indoor playhouses, so that intervals of actual and stage time occur between each, giving the audience and the action pause. Dramatic punctuation is also provided by the *sententiae* – those rhymed aphoristic couplets (usual distinguished in printed texts by the use of italics), which offer a kind of semi-distanced, often out-of-character summing up of a foregoing sequence.

LANGUAGE   Where Shakespeare's language characteristically allows free rein to an audience's imagination, Webster tends to enfold one in his own – leading us into the metaphysical universe where princes' effigies lie on tombs 'as if they died of the tooth-ache', and the doors of death 'go on such strange geometrical hinges / You may open them both ways (IV, ii, 158, 221–2). Taking his commonplace books of others' wisdom and the emblem-books which gave visual substance to such *sententiae*, he creates a kaleidoscopic vision in which verbal and visual imagery inextricably blend.

CONVENTIONS   Dumb-show is used in the scene at the Shrine of Our Lady of Loreto (III, iv), where two pilgrims observe the ceremony of the Cardinal divesting his robes for 'the habit of a soldier' and the banishment of the Duchess and Antonio. Other 'shows' include the waxen corpses, the dead man's hand, and the bizarre masque of the madmen.

STAGE PRACTICE   It may have been possible for the lighting required for indoor performances at the Blackfriars to have been lowered for such 'dark' scenes as the tormenting of the Duchess in her chamber.

In performance

The Duchess of Malfi evidently kept its place in the repertoire of the King's Men following its first stagings at the Blackfriars and the Globe, at least until a performance before the King in 1630. But although revived regularly after the Restoration, it survived into the following centuries only in adaptations. These included Theobald's *Fatal Secret* of 1735 and a version by R. H. Horne successfully produced by Phelps at Sadler's Wells in 1850. William Poel presented a more accurate version of the text in 1892, as did a Phoenix Society production at the Lyric, Hammersmith, in 1919. Such 'little' theatre productions kept the play alive between the wars, but it was George Rylands' staging at the Haymarket in 1946, with John Gielgud as Ferdinand, Peggy Ashcroft as the Duchess and Cecil Trouncer as Bosola, which first struck a chord with postwar audiences. Notable among over fifty productions in the following six decades were those by John Bury for Theatre Workshop at Stratford East in 1957; by Donald McWhinnie for the first London season of the RSC at the Aldwych in 1960, with Peggy Ashcroft reprising the Duchess; by Peter Gill and William Gaskill at the Royal Court in 1971, with Judy Parfitt as the Duchess and Victor Henry as Bosola; by Clifford Williams for the RSC at Stratford later in 1971, with Judi Dench and Geoffrey Hutchings; by Adrian Noble at the Roundhouse in 1981, with Helen Mirren and Bob Hoskins; by Philip Prowse for the National Theatre in 1985, with Eleanor Bron and Ian McKellen; by Bill Alexander for the RSC at the Barbican Pit in 1990, with Harriet Walter; by Declan Donnellan, for Cheek by Jowl in 1996; by Gale Edwards for the RSC at the Barbican in 2000; and by Phyllida Lloyd at the National in 2003, with Janet McTeer.

Women Beware Women
Thomas Middleton

c. 1621

Sources

The elopement of Bianca Capello, her subsequent affair with
Francesco de Medici, and their mysterious deaths were given
narrative form in Celio Malespini's *Ducento Novelle* (1609),
and more recent English accounts may have been available to
Middleton in manuscript. The sub-plot derives from a French
source of 1598, translated into English as *The True History of
the Tragic Loves of Hipolito and Isabella Neapolitans* in 1628.

The story

When Leantio, a banker's clerk, brings home his bride, the
beautiful and socially superior Bianca, his surprised Mother is
sceptical of the success of the match, but does her best to keep
Bianca safe indoors in her son's absence. However, the lasci-
vious Duke catches Bianca's eye as she watches a passing procession, and he seeks the help of a courtier, Guardiano, and
Livia, a friend of the Mother's, in plotting her seduction. As
Livia distracts the Mother over a game of chess, the Duke
seizes his chance and wins Bianca's compliance with promises
of fortune. Meanwhile Livia's niece Isabella has been told by
her father, Fabritio, that she is to marry Guardiano's nephew,
a rich but foolish Ward. Livia's brother, Hippolito, having
confessed to her that he harbours an incestuous love for their
niece, Livia persuades Isabella that Fabritio is not her real
father, and suggests that marriage to the Ward would be a
good cover for permitting her to return Hippolito's affections.
Leantio, distraught at his wife's unfaithfulness, also turns
to Livia, and the two become lovers. The Duke has bought

off Leantio with a court sinecure, but now comes into conflict with his brother, the Cardinal, over his adulterous affair, and, wishing to be free to marry Bianca, orders Hippolito to murder her husband. The grief-stricken Livia retaliates by revealing the incestuous relationship between Hippolito and Isabella, to her niece's dismay and the fury of Guardiano. Despite an outward show of reconciliation, Livia, Isabella, Hippolito and Guardiano plot their revenges under cover of the masque to be staged during the celebrations of the Duke's marriage to Bianca; but the plots miscarry, resulting in their own deaths as well as those of their intended victims. Only the Cardinal is spared, to utter a pious pronouncement over the bloody scene.

The author and his work

Born in 1580, the son of bricklayer who made himself a gentleman, Thomas Middleton went to Queen's College, Oxford, in 1598, but apparently did not complete his studies, either because he was already intent on a literary career or because he needed to assist his mother in a protracted dispute over the family property. By the time of his marriage in 1602 his career in the theatre had evidently begun. Henslowe's 'diary' of that year records him as collaborating on three plays, now lost, though a fourth, his first independent work, *The Family of Love*, a comedy for the Admiral's Men, has survived. He went on to write around fifty theatrical pieces, some collaborative, variously for the leading adult and children's companies and the City of London, whose civic chronologer he became in 1620. He was among the first practitioners of 'city comedy', his works in this satiric mode including *Michaelmas Term* (1605), *A Mad World My Masters* and *A Trick to Catch the Old One* (c. 1605–6), *The Roaring Girl* (with Dekker, c. 1608: see p. 139) and *A Chaste Maid in Cheapside* (c. 1611). His tragi-comedies include *The Witch* (c. 1614), *A Fair Quarrel* (with Rowley, c. 1615) and *The Old Law* (1618). *The Revenger's Tragedy* (1606: see p. 123) may be his, but his two great tragedies, *Women Beware Women* and *The Changeling* (with William Rowley, 1622: see p. 225), are both thought to date from later in his career. His output also included masques, civic pageants and the anti-Spanish political satire *A Game at Chess* (1624), which enjoyed an unprecedented run of nine consecutive performances at the Globe before it was suppressed. Middleton died in 1627.

The historical context

Feminine morality was a dominant interest of the Jacobean theatre in the years preceding *Women Beware Women*. From 1619 and 1620 alone we find such titles as *All's Lost by Lust*, *The Fatal Dowry*, *The Woman's Mistaken*, *The Double Marriage*, *The Virgin Martyr* and *The Costly Whore*. King James actually issued an instruction to his clergy in 1620 to 'inveigh vehemently against the insolence of our women'; and it was in this year that the intermittent pamphlet war over the dignity and status of women reached its height, in the pamphleteering confrontation between *Haec Vir*, an effeminate male with courtly characteristics, and *Hic Mulier*, a supposedly 'mannish woman'. An anonymous Queen Anne's play, *Swetnam the Woman-Hater*, also reached print in 1620 – its villain the misogynistic Joseph Swetnam, author of an *Arraignment of Lewd, Idle, Froward, and Unconstant Women* (1615). This had already been pugnaciously rebuked in prose by Constantia Munda's *The Worming of a Mad Dog* (1617) and Daniel Tuvil's *A Sanctuary for Ladies* (1616), which almost asserted the equality of the sexes. But the nature and status of women was not the only or indeed main concern of 1621. That year also saw a newly assertive parliament, which challenged Buckingham, the King's favourite, and impeached the Lord Chancellor; and James' pro-Spanish foreign policy saw his own popularity waning. The King was now aged fifty-five – making double-edged Bianca's remarks (I, iii, 92–4) on the Duke's 'wisdom' on reaching that age (though philandering with women was not, of course, among the royal vices).

The world of the play

Women Beware Women takes place in a confluence of Middleton's imagination between the City of London and the Dukedom of Florence. The procession in which Bianca catches the Duke's eye is surely, in Middleton's, akin to the Lord Mayor's Show and – with its 'variety of music and song' (I, iii, 102) – to the pageants he himself wrote for the City. It is not (or not until the last act) the world of the Italianate court, familiar in Jacobean tragedy, in which a declassed malcontent controls and loses control of events. For Middleton's social spectrum here is both wider and more precisely defined: from the humble, clerkly bourgeoisie whence Leantio and the Mother spring, and whose trappings Bianca comes to despise; through the genteel fringes of the nobility which was Bianca's and is Livia's milieu; to the devious world of the Duke himself – redolent as much of the boardroom as the throne room, its power secured not by divine right but worldly wealth.

When Bianca claims that the Duke was gazing at her, and the Mother delivers the rebuke that 'the look he casts / Is at his own intentions, and his object / Only the public good' (I, iii, 110–12), her words convey the deference of one who 'knows her place': their irony is for the action to reveal. For there is little here of the 'public good' or indeed of any matter of state, and only the Cardinal's pieties make even a perfunctory connection between public and private morality. The exercise of power is to satisfy lust – and power over women is a male prerogative. In the opening scene Leantio glories in his acquisition of Bianca in such terms that it is clear her class has been as much her attraction as her beauty: she is his 'trophy wife'. It is in Fabritio's power as a father to dispose of Isabella at will, just as it is in Hippolito's to abuse his niece. Class differences are also crucial: if Leantio had abandoned his job to keep his wife happy, it would have reduced her to greater poverty; for Bianca, as a gentlewoman, could not (does not know how to) work, and, there being no daytime television, the best that a wife indoors can do is stare out of the window at a passing show. Later, having grumbled at length to the Mother that Leantio cannot refurbish their home according to the latest fashions (III, i), she accepts the higher price the Duke will pay for her honour, and transfers her domicile as well as her affections to the court. If she is to be a chattel, at least the household goods will be of a better class.

The Duke thus secures Bianca through the operation of market forces; and Leantio is bought off his cuckoldry by an 'employment' no better paid than his own, but which means, since he no longer has to work, that he is now a gentleman. The Duke has used no physical force in raping Bianca or bribing her husband; but the threat is always there – has indeed been made to Bianca should she fail to comply – and is soon to be actualised in Hippolito's murder of Leantio. This he commits at the Duke's behest not (as he claims) to redeem Livia's honour, still less from moral outrage, but, as Margot Heineman observes, from 'pure savage snobbery' at a noblewoman's dalliance with a clerk and 'personal greed' at the prospect the Duke holds out of finding his sister a good match.

All the women of the play seek in vain for independence from the prevailing patriarchy. Bianca's elopement to avoid her father's choosing her a husband only lands her in a different kind of trap (Una Ellis-Fermor attributes her silence in the opening scene to 'an enchanted meekness of devotion'; to me it seems more like a dawning, sulky awareness of her social and sexual degradation). Isabella's seeming obedience, to disguise her intended adultery, results only in her being duped into an incestuous liaison. Livia enjoys the independence of a widow turned procuress – that is, she is free, but only to put other women under male control (even that degree of freedom frightens the Duke, who suggests that he find her a husband to tame her). Although Livia is given some persuasive protofeminist insights, and there is impressive emotional force in her love for Leantio (which Howard Barker made the wellspring of his 1986 adaptation), her truth-telling is compromised by her profession – as is Leantio's gentility by his dependence on her for its accoutrements, which dwindles his status back to its class origins. The handsome bank clerk has merely turned toy-boy to a wealthy older woman (an ironic inversion of the 'expected' circumstance of the Duke and Hippolito being far older than their mistresses).

Livia's wealth enables her both to patronise the Mother (her 'Sunday-dinner and Thursday-supper woman') and to play hostess to the Duke – she is a go-between in a social as well as a sexual sense. That she and the Mother play and discuss chess during the rape scene (foreshadowing the black and white pieces who act out Middleton's *A Game at Chess* a few years later) is not just metaphorically appropriate, but entirely in keeping with the niceties of the class relationships involved. T. S. Eliot's description of Middleton as a 'seventeenth-century Ibsen' is especially appropriate to the powerful blending of naturalism and symbolism in this scene. No less aptly might the character of Bianca be said to prefigure both Ibsen's Hedda Gabler, in her implosive, compromised passion, and his Nora from *A Doll's House*, in the acquiescent domesticity on which she at last slams the door.

Middleton is said to have been the puritans' favourite (or least unfavourite) dramatist, and his later plays have even been described as tragedies of predestination. This would leave no room for Bianca or indeed any of the characters to behave differently; but the determinism at work here is again closer to Ibsen's than Calvin's, in that the play exemplifies the pressures that birth and circumstances impose on behaviour. Bianca is not predestined, but she is irresistibly predisposed.

Comparing the complex staging demands and the murderous mixed-means of the climactic masque with the straightforward (though no less fatal) stabbings of *The Spanish Tragedy* and *The Revenger's Tragedy*, Margot Heineman wryly comments: 'The Duke complains that something has gone wrong with the programme notes and dies still trying to understand the allegory.' And while in one sense the final act does turn the wedding masque into a descent into hell – much criticised for its apparent near-farcical excess – in another it is not so much an allegory without annotation as a masque which breaks that already archaic form, and makes of it (like the game of chess) an in-yer-face metaphor for the 'real-life' action.

And so, in an age when, in a real courtly masque, the most notorious lecher could still be called on to spout a virtuous homily, the procuress Livia is cast in the role of Juno Pronuba, the marriage goddess. She is poisoned by Isabella with a 'precious incense' – the punning closeness of 'incense' and 'incest' being readily recognisable to a Jacobean audience – while Isabella falls to her own death through a gaping trap; Hippolito commits a phallic suicide by impaling himself on a guard's sword; and the Duke and Bianca choke on 'nectar' spurned by its intended victim, the Cardinal. And the wealth that underpins power is given both symbolic and material form when Livia kills Isabella with a 'lapful' of 'burning treasure' from 'our brother Jove' – an allusion to Jove's having taken the form of a shower of gold in his rape of Danae (V, ii, 115–22). The excess lies not in the masque, but in the lives of its dancers and its 'noble' audience.

The playwright's craft

FORM   It has been variously suggested that *Women Beware Women* is a 'romantic tragedy', in that it begins where romantic comedy often ends (in true love triumphant in defiance of parental obstacles) only to reveal that marriage can be no less an imprisonment; or a 'city tragedy', in that it employs the milieu and explores the assumptions of city comedy, but rejects its happy ending – though some see the climactic bloodbath as itself parodic. Nicholas Brooke interestingly proposes that the play shifts in genre as it ascends the social scale, 'from comedy through high comedy to tragi-farce'.

LANGUAGE   The prevailing imagery is that of consumption – of the appetite for sex reflected in the appetite for food – and of property, with treasure and jewels kept safe under locks and keys. But Middleton's language (especially compared with Webster's) is simple, practical and spare – almost, indeed, puritanical. The dominant metaphors, as discussed above, are reflected in the action rather than through verbal elaboration.

STAGE PRACTICE Of the play's two great set-pieces, the first, the playing of a game of chess by Livia and the Mother, would have taken place on the lower stage, while the Duke was talking with Bianca on the upper. The second, the climactic masque, is in one sense a highly conventional means of wrapping up a tragedy through plotful play-acting, in another a parodic (as it were, post-early modern) commentary on its own form and the play's content, both distancing and underlining its horror. The play is unusual in offering no fewer than four major roles for women, suggesting unusual strengths (or an unusual strain) on the acting company's resources.

In performance

Though a prefatory verse to the first printed edition of 1657 claims 'Never came tragedy off with more applause', we have no other evidence about the play's staging before the Restoration and none for its revival afterwards, until a student production at Reading University in 1962. Later that same year the play was directed by Anthony Page, with Nicol Williamson as Leantio, during the RSC's season at the New Arts Theatre. A production by Gordon McDougall at the Traverse Theatre, Edinburgh, in 1965 was sandwiched between this and a second RSC revival, directed by Terry Hands, seen in Stratford and at the company's then base in London, the Aldwych Theatre, in 1968–69, with Richard Pasco as Leantio and Judi Dench as Bianca. In 1986 the Royal Court Theatre staged a version of the play of which the first half was a condensation of the first three acts, while the second, with a completely new ending, was entirely the work of the adaptor, Howard Barker. John Adams directed the play at the Birmingham Rep in 1989, and Christopher Geelen staged a modern-dress version with the Buttonhole Theatre Company in 1994, but the play has yet to find a secure place in the contemporary repertoire.

A New Way to Pay Old Debts
Philip Massinger

c. 1621

Source

The main plot derives loosely from that of Middleton's *A Trick to Catch the Old One* (1605); the sub-plot is Massinger's variation on the theme of young love triumphing over parental plans.

The story

Young Welborne is penniless, having squandered his inheritance – partly through his own profligacy, but also through the wiles of his uncle, Sir Giles Overreach, who has advanced him money only to secure possession of his estates. Minor creditors, such as the innkeeper Tapwell and his wife Froth, have also turned against him – provoking Welborne to angry violence, from which he is dissuaded by the arrival of his friend Alworth. Alworth is in love with Overreach's daughter Margaret but, being a mere page to the noble Lord Lovell, has no hope of her hand – especially since Overreach plans to ennoble his heirs by securing a match between Margaret and Lovell himself. Alworth's rich stepmother is still in mourning for her husband (much to the dismay of her servants, who feel they are wasting their skills to entertain the freeloaders clustering to her table) and is at first haughty when visited by the 'debauch'd' Welborne; but she is won over by his clear repentance and innate nobility, and in a whispered conversation agrees to help him recover his fortunes. Their plan becomes clearer when Welborne tells Overreach's factotum Marrall that he can secure him a seat at Lady Alworth's table, where her favour towards Welborne convinces Marrall that she intends to marry him. Marrall's obsequiousness towards Welborne earns him a beating from the disbelieving Overreach. Alworth and

Lord Lovell are meanwhile journeying to Sir Giles' house, where Lovell promises to help Alworth win his beloved. Margaret's reluctance to accept her father's choice of husband angers Overreach, but having been told of the plot by her supposed suitor she pretends compliance, while her father agrees to Alworth serving as a messenger for his master. Sir Giles is astonished when Lady Alworth arrives to pay her compliments to Lovell in the company of Welborne, to whom she shows clear favour, and whom he accordingly invites to dine (in place of the aptly named Justice Greedy, who has to resign himself to the kitchen table). By boasting of lands he will secure from others, Overreach reveals all his extortionate wiles to Lovell, who in an encounter with Lady Alworth exchanges a vow of mutual assistance in their plotting. Overreach having given money to his nephew – unsecured, in anticipation of battening on his estates once he is married – Welborne repays his creditors, while Alworth, now with free access to Margaret, secures a note from her father to a parson to marry her to its bearer. No sooner has Sir Giles become aware that the servant and not the master has married his daughter than he is stripped of his security over Welborne's properties by a device of Marrall, who now determines to change his allegiance. Driven mad, Overreach is packed off to Bedlam, Lady Alworth agrees to marry Lovell, and Welborne resolves to redeem his reputation by serving with Lovell's regiment in the Netherlands.

The author and his work

Born in Salisbury in 1583, the son of a confidential agent to the Earl of Pembroke, Massinger attended Oxford University, but left in 1606 without a degree. By 1613 he was working for Henslowe, to whom he had apparently appealed for help with his debts. He wrote over fifty plays, at first in collaboration, variously with Dekker, Richard Daborne, Nathan Field and, increasingly, John Fletcher, whom he succeeded as principal dramatist for the King's Men in 1626. Among his collaborations were *The Fatal Dowry*, with Field (*c.* 1619), and *The Custom of the Country* (1620). His later, independent works included other comedies such as *The Parliament of Love* (1624) and *The City Madam* (1632); the tragi-comedies *The Maid of Honour* (1621), *The Renegado* (1624) and *The Bashful Lover* (1636); and the tragedies *The Duke of Milan* (1621), *The Roman Actor* (1626) and *Believe as You List* (1631). He died in 1640.

The historical context

As James' reign drew to its close, his unpopularity increased. This was due in part to his half-hearted intervention in the war in the Palatinate and his favourite Buckingham's negotiations for a Spanish marriage for Prince Charles, but also in part to an accumulation of longer-standing grievances. In 1621, the year of a parliamentary 'Grand Petition' which the King tore from the records, Sir Giles Mompesson and a magistrate acting as his agent were convicted of extortion and corruption in the exercise of Mompesson's patent for the licensing of inns, and both were stripped of their knighthoods, as was Sir Giles of his additional monopolies over licensing the manufacture of gold threads and charcoal-making. Such abuse of monopolies was increasingly a cause of parliamentary criticism and popular grievance, for just as the King had authorised acting only under the grant of 'letters patent' from the Crown, so also a 'patent' might bestow a monopoly, either upon a royal favourite or in return for ready money (later, a bill to abolish the 'mountains of monopolies' was among the earliest concerns of the Long Parliament in 1640). Our Sir Giles and his tame Justice Greedy, while similarly exploiting the Tapwells and their kind, seek also to seize land, and not only from the nobility but from the poor – Overreach boasting of being a 'grand encloser / Of what was common, to my private use' (IV, i, 124–5), a reference to the practice of enclosing what had been common land. The sense of a King alienated from his people reflects such grievances in a play by the innately conservative Massinger as by the more free-thinking Middleton.

The world of the play

A New Way to Pay Old Debts is set not in London but among the rural gentry of Nottinghamshire; and its world (although the happy outcome to the plot conceals it) is recognisably one in which the old social order is in decline, as the power of the nobility, rooted in landed estates, confronts and is often ensnared by the power of money derived from trade and from the manipulation of money itself. At the same time, Overreach's greed for land, and his almost pathetic ambition to join the nobility even as he beats it, reflects the reality that liaisons between 'money' and 'land' were often arranged to rescue the nobility from its debts. (Indeed, that Overreach is uncle to the significantly named Welborne indicates that he already has a foot on the ladder, presumably through just such an expedient match and the purchase of his knighthood.)

Later, in The City Madam, Massinger was a little more sympathetic to social mobility; but here, in contrast with Middleton's cityscapes of shifting allegiances, the rustic milieu is one in which every character but Overreach, down to the most menial of the servants, believes absolutely in maintaining the existing hierarchy. Even Sir Giles' own daughter Margaret realises that she, being 'of low descent, however rich', would be ill-suited to a husband of noble birth (III, ii, 198). In a passage of astonishing contempt not for the girl herself but for her class, Lovell angrily asserts that such a match would 'adulterate my blood' (IV, i, 219–27). But she is an acceptable match for Alworth, whom Lovell distinguishes from lesser servants as 'a gentleman by want compelled to serve me' (III, i, 28). Also humbled from high rank is the Lady Downfall'n, unseen in the play but mentioned by Margaret, her mistress, as better fitted 'for a companion, / Not as a servant' (III, ii, 38–9); while Lady Alworth's kitchen skivvies delight in class-conscious mockery of Marrall's table manners.

In contrast to Marlowe's Barabas or Jonson's Sir Epicure Mammon, Overreach is (as Eliot put it) 'the terror of a dozen parishes instead of the conqueror of the world': and in this sense Sir Giles is not an overreacher at all, since he is keeping his extortions cannily in bounds – even preferring to hide behind Greedy, his tame magistrate, so that 'in being out of office, I am out of danger' (II, i, 14); and he is mean-minded if canny in seizing his neighbours' lands by forcing them to sue him and ruin themselves with the costs (II, i, 34–68). His weakness – which he shares with Barabas and Shylock – is his daughter, though his concern for her future is inspired not by love but by the desire to see his name nobly perpetuated.

It is thus in his social ambitions that, in Massinger's eyes, Overreach is excessive – in aspiring to the aristocracy 'though I come from the city' (II, i, 81). Thus, his crimes are seen not so much as against the public good as against the established order. Some modern critics have discovered a 'secret' play in which Massinger is critical of the bonding of aristocrats against *arrivistes*; if so, the secret is well concealed. But with a noble Lord and a noble Lady in league against Overreach, there is never any doubt as to his downfall, and only the apoplectic manner of his departure offers any real surprise. His successful snares – unlike those of Barabas, in which the audience is allowed guilty complicity – are in the past, as he falls unerringly into the traps set by others. And while Barabas' boasts are tinged with an ironic mockery of his audience and himself, Sir Giles' are straight-faced and (whether directed at Marrall or Lord Lovell) doomed to be counter-productive.

So how is it that *The Jew of Malta* disappeared from the living repertoire for over three centuries while *A New Way to Pay Old Debts* became a theatrical standby? Although the play clings so firmly to the values of a declining social order, the very insistence of its affirmations lends many of its scenes the kind of declamatory self-awareness that was to distinguish the sentimental comedy of the eighteenth century – as witness the mutual admiration between Alworth and Margaret (IV, iii) and the moralising exchanges which constitute foreplay for Lovell and Lady Alworth (IV, i, 158–248) – while the villainy of Sir Giles is so one-dimensional as to anticipate melodrama. In both instances, there is little gap between what is said and what is felt: everything is on the surface, and everybody is either good or bad (or safely below stairs), with the exception of the prodigal Welborne, whose plight sets everything in motion but whose very name is an assurance of his ultimate redemption. His cravings open the play ('No booze? Nor no tobacco?'), and he is soon involved in starting a brawl; yet his dissolute habits and streak of violence (from which Alworth has to restrain him) are excused almost instantly in Lady Alworth's eyes by his declaration, 'The blood that runs in this arm is as noble /As that which fills your veins' (I, iii, 88–9). Indeed, the widow's transition from deep mourning to vivacious *faux* mistress is so abrupt that Massinger cannot rise to its rhetorical demands, cloaking Welborne's persuasions in a whisper (I, iii, 124).

We have many, varied glimpses of what Massinger regards as traditional verities. It is clear from the kitchen talk that Lady Alworth still offers hospitality, not only to the neighbours who gormandise in her widowly absence, but to the poor who are allowed to feed from the leftovers. Lord Lovell feels constrained to offer an elaborate defence of his decision to marry a widow (V, i, 48–66) as if the traditional typology (most famously embodied in Chaucer's Wife of Bath) self-evidently required such an apologia. And when a tailor among Welborne's creditors assures him, 'I ask no interest, sir,' (IV, ii, 96) this is a surely an intended affirmation of the Church's long-standing but outmoded condemnation of usury.

In some of his other plays Massinger appears critical of the monarchy – as he is implicitly here, against the King's dependence on farming out monopolies. Yet he finds Welborne's prodigality offensive not because nobility enables such behaviour but because such behaviour betrays nobility, and so, as in Welborne's case, unthreatening to the hierarchy so long as it is remedied. Indeed, it reinforces the hierarchy, by showing that the fault lies with the upstart Sir Giles. As Philip Edwards pertinently suggests, the play can 'be seen as a kind of therapeutic rite, in which a social class finds satisfaction in making a model of what it most fears and then destroying it'.

The playwright's craft

FORM   This is a comedy of the romantic kind in that it ends with the redemption of the prodigal and the celebration of two marriages. But the play is singularly unfunny, and such would-be butts of satire as Greedy and Marall do little to add humour, either in the Jonsonian sense or our own. Sir Giles is a villain in a proto-melodramatic, not a comic mould.

STRUCTURE   The opening scene is reminiscent of Jonson's *The Alchemist* in staging a slanging match which modulates into useful exposition; and I, ii, is also replete with information amidst the servants' kitchen grievances. But the play is rather prematurely directed towards its happy ending once Lady Alworth and Lord Lovell have taken sides with Welborne and young Alworth, and we necessarily become less concerned with the mechanics of the plot than the emotional colouring of the dialogue.

LANGUAGE   As reflected in the structure, liveliness in language is reserved for the lowlier characters, their betters tending to reflective rather than active dialogue – typified by the exchange of courtly compliments between Lovell and Alworth which constitutes almost the entirety of III, i. But in this deeply class-conscious play, Massinger strikes one egalitarian note – allowing his servants, publicans and sinners the use of blank verse alongside their betters.

CONVENTIONS   The names of all the main characters (give or take Margaret's hapless paternity) tell us exactly what we expect and should be thinking of them – the use of such 'charactonyms' not uncommon in the Jacobean drama, but more pervasive after the Restoration.

STAGE PRACTICE   The fluidity of movement between locations roots the play firmly in Jacobean conventions, in contrast with the relative scenic specificity of Restoration drama.

In performance

The play appears to have remained in repertoire under successive managements at the Phoenix in Drury Lane and at Salisbury Court until the closure of the theatres in 1642. Unlike many plays of the period, which were revived during the Restoration only to decline in favour, *A New Way to Pay Old Debts* had no further recorded productions in London until its staging by Garrick at Drury Lane in 1748. There were then further occasional revivals in London and the provinces until 1781, when John Henderson played Overreach at Covent Garden and John Philip Kemble gave in Edinburgh the first of what were to be many performances in the role; but it was Edmund Kean who brought to it his own strange fire after first playing Overreach at Drury Lane in 1816. His performance anecdotally reduced Byron to convulsions, and more revealingly disturbed Kean's fellow actor with the energy of its communicated evil. Until the 1880s the play remained a stock piece for repertory companies, and attracted leading actors including Charles Kean, Samuel Phelps and Edwin Booth. It received less attention in the last century, though there were revivals at the Birmingham Repertory Theatre in 1914 and at the Old Vic in 1922, and Donald Wolfit restored something of the play's barnstorming reputation on tour in 1950. The only major subsequent revival has been by the RSC, under the direction of Adrian Noble in 1984, at The Other Place in Stratford and the Barbican Pit in London. In the words of Jack Tinker, Emrys James' Overreach could 'turn purple with apoplexy behind his hand and emerge a second later smiling the serene, cold grin of a raving shark'. Michael Coveney agreed: 'It is a charged and driven performance, one that cracks . . . into a fractured rage and panic.' Martin Esslin, who also praised Miles Anderson's 'nice blend of dissipation and inborn nobility' as Welborne, considered this 'one of the finest productions the RSC has ever offered us'.

The Witch of Edmonton
Dekker, Ford and Rowley

1621

Source

While the Cuddy Banks sub-plot is original, the Thorney–
Winnifride thread bears some similarities to the sub-plot of
Rowley's *All's Lost by Lust* (1619). The Mother Sawyer plot is
remarkably faithful to its source – Henry Goodcole's pamphlet *The Wonderfull discoverie of Elizabeth Sawyer a witch, late
of Edmonton, her conviction and condemnation and death. Together
with the relation of the Divels accesse to her and their conference
together*, published just eight days after the real-life Mother
Sawyer was hanged at Tyburn on 19 April 1621.

The story

Young Frank Thorney, believing himself father of the baby
expected by his fellow-servant Winnifride, has secretly married
the girl to save her from disgrace. On Frank's departure it
becomes clear that their master, Sir Arthur Clarington, is the
real father of the child; but to Clarington's angry surprise
Winnifride declares that she intends to stay faithful to Frank.
Frank's father, in financial difficulties, wants him to marry
Susan, daughter of the rich but down-to-earth yeoman farmer,
Old Carter. Susan is herself in love with Warbeck, whose
friend Somerton is enamoured of her sister Kate. Frank persuades his father that rumours of his marriage with Winnifride
are untrue, and it is agreed that Susan and Frank will marry
next day – with the dowry paid down at once. Mother Sawyer
bemoans the abuse that her neighbours, who believe her to be
a witch, heap on her for their own faults and misfortunes. Old
Banks, on whose land she is gathering kindling, beats her,
and, cursing him, she wishes she were indeed a witch. Banks'

clownish son Cuddy and his friends now arrive, discussing their plans for a morris dance, and they too mock Mother Sawyer. The Devil appears to her in the form of a dog, and they seal a pact with her blood. And so, when Cuddy returns, hoping that the 'witch' may be able to help him to woo Kate Carter, Mother Sawyer pretends willingness to do so; but the hapless Cuddy almost drowns in a pond when he tries to pursue a spirit in the form of his beloved. Susan, anxious about Frank's moodiness, and fearing he has arranged a duel with Warbeck, determines not to leave him alone until the quarrel is reconciled. Frank plans to flee abroad with Winnifride, now disguised as a male servant, and, failing to persuade Susan to leave him, stabs her with a knife. As she lies dying, he reveals the truth, whereupon Susan welcomes her fate. Unaware of all this, Clarington, with Warbeck and Somerton as guests, watch the morris men perform their dance – in which they are joined by the Dog, now Mother Sawyer's 'familar'. Constables enter to arrest Warbeck and Somerton, whom Carter and Thorney have been persuaded are Susan's murderers. Old Banks and his neighbours set fire to the thatch of Mother Sawyer's hovel, but are prevented from inflicting violence on her, and she contemptuously asks her inquisitors 'who is not' a witch in this proud and sinful world. Encouraging the 'recovering' Frank to eat, and using his knife to carve a chicken, Kate Carter finds it stained with her sister's blood. As she leaves to inform her father, the spirit of Susan appears to Frank, who confesses to the murder when the disguised Winnifride arrives at his bedside. Mother Sawyer, abandoned by the Dog – who tells her that she is 'ripe to fall into hell' – is hauled off to jail. Failing to persuade the Devil to 'become an honest dog', Cuddy tries to drive him away. In the final scene, as Thorney and Carter watch Frank prepare to meet his death, Mother Sawyer also appears, still cursing, on her way to execution. The penitent Frank reconciles himself with Winnifride, and even Carter finds himself weeping. Kate and Somerton are to be married, and the sorrowing Winnifride is invited by Old Carter to share their home.

The authors and their work

For Ford's life, see under *The Broken Heart*, p. 234; and for Dekker's, under *The Shoemakers' Holiday*, p. 65. William Rowley, the third collaborator on *The Witch of Edmonton*, was probably born around 1585, but little else is known about him until his earliest, collaborative plays (for Queen Anne's Men) reached the stage between 1607 and 1609 – among them *The Birth of Merlin* (*c.* 1613), attributed jointly but improbably to Shakespeare in the earliest surviving edition. In 1609 Rowley joined the Duke of York's (later Prince Charles') Men as an actor, taking mainly comic roles. *A Fair Quarrel* (1617), for which Rowley wrote the sub-plot, was the first of his fruitful collaborations with Middleton, of which the most important was *The Changeling* (1622: see p. 225). He played the clown in Middleton's *The Inner Temple Masque*, as in his own *All's Lost by Lust* (both 1619) – his single, hyperbolic attempt at tragedy without a collaborator – and he no doubt took the role of Cuddy Banks in *The Witch of Edmonton*. In 1623 he joined the King's Men, collaborating with Middleton on the tragi-comedy *The Spanish Gipsy* (1623) and with Webster on the comedy *A Cure for a Cuckold* (1625), in which he played the popular clown Compass. In the same year he wrote independently the comedy of city life *A Woman Never Vexed*, one of the last of about fifty plays with which his name was associated, of which only sixteen have survived. Perhaps recognising his own limitations as a writer in his readiness for collaboration, he was happiest as a contributor of comic sub-plots, in a number of which he himself appeared as clown – apparently physically suited to his role as Fat Bishop in Middleton's political satire *A Game at Chess* (1624). He died in February 1626.

The historical context

Witchcraft never aroused such a hysterical public response in England as it did in continental Europe, where literally millions were executed for the alleged offence. While there were around a thousand executions of so-called witches in England between 1542, when witchcraft became a punishable offence, and 1736, when it ceased to be so, this figure was exceeded in just one year in a single Italian city (that of Como, in 1524).

It has been argued that, before Henry VIII repudiated the authority of the Pope, the people felt sufficiently protected by the rituals and dogmas of the Catholic faith against the powers of witchcraft. Yet neither the old Catholic authorities nor the new, state-controlled Church of England seem to have been very active in prosecutions for witchcraft, and the death penalty was seldom exacted under Elizabeth, even during a brief upsurge of witch-hunting during the 1580s. But James, himself author of a treatise on *Demonology* (1597), was a firm believer in its powers, and an Act of 1604 both increased the penalties and made proof easier to come by – for example, the possession of a supposed 'familiar' now being regarded as a crime in itself rather than as one possible sign of guilt. Even so, between 1616 and James' death in 1625 there were only five executions for the offence – one of these being that of the actual Mother Sawyer, in 1621.

The world of the play

Although Edmonton is now scarcely distinguishable amidst the urban sprawl of outer London, it was of course still an isolated rural village at the time of the real-life Mother Sawyer. No doubt it was on account of the topicality of her trial and execution that she became one of the lowliest characters to give her name to a play; for her part in its action is less central than, say, that of Frank Thorney, or even the clownish Cuddy. However, it is one of the remarkable features of the play – not least because its various elements were the work of three different authors – that the various levels of its action merge almost seamlessly to create a distinctive theatrical world. And no less remarkable, though unobtrusive, is the play's reflection of both the supposed fixity and actual fluidity of its characters' social standing. Sir Arthur Clarington, as a wealthy local landowner, also heads the magistracy, and so can create his own rule of law; but while his seduction of his servant, Winnifride, sets the play in motion, his subsequent part in its action is far less prominent than that of Overreach in *A New Way to Pay Old Debts* – nor are there, as in Massinger's play, higher-ranking aristocrats to bring him to order. In fact, the play is unusual for the socially inferior status of most of its characters. Frank Thorney is presumably sent to serve Sir Arthur as some sort of manager or steward by a father who is finding it hard to preserve his own status as a gentleman; but Old Carter rejects Old Thorney's commendation of him as a 'gentleman', preferring the dignity of an 'honest Hertford-shire yeoman' (I, ii, 1–6) who is proud to work for a living.

Frank Thorney is thus cast adrift socially – the equal both of his lowly fellow-servant Winnifride and of Susan Carter, from whose father's upward mobility his own father hopes to benefit. Similarly, Old Banks mixes comfortably with both the impoverished gentleman Thorney and the wealthy yeoman Carter, though he himself is a mere tenant farmer with no hope of owning his own land – while his son Cuddy has drifted into the company of the local lads, and is evidently regarded even by them as something of a clown – which is, of course, how he functions theatrically.

The play also shows an unusually complex attitude for its time towards witchcraft. As Mother Sawyer's opening speech indicates (II, i, 1–15), she has been abused for being a witch long before she actually turns in desperation to the Devil, and her neighbours have thus been blaming her for their own follies or misfortunes without any real cause for grievance. Even after her pact with the Devil, she becomes a convenient focus for any guilt others wish to shift – as when Old Carter accuses her of bewitching Frank, and she responds by asking, 'Is every devil mine?' (V, iii, 28–30). But the better educated members of society, such as Sir Arthur and the Justice, are far more sceptical than Banks and his neighbours about Mother Sawyer's guilt, and it is, significantly, Old Banks who takes the initiative in seeking a warrant for her arrest (IV, i, 255–7).

Mother Sawyer has thus become a 'common sink' not only for the 'filth and rubbish of men's tongues / To fall and run into', but for their every guilt as well. As she asks Sir Arthur Clarington and the Justice, 'Dare any swear I ever tempted maiden, / With golden hooks flung at her chastity, / To come and lose her honour, and being lost / To pay not a denier for't?' (IV, i, 141–4). 'By one thing she speaks / I know now she's a witch,' responds Clarington, secretly fearing that the allegation is a reference to his seduction of Winnifride. Thus, what tips the scales in his 'educated' mind against Mother Sawyer is, ironically, a superstitious sense that she is aware of his own guilt.

In this 'community severely disrupted and disturbed by the evil in its midst', as Kathleen McLuskie calls it, Clarington deceives Frank, Frank deceives Susan, and the Devil deceives Mother Sawyer and the lovelorn Cuddy. Against this, the women characters display different kinds of loyalty: Winnifride and Susan towards Frank, and Mother Sawyer towards the Dog – as an object of real affection, not merely an instrument for mischief. In each case, of course, the loyalty turns out to be misplaced. Nor are the apparently sympathetic characters in the Banks sub-plot without blame. It is, after all, they and their friends and neighbours who are the 'tattling gossips' so feared by Winnifride in the opening scene (I, i, 3), while Mother Sawyer is already the victim of their casual slanders as she is to become the object of their witch-hunt, when they set fire to her thatch and call for the burning of the wretched woman herself (IV, i, 1–21).

Even Old Carter is less than the man of his word he proclaims himself, conveniently overlooking his promise to Warbeck in his preference for Frank as suitor to Susan, and, indeed, in his disturbing rejection of his dead daughter. Carter is well aware of the power his money allows him to wield: it is this power which drives Frank Thorney into his bigamous marriage and so into murder, just as it is money which enables Clarington to shrug off his responsibilities with the payment of a fine he can readily afford.

It is in its balancing of social pressures against individual responsibility that one is most fully aware of the play's internal coherence. The apparent diversity of its three levels of action is in this sense not merely explicable, but crucial to our sense of how that balance may be shifted by wealth and by social standing – or tilted fatally against the likes of Mother Sawyer, who try but fail to ignore the moral values and hypocrisies of their society. This is, then, a complex picture of a small rural community in which most of the characters are subject to social or economic pressures it is hard for them to resist. And so they come to share a portion of the guilt for the spread of evil in their midst: the Devil simply has to await his call.

The playwright's craft

FORM   The first title-page describes the play as 'a known true story, composed into a tragi-comedy' – though the murder of Susan and executions of Frank and Mother Sawyer would belie the latter genre by most standards of the time, while, as in *Arden of Faversham*, the characters lack the nobility proper to tragedy itself. The play happily rebuts easy categorisation.

LANGUAGE   After the high emotions expressed through blank verse in the first scene, we may note how naturally prose is then used for establishing the 'blunt' character of Old Carter and discussion of money matters, while the romantic exchanges of the young couples switch back to verse. Sometimes, prose and verse are used for different effects by the same character: thus, Mother Sawyer in II, i, uses verse for her opening soliloquy but 'descends' into prose for her exchanges with Old Banks. Only the low-life characters of Cuddy and his friends speak in prose throughout the play.

CONVENTIONS   While three elderly fathers figure prominently in the action, there is, typically for plays of the period, a notable absence of mothers (young girls are, of course, more readily imitable by boy actors than mature women).

STAGE PRACTICE Despite its original performance in a 'private' or indoor theatre, the play would not have made much call upon the relatively more sophisticated resources of such houses, though trickwork for the devil's scenes would have been more conveniently accomplished. Music would have been integral to the morris dance, its traditional accompaniment a pipe and tabor, though here a fiddle is also required.

In performance

The Witch of Edmonton was written for Prince Charles' Men, who gave the first recorded performance at Court on 29 December 1621; but it would first have been played earlier in that year at the company's regular playhouse, the Cockpit in Drury Lane. The Phoenix Society mounted the first modern production at the Lyric Theatre, Hammersmith, in 1921, with Mother Sawyer played by Sybil Thorndike – who, according to *The Times*, 'made the mistake of dressing and acting the witch like something out of *Macbeth*'. A revival at the Old Vic in 1936 was not a success with audiences, in spite of a performance from Edith Evans in which, as Audrey Williamson wrote, she played 'with the cankerous malice and glimmer of pity the part demands'. Reviewing Bernard Miles' production at the Mermaid in 1962, Martin Esslin welcomed the play as 'combining reportage with poetry', with Ruby Head's performance bringing out 'the suffering, downtrodden and frustrated human being in the witch'. In Barry Kyle's production for the RSC at The Other Place in 1981, Miles Anderson's Devil, according to Christopher Hudson, 'licks and crawls like a dog but speaks in chillingly cultured tones: the perfect foil to the crackling spitefulness of Miriam Karlin's Sawyer'. Robert Cushman felt that Karlin's performance had brought out 'both the suffering and the malice' in the role. Later revivals were directed by Helen Fry at the Hen and Chickens pub theatre in 1992, and by Simon Cox at Southwark Playhouse in 2000.

The Changeling
Middleton and Rowley

1622

Source

The main plot derives from Book I of John Reynolds' *The
Triumphs of God's Revenge against Murther* (1621). The sub-
plot of assumed madness is original.

The story

Alsemero, a traveller visiting the castle of Alicante, has fallen
in love with Beatrice-Joanna, daughter of the governor, Vermandero. She responds to his advances, without telling him
she is already betrothed to the wealthy courtier Alonzo, but is
scornful of De Flores, an ill-favoured though cunning servant
of Vermandero, who is also in love with her. Learning of the
forthcoming marriage, Alsemero gives up hope of Beatrice,
but is persuaded to stay for the celebrations. Beatrice now
pretends warmth to De Flores to persuade him to rid her of
Alonzo, whose brother Tomazo now suspects her change of
heart. The jealous old doctor Alibius, warden of a madhouse,
discusses with his servant Lollio how best to keep his young
bride Isabella faithful to him – while a new patient, Antonio, is
already intent on wooing Isabella, under cover of madness.
Pretending to take Alonzo on a tour of the fortifications, De
Flores kills him, and cuts off his ring-finger as proof of the
deed. Beatrice is horrified when confronted by the token – the
more so when De Flores tells her that he wants her body, not
her money, as his reward. Lollio introduces Isabella to another
counterfeit madman, Franciscus, also intent on her seduction.
Lollio overhears Antonio telling her of his deception, which
she rebuffs but agrees not to reveal. In dumb-show, Vermandero, fearing the worst from Alonzo's apparent flight, agrees

to Beatrice's betrothal to Alsemero. Learning that he intends to test her virginity, now lost to De Flores, Beatrice applies the test to her maidservant Diaphanta, whom she bribes to take her place on the wedding night. The absent Franciscus and Antonio fall under suspicion of doing away with Alonzo, while Alsemero is told by his friend Jasperino of a compromising conversation overheard between De Flores and Beatrice. Subjected by Alsemero to the test of virginity, Beatrice has noted the symptoms of chastity shown by Diaphanta, and is able to simulate them to her husband's satisfaction. Concerned at Diaphanta's failure to return from the marriage bed, Beatrice has De Flores start a fire in order to arouse the company and kill Diaphanta to ensure her silence. Isabella shames Alibius by showing how she has remained faithful under siege from Franciscus and Antonio, who are hauled off by Tomazo as complicit in Alonzo's death. But, confronted by Alsemero and Jasperino, Beatrice confesses to her part in the murder and to her adultery with De Flores, who inflicts fatal wounds on himself and his mistress – 'beauty changed', as Alsemero puts is, 'to ugly whoredom'.

The authors and their work

For Middleton's life, see under *Women Beware Women*, p. 202; and for Rowley's, under *The Witch of Edmonton*, p. 219.

The historical context

The apparent source for the main plot of *The Changeling* was one of the 'histories' in a popular (and long-reprinted) series, *The Triumphs of God's Revenge*. But the play echoes events closer to home than Alicante, which had had their beginnings in 1606 when the Earl of Essex (son of Elizabeth's erstwhile and recently executed courtier) was married at the age of fifteen to Lady Frances Howard, two years his junior. By 1611 Frances had become mistress of the King's favourite, Robert

Carr, newly created Earl of Somerset, and was soon trying to hire assassins to do away with her husband, while seeking out obscure medicines to keep him impotent. Carr's adviser and confidant Sir Thomas Overbury opposed the affair and, when a divorce from Essex was sought in 1613 to enable the couple to marry, he refused a foreign mission intended to buy his silence, and was sent to the Tower. There, in September, he died, while a commission appointed by the King solemnly considered whether Frances was a virgin (an unconsummated marriage being easier to annul). A panel of midwives dutifully attested to her virgin state, of which even the Archbishop of Canterbury had doubts, and there were rumours of a substitute having been employed. The lovers were married that December, but two years later allegations surfaced that Overbury had been poisoned at the instigation of Frances, and eventually all those involved were arraigned – in reverse order of their social standing. Frances was at last tried and found guilty, as finally was Carr, by a tribunal of fellow-peers, both being condemned to death. The first and lowliest conspirator had said, in entering his own plea, that he hoped he would not be helping to 'make a net to catch the little birds, and let the great ones go'. In the event the 'little birds' were all executed, and the 'great ones', after spending a few years in the Tower, were released into safe (though estranged) obscurity. Beatrice-Joanna seems to have shared with Frances Howard a not unreasonable belief that her social status would keep her immune from justice – and that some morning-after trick could be devised to recover her mislaid virginity.

The world of the play

Middleton (in this case in remarkably seamless partnership with Rowley) never overlooks the minutiae of social life in his plays. This is most obvious in his comedies, of course; but *Women Beware Women* spanned a whole spectrum of urban society, and while *The Changeling* is less encompassing, its strange play-worlds are connected both to each other and to the wider world beyond. Alsemero is that rare but distinctive Jacobean figure, the traveller, who talks now of coming 'home' to marriage (I, i, 9). But 'home' in this play is a 'citadel . . . plac'd conspicuous to outward view, / On promonts' tops' (I, i, 165–7), with its nearest neighbour a lunatic asylum – the one presumably as difficult to get into uninvited as the other is to leave. No wonder, then, that Beatrice-Joanna is intensely repelled yet fascinated by De Flores, so constant and unavoidable is his presence in Vermandero's claustrophobic citadel. And no wonder that Antonio and Franciscus take their chance amongst the madmen to vary the monotony, when the old doctor in charge weds a beautiful young bride. Such would be an over-literal approach to most Jacobean tragedies; but I suspect that Middleton would have taken such contingencies into account – while his play is arguably not a tragedy at all.

The opening scenario of the main plot and sub-plot of *The Changeling* might, indeed, be of a romantic comedy: a feisty heroine, Beatrice-Joanna, comes to bemoan her father's choice of bridegroom, while a young wife, Isabella, is yoked to an elderly husband from whose clutches gallants are eager to snatch her. Wily servants, in the persons of De Flores and Lollio, are even on hand to assist. But such expectations are disappointed – and Middleton and Rowley continue to disrupt most conventions on which they seem to call. The contrasting worlds of their play are not of court and country, or of city and court, but of castle and lunatic asylum. Straying from one to the other, Isabella's would-be gallants provide an initially tenuous link, when their absence from Alicante causes them to fall under suspicion of Alonzo's murder; but Tomazo, as if plucked from the revenge tradition to seek retribution for his brother's death, only makes a fool of himself by hauling them back for arraignment just when the guilt of De Flores and Beatrice is coming to light. And De Flores, apparently fitting the mould of malcontent, bursts its bounds to become the lover rather than the instrument of his mistress. Even when the plots finally merge at the close, and Isabella's foolish husband appears to have learned a comedic lesson in how to treat a young wife, around them a different generic game is being played out – one of guilt and retribution, in a play which, if a tragedy, allows neither nobility of stature nor self-recognition to its tragic heroine, who dies no better aware of herself than when she first found murder a convenient means of gratifying her desires.

De Flores has little existence beyond the moment, living and acting in a flow of existential immediacy. There is no sense (as with, say, Flamineo in *The White Devil*) of a familial or social background having helped to shape him or, as with Iago, of a psychic energy that drives otherwise inexplicable actions. Unlike his mistress, De Flores calculates consequences, but he loses clarity as well as conscience in his fixation with possessing her. The ringed finger that he brings to Beatrice (which is, of course, replete with a symbolism that hovers ambiguously between signifying castration and sexual potency, like the dropped glove that Beatrice refuses to accept from his hands earlier in the play) is a rare moment of realisation for Beatrice. 'Bless me, what hast thou done?' is her genuinely startled response (III, iv, 29), as if the token is more terrible than what it signifies. Then, as Beatrice becomes aware that De Flores seeks the reward not of her purse but her person, it dawns no less humiliatingly on De Flores that he has been treated, despite Beatrice's pampering persuasions, not as a potential lover but a hired hit man.

Her appalled realisation is of course heavy with irony in its reflection alike of her warped moral sense – that De Flores could be 'so wicked . . . To make his death the murderer of my honour!' – and of the incongruous social snobbery of her appeal: 'Think but upon the distance that creation / Set 'twixt thy blood and mine' (III, iv, 120–31). But soon Beatrice has persuaded herself that she is beholden to De Flores for preserving the very 'honour' he has by now besmirched: 'I'm forced to love thee now, / 'Cause thou provid'st so carefully for my honour' (V, i, 47–8) – which he does by committing the second murder, that of Diaphanta. Perhaps one reason that we see so little of De Flores beyond his relationship with

Beatrice is because he functions dramatically as a mirror which presents her with an image of a truth she is unable to see in herself – and as 'foul villain' and 'fair murderess' conjoined (III, iv, 141–2) they become one at last in death.

Beatrice-Joanna, then, embodies a kind of perverse innocence that is almost psychopathic in its ego-driven amorality, Even at the end, when all is known, she appears to anticipate Alsemero's forgiveness, since the murders were committed to enable their love. She still believes that her 'honour' is somehow intact – not so much unconscious of how she had earlier pleaded with De Flores to preserve that same honour, as able to adapt her perception of the word to its loss. If *Hamlet* is in part a tragedy of a character who thinks too much before he acts, *The Changeling* gives us in Beatrice a character who scarcely seems to think at all, so fixedly are her preconceptions made to justify her desires, and so readily does she adapt those preconceptions to what she has done – not so much accepting the consequences as absorbing them.

Though *The Changeling* was staged not long after Ford's *New Way to Pay Old Debts*, Middleton and Rowley are writing of changing times and with more alert moral perceptions – compare their authorial attitude when Beatrice appeals to De Flores to remember their difference in blood with Ford's to Alworth, as he lords it over Margaret. This may bring the play into better focus for our own times, but it grants us few certainties. Is Vermandero, in Trevor R. Griffiths' words, 'a decent man, a careful father trying to do his best for his daughter', or, as feminist critics have it, a patriarchal tyrant imposing a husband on Beatrice for his own economic convenience? He is, of course, both; just as Isabella is at once an oppressed victim and the triumphant standard-bearer of a sterner morality than her male 'betters'; while Alsemero is both a man of rectitude and an opportunist, willing to kill a rival in a duel and to humiliate his bride with his absurd virginity test.

This, perhaps, suggests a wider significance to the play's title than the usual roll-call of possible 'changelings'. Yes, one of the several Jacobean senses of 'changeling' was 'a fickle woman', and if this is the primary sense intended, the application to Beatrice is clear – while in the more usual sense Antonio remains chief claimant to the role. But most of the characters are in some sense 'changed' in the course of the action – De Flores from 'honest' to 'horrid villain' in the eyes of the world, from near-ogre to trusted lover in those of Beatrice; Diaphanta from chaste maid to substitute bride; Alibius from tyrannical husband to tolerant partner; even Tomazo, from brave avenger to bumbling sniffer after red herrings. Some of these changes are real, some only perceived – but all have to do with the changing times and attitudes which Middleton recognised and dramatised more perceptively than most of his contemporaries.

The playwright's craft

FORM *The Changeling* has travelled about as far as tragedy could go before the Restoration refashioned it. Leo Salingar prefers to call it one of the first 'dramas of domestic life', in a line that looks forward to the problem plays of Ibsen rather than the 'heroic' or 'sentimental' modes that came between.

STRUCTURE Note how the crucial encounters between De Flores and Beatrice, before and after Alonzo's murder, are interrupted by the asylum scene in which Isabella rebuts the attentions successively of Antonio and Lollio (II, ii–III, iv).

LANGUAGE Though typically flexible and colloquial in their use of blank verse, the authors here introduce recurring words and related ideas – notably concerning 'blood', 'will' and 'service' – which the main characters all employ, often in ironically different senses, sometimes self-unaware, sometimes as intended puns. Words in this play are also 'changelings'.

CONVENTIONS Middleton is a master of 'asides', which in the crucial scenes between De Flores and Beatrice explicate the crossed purposes between them, while also showing, as

N. W. Bawcutt puts it, how the characters 'are isolated from each other, withdrawn into a private world of reverie and pre-occupation'.

In performance

Although other evidence suggests the play's popularity with audiences, the only recorded contemporary performance of *The Changeling*, two years after it was licensed, was at court, in 1624 – as was the last for almost three centuries, in 1668. The first known modern London revival was by the amateur First Folio Club in 1950, since when at least fifty further productions have been staged, establishing the play's claim to its place in the repertoire. The first professional revival, directed by Tony Richardson at the Royal Court Theatre in 1961, was brought forward in time to the Spain of Goya, with Mary Ure as Beatrice achieving, in Peter Roberts' judgement, 'a good measure of the character's childlike selfishness'. Frank Evans directed the play for the Oxford Stage Company in 1966, and Philip Prowse for the Glasgow Citizens' in 1976. Peter Gill's revival for the Riverside Studios, Hammersmith, in 1978 was followed within a month by Terry Hands' production for the RSC at the Aldwych, in which Emrys James, playing De Flores to Diana Quick's Beatrice, was, in Benedict Nightingale's description, 'a seducer who somehow manages to make menace tender and implacable sensuality gentle'. Ten years later, in a production by Richard Eyre for the National Theatre which transplanted the action to a nineteenth-century Spanish slave colony, Miranda Richardson's Beatrice was, according to Peter Kemp, a 'semi-psychotic' who 'always heads towards the nearest temporary escape route' – though Kate Kellaway found an 'incandescent quality' in her face. Michael Attenborough directed the play for a second RSC production in its Swan Theatre in 1992, which transferred to the Barbican Pit in 1993. Robert Gore-Langton described Michael Storry's De Flores as conveying 'a sense of the psychotic by being so earnestly pleasant and reasonable'.

John Ford
The Broken Heart

c. 1629

Source

Unusually among his contemporaries, Ford drew on his own imagination rather than previous fictions or reports of actual events for the plots of his tragedies.

The story

Penthea has been coerced by her brother Ithocles into marriage with the elderly Bassanes, who is much given to jealousy – especially of her former lover, Orgilus, who declares his intention of leaving Sparta for Athens, having obtained a vow from his sister Euphrania not to marry without his consent. Ithocles and his friend Prophilus, returning after a great victory over Messene, are welcomed home by the Spartan king, Amyclas, his daughter, Calantha, and his counsellors, Orgilus' father Crotolon among them. Orgilus has in fact remained in Sparta, disguised as a disciple of the philosopher Tecnicus. Penthea, summoned to the palace by her brother, meets Orgilus in the gardens, where he reveals his true identity; but although confessing to love him, she virtuously spurns the consummation he desires. Prophilus has meanwhile been paying court to Euphrania who, with her father's support, agrees to marry him if Orgilus also consents. Ithocles professes contrition to Penthea for his treatment of her, and declares his love for Calantha – whom her father hopes to marry to the visiting Nearchus, King of Argos. They are interrupted by Bassanes, jealous that their relationship is incestuous. Penthea, fearful of dying from despair, fulfils her promise to her brother to plead his cause with Calantha, who is moved by her plight but appears non-committal – until, while walking with Nearchus, she shows favour to Ithocles by throwing him a ring. This prompts a jealous dispute between the rivals, which Orgilus helps to smooth over. Amyclas falls suddenly ill, and Tecnicus interprets an ambiguous Delphian oracle which does not bode well for his kingdom. While the marriage of Euphrania to Prophilus is to proceed, and Amyclas gives his consent to the match between Calantha and Ithocles, Penthea has been driven mad by her despair and, although Bassanes is now truly repentant of his jealousy, she starves herself to death. As Orgilus and Ithocles sit by her corpse, Ithocles is trapped in his chair by Orgilus, who stabs him to death, which Ithocles professes to welcome. Calantha, presiding at the wedding celebrations, is brought news of the deaths of her father, of Penthea, and of Ithocles, all of which she receives while continuing almost manically to dance. Sentenced to death, Orgilus opens the arteries in his arms. Calantha, having made provision for the future – bestowing Ithocles' estates upon Prophilus, and proclaiming Nearchus as next King of Sparta – weds the dead Ithocles by placing her mother's ring on the finger of the corpse. Kissing his dead lips, she too dies – of a broken heart.

The author and his work

John Ford was baptised in Ilsington, Devon, in April 1586, son of a small local landowner. He was admitted to the Middle Temple to study law in 1602, and (apart from two years exclusion for debt) appears to have been in residence most of his life, presumably practising law. Of his early, occasional pieces, none were for the stage, and it was not until 1621 that he collaborated with Dekker and Rowley on *The Witch of Edmonton* (see p. 217), his first known play of around twenty. Probably between 1625 and 1633 he wrote *The Lover's Melancholy* (a tragi-comedy indebted to Burton's *The Anatomy of Melancholy*, and interesting for its sense of the personae in which people entrap themselves) and *The Broken Heart*, both for the King's Men. Then, for the Queen's company, playing at the Phoenix, came *'Tis Pity She's a Whore* (see p. 241); an historical

tragedy *Perkin Warbeck*; *Love's Sacrifice*, a tragedy of passionate but chaste love reconciled in death; an ironically bawdy
tragi-comedy, *The Fancies Chaste and Noble*; and the romance
The Lady's Trial. Like Jonson, Ford seems to have taken unusual care over the publication of these, his published plays,
viewing them as literature rather than ephemeral entertainments. He is not heard of after 1640.

The historical context

Ford looks both back and forwards in *The Broken Heart*. His
plot has no basis in the historical Sparta, but the play is suffused with the kind of moral austerity and stoic resignation in
adversity for which this small but powerful Greek province
was both famous and reluctantly admired by its Athenian near-
neighbour – unlike which it remained faithful to a tradition of
kingship. But the play also anticipates the 'heroic drama',
which was to preoccupy tragic playwrights in the aftermath of
the Restoration with its twin themes of 'love and honour'.
This may in part reflect the ambitions of Queen Henrietta
Maria, after the accession of her husband as Charles I in 1625,
to create, by contrast with the dissolute Jacobean court, one
which revivified the late-medieval concept of courtly love, with
its roots in the platonic belief in the precedence of ideal forms
over 'real' and of spiritual over physical love. Of course, for the
canny Queen this was directed to the building of a power base
at court, and she even encouraged 'courtier dramatists' into
her circle. Ford was not among these, but the motto included
on the title-page of this as of most of his plays was both an
anagram of his own name and an apt description of a favoured
courtly theme – *fide honor*, or 'honour through fidelity'.

The world of the play

The world of *The Broken Heart* is, by comparison with that of
other recent tragedies, strangely static. Many of the events on
which it hinges have occurred before the play begins, and

characters undergo changes of heart for their past errors unusually early in the action. We do not even see Ithocles until
he has become ashamed of enforcing his sister's marriage to
Bassanes – who himself is given two acts instead of the usual
last-minute few lines (like Alibius in *The Changeling*) to repent
his excessive jealousy. And Orgilus casts off his disguise before
it has had much impact on the plot, resolving, rather ambiguously, to 'stand up like a man' (II, iii, 125). Thereafter he
largely keeps his own counsel – presumably since to share his
feelings with the audience would mute the shock value of his
murder of Ithocles, to whom he has appeared reconciled.

There are few grand declarations of feeling in *The Broken
Heart*, but many elliptic emotional concealments. Sometimes
these are intentional deceptions, of which Armostes (doubting
Orgilus' reconciliatory words) warns Ithocles: ''Tis the tongue
informs our ears. / Our eyes can never pierce into the thoughts,
/ For they are lodged too inward' (IV, i, 16–18). Sometimes
they are the understated ways through which deep feelings
find expression, as when Calantha can only admit her love for
Ithocles in a throwaway gesture. But more often they hide
what Calantha calls 'the silent griefs which cut the heart-strings'
(V, iii, 75) – here describing the stifling of her own feelings
about the last-act deaths until she is ready to make her dispo-
sitions and die, it seems of a self-willed broken heart. And
Penthea's pent-up miseries fester into despair, at last finding
an outlet in madness in that extraordinary scene (IV, ii) witnessed by her husband, lover and brother.

These are not criticisms of the play, any more than one
would criticise, say, the climax of *Brief Encounter* for emotional
restraint, because emotional restraint is what the film is about.
Thus, *The Broken Heart* is at once very Spartan and close to
modern Englishness in its characters' concern to keep their
feelings buttoned and their upper lips stiffened – arguably a
wearisome quality in English drama of the mid-twentieth
century, but distinctive and quite refreshing in English drama
of the Jacobean or Caroline age. And Ford gives us not only
the emotional evasions of repressed feelings, but the self-

fashioning through which his characters display their faces to the world. Penthea, fearful of loss of self-control, delivers to Calantha not a woman-to-woman supplication but an allusive 'bequest' (III, v). Orgilus, most contained of all, maintains his outward show to the end, choosing to die by bleeding to death before the assembled company – achieving a theatrical effect which his disguise failed to sustain. Even Bassanes is careful to keep his jealousy indoors – indeed, is shocked into the self-realisation necessary for reform when he allows it to be displayed before others, and sees that it is destroying the wife to whom he is unable to express love. (As loquacious in his guilt as in his oppression, he earnestly sets out to make amends, and his efforts are recognised when Calantha bestows on him the marshalship of Sparta.)

Even in his death throes, Ithocles cannot help admiring the figure he cuts in the set-piece trap Orgilus has arranged, and (as his murderer later recounts) 'Proclaim'd his last act triumph over ruin' (V, ii, 43). Bassanes also uses 'triumph' – which for Jacobean audiences would connote a theatrical spectacle – to describe Orgilus' suicide, which he predicts will be celebrated by future poets to become 'the writer's glory and his subject's triumph' (V, ii, 134); and he is still thinking theatrically after Calantha's death (which has of course been carefully stage-managed by herself): 'O royal maid, would thou hadst miss'd this part; / Yet 'twas a brave one' (V, iii, 96–7).

There are no villains in this play any more than there are heroes, or even anti-heroes. True, Orgilus commits an ignoble crime, and is punished for it. Rather tenuously, his is an act of revenge – at least, it is apparently determined by his sister's pointing to Ithocles as the cause of her madness – but the other deaths occur as a consequence of character, not in a climactic bloodbath. Even the shadowy figure of Amyclas may be said to have died of his own inner dread – a consuming fear of the Delphic oracle. But if this is a proto-problem play rather than a tragedy, Ford is dramatising the problem – that of the moral status of loveless marriage – not offering or implying a solution. Orgilus and Penthea believe their prior betrothal makes them truly 'married'; but Penthea, though she declares herself a 'whore' living in 'adultery' with Bassanes (III, ii, 74–5), will not take the further step Orgilus desires – to 'possess my wife' (II, iii, 71). In comedy, marriage to an unloved but 'suitable' partner is thwarted precisely because it was seldom so in real life – though usually leading to quiet despair rather than tragic death.

Ford does seem to have had a special sympathy for women made powerless by the patriarchal society of the time, and is also reluctant outright to condemn forms of love which transgress the moral proprieties. Though incestuous feelings between Ithocles and Penthea exist only in Bassanes' obsessed imagination, there are hints that Orgilus feels more than brotherly love for his sister (as does Giovanni for Annabella in *'Tis Pity She's a Whore*). Not only does he usurp his father's prerogative in demanding to approve Euphrania's choice of husband, but he is a voyeuristic presence in her dealings with Prophilus, and in disguise agrees to act as a go-between. None of these elements proves more than marginally relevant to the plot, but they may provide clues to our understanding of Orgilus' psyche and his burning, deeply concealed anger.

Indeed, that such plot elements appear to lead nowhere suggests either that Ford was a careless craftsman (as Eliot believed) or that he included them as psychological pointers rather than as contributing to the 'unity of action' some have found in the play – and others duly disputed. But debates over whether *The Broken Heart* is a forerunner of the neoclassical French tragedies of Corneille and Racine are pointless for English audiences, who have seldom responded to either; it is more helpful to be open to the idea that Ford is stretching the boundaries of the form, enabling a response that combines a sense of the emotional inevitability of a tragic outcome with an intellectual questioning of its cause.

The playwright's craft

STRUCTURE We note how the focus of the action shifts throughout the play between Orgilus, Ithocles, Penthea and

Calantha, the four characters who are to die – their deaths also spaced carefully, so that each is its own set-piece rather than a last-act domino effect. Music plays a part in 'displaying' the action at important moments, and Ford is very detailed in his stage directions when a specific visualisation is required: see, for example, the instructions which open Act V, Scene iii.

LANGUAGE   Charles Lamb's verdict of 1808 remains apposite: 'He sought for sublimity not by parcels in metaphors or visible images, but directly where she has full residence, in the heart of man; in the actions and sufferings of the greatest minds.' Nor has Swinburne's description of 1871 dated: 'At all times his verse is even and regular, accurate and composed; never specially flexible or melodious, always admirable for precision, vigour and purity.'

CONVENTIONS   The disguise convention in the play is deployed only to be quickly abandoned. Similarly, the character whose role appears to be that of detached observer of events, Tecnicus, serves briefly as mentor to Orgilus, returns to interpret the oracle – itself a familiar feature of plays set in the ancient world – and then departs, for Delphi or death or both. His homily on the nature of honour (III, i, 31–51) appears to be a crucial statement of Ford's theme; but it is delivered to Orgilus, who gives it his approval and then proceeds to act in a contrary manner. Act V, Scene ii, begins with music for a wedding celebration – a convention from comedy which is here the accompaniment to a macabre roll-call of deaths. In short, as so often in the play, the familiar is called into question rather than functioning in the expected way.

STAGE PRACTICE   As Keith Sturgess has pointed out, the emotional restraint of the play would have called on the more intimate style of acting to which the King's Men would by now have accustomed themselves for their indoor playhouse, the Blackfriars. He notes, too, how many scenes call for chairs, and that other scenes could also be played seated – making more integral the use of the trick chair which traps Ithocles in IV, iv (a demanding project for the stage carpenter). The play would still best be seen in a small-scale or studio theatre: there are few swathes of frantic activity or great emotional outbursts, but many personal, close-up encounters between small groups of characters.

In performance

The attribution of *The Broken Heart* to the King's Men on the title-page of the first (and only) quarto of 1633 would place it in the earlier part of Ford's career, suggesting a first staging around 1629 at the Blackfriars. No more is heard of the play until 1898, when a pared-down text was staged by Poel's Elizabethan Stage Society in St George's Hall, perhaps providing impetus for a revival by the Mermaid Society at the Royalty Theatre in 1904. A single student production is recorded in 1959, before Laurence Olivier gave the play unwonted prominence by including it in his inaugural season at the Chichester Festival Theatre in 1962. Kenneth Tynan reserved his praise for Rosemary Harris' 'calm, unpainted Penthea, looking at once ravaged and ravishing'. He dismissed Joan Greenwood's Calantha as 'a stoical heroine reduced to the stature of a baritone Joyce Grenfell', and bemoaned Olivier's playing of Bassanes as 'a sombre old victim bound for slaughter, too noble and too tragic ever to be funny'. The play then disappeared from the live repertoire until 1994, when no fewer than three productions were staged – Daino Fainaro's at Arts Threshold, Jonathan Church's at the Lyric Studio, and Michael Boyd's for the RSC at the Swan Theatre in Stratford, a production which for Michael Billington confirmed 'that the power of stoicism derives from the intensity of feeling it conceals'. There was general praise for Emma Fielding's Penthea – a 'study in blasted feeling', as John Peter wrote. 'Her tight, white face suggests a long familiarity with pain, and her supple voice encompasses Ford's whole range of the poetry of doom with all the confidence of great music.'

John Ford
'Tis Pity She's a Whore

c. 1633

Source

There are, unsurprisingly, analogues to be found in a number
of earlier tragedies and tales of incest but, superficial resemblances apart, the plot appears to have been Ford's invention.

The story

Friar Bonaventura is horrified by the admission of the young
Giovanni, to whom he is confessor and tutor, that he is in love
with his own sister, Annabella. Soranzo, a nobleman of Parma,
and Grimaldi, a visitor to the city from Rome, are rival suitors
for Annabella; and her father, Florio, has to rebuke Soranzo's
servant Vasques and Grimaldi for quarrelling over her in the
street. Annabella and her old nurse Putana are watching from
the balcony, but the girl shows little interest until she sees
Giovanni arriving below. When he confesses that he loves her,
Annabella reveals that she returns his feelings, and they swear
an oath of fidelity. Although he has already promised Annabella to Soranzo, Florio tells his friend Donado that he has no
objection to his foolish nephew, Bergetto, also becoming a
suitor. Giovanni and Annabella emerge from consummating
their love, to which Putana gives her blessing. Florio introduces to his daughter Richardetto, a visiting doctor, and his
niece Philotis. Hippolita, Soranzo's former mistress, abuses
him for his desertion, but is calmed by Vasques, who offers
help in her plans for revenge. When Richardetto and Philotis
are alone, it turns out that the supposed doctor is Hippolito's
cuckolded husband, whom she had supposed dead. He is now
seeking his revenge on Soranzo, and agrees to give Grimaldi
a poison for the tip of his rapier, to make certain of his rival's

death. Bergetto is treated kindly by Philotis when he is hurt in a brawl, and decides that he prefers her to Annabella. The Friar condemns Giovanni for his incest, and warns him that Annabella must be married; but when Soranzo pays court to Annabella, secretly watched by Giovanni, she rebuffs him. She is taken ill, and Putana tells Giovanni that she is pregnant. The Friar terrifies Annabella with a vision of Hell, and she agrees to a marriage. Bergetto and Philotis are planning to marry secretly, but Grimaldi mistakes the simpleton for Soranzo: he kills him, and finds sanctuary with the Cardinal. During the wedding celebrations of Annabella and Soranzo, Hippolita, after presenting a masque, tries to poison Soranzo, but Vasques tricks her into taking the poison herself. Richardetto advises Philotis to become a nun, and she departs. Discovering Annabella's pregnancy, Soranzo threatens to kill her if she does not reveal the child's father, but Vasques dissuades him from violence and by guile persuades Putana to reveal the secret, then orders hired banditti to put out her eyes. Annabella asks the Friar to deliver a letter to Giovanni, written in her blood, urging repentance. Invited to Soranzo's birthday celebrations, Giovanni stabs Annabella after a last bedroom tryst, then appears to Soranzo and his guests with her heart on his dagger. Florio dies of shock, and Soranzo is killed by Giovanni before being slain himself by Vasques and the banditti. The Cardinal banishes Vasques and seizes the estates of the deceased for the church.

The author and his work

For Ford's life, see under *The Broken Heart*, p. 234.

The historical context

The Christian Church originally prohibited marriages between cousins as well as siblings, and although the former were allowed by the Church of England under the 'Table of Consanguinity' appended to the Elizabethan Book of Common

Prayer, and remain permissible under English law, marriages between cousins are prohibited as incestuous in a majority of states in the USA. So the religious and legal understanding of what constitutes incest has always been subject to social pressures and needs, and has varied considerably through history. When Giovanni calls Annabella his Juno – Jupiter's sister as well as his wife – it thus reminds us that incest was commonplace in classical mythology, as it is in many myths of origin. And from the Egyptian pharaohs to the Roman emperors to the Habsburgs it has been practised to serve the interests of dynastic continuity – but, as the hereditary ailments prevalent in European royal families bear out, arguments against the marriage of close blood relations have a medical as well as (or perhaps underlying) a moral basis. At the other end of the social scale, intermarriage of close relatives in small, isolated communities has often been the cause of hereditary disease or genetic defects. Among the nobility and gentry, increased mobility was by Ford's time making close intermarriage less common – but Soranzo's original cause of fury, that he was to father another man's child, remained a pervasive fear. A main reason for the almost paranoid obsession with female virginity before marriage, and fear of cuckoldry afterwards, was that under the laws of primogeniture the firstborn male inherited his father's title and lands – and so, to judge from the little evidence we have, the obsession was less common among the working classes, where there was little or nothing for anybody to inherit.

The world of the play

The world of 'Tis Pity She's a Whore is that of a provincial city – self-important rather than influential, for no vital affairs of state are settled here, and the Cardinal, merely by his association with Rome, holds effective power, even over the forces of law and order. There are no family feuds, just the expected jealousies over local beauties – and, of course, the adulteries that are the stuff of small-town gossip. Into this placid pool jumps Giovanni, fresh from university and ready to outdo his tutor in conducting a disputation – which, it soon emerges, is an attempt at moral justification for his own incestuous love.

But their debate proves to be, almost literally, peripheral; for the incest, soon broached and consummated, is thereafter, in Martin Wiggins' words, 'on the sidelines of the action'. Neither the Friar nor Giovanni 'speaks at length to anyone but each other and Annabella, while the plot goes on elsewhere'. And so, until the last-act confrontations, life in Parma proceeds much as usual, give or take a little violence on the streets. It is Annabella rather than Giovanni who has to reconcile the normalities of the everyday world with her secret life with her brother, and it is upon her (as the title of the play suggests and as the Cardinal's closing words echo) that the weight of moral censure falls, although it is she who dies repentant and hopeful of Heaven, while her brother, more solipsistic than defiant, no more expects salvation than he fears divine displeasure.

Male ranks close against Hippolita as against Annabella, while Soranzo appears – less hypocritically than self-deceptively – unable to conceive that he is no less guilty of adultery than his mistress or wife. Florio, although he is genuinely concerned that Annabella should marry the suitor of her choice, does not conceal his own preference for a man whose wealth and rank render past misconduct a forgivable sowing of wild oats. And just as double standards operate in matters of sexuality, so they do in offences against the law, as Florio and Donado find when they come up against the Cardinal's blunt refusal to give up Grimaldi for his murder of Bergetto, because he is 'no common man, but nobly born / Of princes' blood' (III, ix, 56–7). While Annabella's body is to suffer posthumous indignities, that of her brother will be buried with the respectable dead – and among the survivors, smugly surveying the carnage, is Richardetto, purveyor of lethal poisons to the nobility. Even a great man's minion, the arch-plotter Vasques, is sentenced only to banishment. Despite his apparent moral neutrality, Ford thus allows us no exemplars of moral probity against which to measure the conduct of the lovers – except the Friar, whose conventional wisdom lies in asserting the infallibility of the Church.

If guilty love is punished, however inequitably, innocent love is simply extinguished. The murder of Bergetto is shocking not just for its unexpectedness, but because comic sub-plots are not usually cut short by casual murder. While Bergetto may be a fool, he is a good-natured fellow, who, as Donado says, 'meant no man harm' (III, ix, 8), and his crush on Philotis is as genuine as her perhaps semi-maternal love for him. His sexual arousal by her kiss clearly astonishes him – and he is no less astonished by the intimations of his own mortality, in a scene which conveys the actuality of death with darkly comic realism rather than self-memorialising rhetoric (III, vii, 8–33).

Although (or because) Bergetto's dying wish that his uncle should 'make much of this wench' is unselfish, it is not carried out; for innocence is not only disposable, but can be easily ignored – its memory, as Florio advises, obliterated by taking a little good wine (IV, i, 22). Directors who choose (as many have) to eliminate this sub-plot altogether, in a vain attempt to bring the Giovanni–Annabella incest into closer focus, fail to recognise that *'Tis Pity* works through just such ironic juxtapositions – between psychological and social realities; between guilt and innocence; and between the symbolic and the actual (Giovanni's obsession with the 'blood' that links him with his sister is thus no less actualised when the dying Bergetto mistakes it for urine than when it drips from Annabella's heart). The oft-noted resemblances to *Romeo and Juliet* – most obviously, the mentoring roles played by a nurse and a Friar – would have been well recognised by audiences of Ford's time, adding a further juxtaposition – between a tragedy caused by falling in love with somebody from the wrong family and one caused by falling in love with somebody from one's own.

Both plays, too, share (and never move beyond) the setting of a small Italian town, whose prominent citizens all know each other and are governed by a shared code of behaviour – which even if breached cannot be ignored. Thus, Giovanni and the Friar, the two characters who keep most distant from the everyday bustle of Parma, still find themselves having to accommodate its normalities. Giovanni's fine words of love are from the first based on a lie – that he has 'asked counsel of the holy church, / Who tells me I may love you' (I, ii, 242–3) – and while even the noxious Richardetto sees a retreat to a nunnery as the 'way to heaven' for his bereft niece (IV, ii, 21), it does not occur to the Friar that Annabella might better save her soul by marrying Christ than save her 'honour' in the eyes of the world by a deceitful marriage to Soranzo.

It would be unhistorical to expect Ford to give us much psychological insight into the roots of the siblings' incestuous love; even so, the extent to which this so speedily becomes a 'given' of the action is surprising. We know Annabella a little the better of the two, since we see her interact with more of the other characters and we witness her growing self-doubt – as also her genuine fear, whether of the Friar's lurid vision of Hell (III, vi, 8–24) or her husband's violence. But the force of this illicit love lies throughout in the rhetoric of its expression rather than in any teasing out of its causes in nurture or nature. The couple have no essence to express beyond the immediacies of passion – which is perhaps why they have proved such tempting vessels for actors to pour themselves into.

In this play, the malcontented servant, although apparently less prominent a figure than a Flamineo or Bosola, remains instrumental to the outcome. The motives of Vasques remain opaque, but he it is who is responsible both for the betrayal of Hippolita's plot and the discovery of the incest – despite whatever set-piece revenge he had planned for the birthday feast being upstaged by Giovanni. The scene in which he wheedles the truth out of Putana is a masterly display of cunning and cruelty. If (as the ambiguity of the Cardinal's reference to 'this woman' makes possible) it is Putana rather than Annabella who is to be 'burnt to ashes' (V, vi, 132–5), the sight of this brutally blinded old crone being dragged away to the stake would make an appropriate climax to a play in which Ford sets sexual and social transgressions in the scales, and leaves his audience to judge which are the more inhuman and inhumane.

The playwright's craft

FORM   Attempts to assign generic labels have varied from finding the play a throwback to the Marlovian tragedy of over-reaching to seeing it as a new kind of 'city tragedy'. Like *The Broken Heart*, *'Tis Pity* is moving beyond tragedy into a more exploratory and (for the audience) challenging mode, which dramatises moral issues as much as personal sufferings.

LANGUAGE   Throughout, from the moment when Giovanni offers Annabella his dagger if she wishes to be sure of his heart (I, ii, 204), through her pert, prophetic comeback to Soranzo's 'Did you but see my heart then would you swear –' with 'That you were dead' (III, ii, 24–5), to Giovanni's final entrance, the difference between the symbolic and actual significance of the human heart is a recurring motif (as further discussed above).

CONVENTIONS   The masque in IV, i, does not (as often) form an integral part of Hippolita's plot, but is simply an excuse to gain entrance to the wedding feast; and the second banquet for Soranzo's birthday (V, vi) is too soon interrupted for music to play a part. It is, indeed, an altogether less prominent feature of this play than of *The Broken Heart*.

STAGE PRACTICE   The brawl between Vasques and Grimaldi not only sustains the pace of the opening after the scene between the Friar and Giovanni, but calls into use the stage balcony, from which Annabella and Putana comment on the action – incidentally getting across some useful exposition. The 'discovery space' would presumably have been required for the Friar's study in III, vi, since he is described as 'sitting' and Annabella as 'kneeling' in the opening stage direction. Annabella is similarly 'discovered' at the start of V, v, where she is described as 'lying' on her bed as Giovanni enters – though the bed itself may well have been rolled or pushed downstage at the start of the scene.

In performance

By 1633, the date of the first quarto edition, *'Tis Pity She's a Whore* was being acted by the Queen's Men at the Phoenix, and was still being played there in 1639, when a legal dispute required a listing of the theatre's repertoire. There were a few revivals early in the Restoration but, unsurprisingly in view of its theme, the play soon fell into disfavour, and was not seen again until 1923, when it was revived for two performances by the Phoenix Society at the Shaftesbury Theatre. It was staged at the Arts Theatre in 1934, and in 1940 Donald Wolfit brought it into his touring repertoire, himself taking the role of Giovanni, with Rosalind Iden as Isabella. Since then the play has been seen in some thirty productions, many by students or in fringe venues. David Thompson directed *'Tis Pity* for the Mermaid Theatre in 1961, and Roland Joffé for a production by the National Theatre's touring company in 1972. The RSC staged the play in its studio theatres, The Other Place in Stratford and The Warehouse in London, in 1977, under Ron Daniels' direction. Ned Chaillet felt that this 'catalogue of bloody sins' benefited 'from its reduction to a chamber play', and found the scenes between Simon Rouse and Barbara Kellerman as brother and sister 'richly believable, erotic both in seduction and murder'. In 1988 Philip Prowse (for the Citizens', Glasgow) and Alan Ayckbourn (for the National) both directed major revivals. Michael Coveney contrasted Prowse's choice of 'going deterministically for a single explanation . . . the stinking corruption of the . . . Catholic church' with Ayckbourn's 'lucid and intelligible' approach – which, however, 'offers no explanations'. David Lan's Young Vic production in 1999 won more general critical approval, pairing what Lyn Gardner called 'a shimmering, brilliant debut' from Eve Best as Isabella with the Giovanni of Jude Law, who, in the words of Roger Foss, took his character 'on a catastrophic emotional journey from insecure but defiant young brat . . . to crazed avenger'. Edward Dick directed a widely praised version at Southwark Playhouse in 2005.

James Shirley
Hyde Park

1632

Source

No sources are known.

The story

Mistress Bonavent's merchant husband is presumed lost at sea; now the seven years he bound her to wait for him have expired, and she agrees to marry Lacy, a longstanding admirer. Her waspishly witty cousin, Mistress Carol, spurns all three of her own suitors, playing off Rider and Venture against one another and offering no kind words to a more serious contender, Fairfield. The 'lost' Bonavent turns up in disguise on the wedding morning, and is humiliated when Lacy forces him into an ungainly dance. Fairfield's sister Julietta appears to reciprocate the love of Lacy's friend Trier, but he plans to test her virtue by telling the amorous Lord Bonvile that she is a courtesan, while asking Julietta to reform the noble rake. Dismissing Rider and Venture, Carol taunts Fairfield until he gets her to swear an oath that she will never love him. The action moves to Hyde Park where, amidst the horseracing and the bets, Bonvile and Julietta remain at cross purposes while Carol continues her verbal fencing with Fairfield: she is unable to tell him that she loves him, and he leaves in disgust. Bonavent appears, and forces Lacy to dance for him at swordpoint. Rebuked by his wife, he gives her a paper revealing his identity, but asks her to keep it secret. Julietta is so angered by Bonvile's continuing importunities that he is persuaded of her virtue, and appears truly contrite. Fairfield and Carol finally reveal their true feelings for each other and agree to marry; but Julietta, discovering that she was being put to the test by

Trier, spurns his explanations and apologies. Bonavent arrives, revealing his true identity, and Lacy honourably resigns himself to the end of his still unconsummated marriage.

The author and his work

Born in 1596 in London, Shirley entered Merchant Taylors' School in 1608, and was apprenticed to a scrivener before attending St Catherine's College, Cambridge, in 1615. After graduating he became Master of St Albans Grammar School, and is thought to have converted to Roman Catholicism; but he was back in London by 1625, when he began what proved to be a twelve-year relationship with the company that was soon to become Queen Henrietta's Men at the indoor Cockpit (or Phoenix). His earliest extant play is a comedy, *Love's Tricks* (1625), and his first known tragedy *The Maid's Revenge* (1626). Later comedies for the company included *The Wedding* (1626), *The Witty Fair One* (1628), *The Changes* (1632), *The Ball* (1632), *The Gamester* (1633) and *The Lady of Pleasure* (1635), while among his tragedies and tragi-comedies were *The Grateful Servant* (1629), *The Traitor* (1631) and *Love's Cruelty* (1631). In 1634 he was admitted to membership of Gray's Inn, the records describing him as 'one of the valets of the chamber of Queen Henrietta Maria'; and his masque *The Triumph of Peace* was performed at court in that year under the auspices of the Inns of Court. The tragi-comedy *The Duke's Mistress* was the last of his plays to be performed by Queen Henrietta's Men, shortly before the plague closure of 1636–37. He then departed for Dublin, where he remained until 1640, writing for the new theatre in St Werburgh Street. The comedy *The Constant Maid* and the tragi-comedy *The Doubtful Heir* were probably first seen in Dublin in 1638, but the latter was also staged in London by the King's Men in 1640, by which time Shirley had returned to become regular dramatist for that company following Massinger's death in March. His work for the King's Men included the tragi-comedy *The Imposture* and the comedy *The Country Captain* (both 1640); the comedy *The Brothers*

and the tragedy *The Cardinal* (both 1641); and the comedy
The Sisters and the tragi-comedy *The Court Secret* (both 1642) –
the pattern of two plays a year probably his expected con-
tractual obligation. But the last of these plays remained un-
performed, owing to the closure of the theatres on the outbreak of the Civil Wars in September. In these he fought on
the King's side, afterwards returning to London, where he
lived quietly and fairly prosperously as a schoolmaster. He
died with his second wife Frances in 1666, apparently after a
miserable flight from the Great Fire of London.

The historical context

The decade or so following 1629, when Charles I began his
ill-fated experiment in personal rule, were lived rather less in
the shadow of the Civil Wars than tradition retrospectively
assumes. Most parliamentary and extra-parliamentary criticism
tended to look back rather than forwards – often contrasting
the new monarch's behaviour unfavourably with the cult
figure of Elizabeth. Few of the forces in opposition to the
King questioned the legitimacy of his office until very late
indeed: they wanted reformation, not revolution. Even class
warfare was as subtextual in Caroline society as in Shirley's
play, where a merchant gets his revenge on a gentleman who
has humiliated him (and gets the girl as well), while a member
of the nobility is sternly reminded that his social obligations
come before his pleasures. If Jacobean 'city comedy' was precisely that – its local colour that of the old City within the
walls – the focus has now clearly shifted to the emerging
West End, whose inhabitants sought means of whiling away
the leisure which was the mark of their gentility. In Hyde
Park, first opened to the public around the time of our play,
they found a semi-rural resort conveniently close at hand –
not so much as a place for exercise as for social mingling, for
sipping syllabub, and for gambling on the athletic prowess of
the footmen and jockeys who competed in the racing which
quickly became popular there.

The world of the play

From its title, *Hyde Park* might appear to be an upmarket version of *Bartholomew Fair* in which milkmaids, jockeys and running footmen are permitted only to play walk-on (or run-on) parts. And within the more limited social range on which he focuses, Shirley is just as intent as Jonson on observing the way in which people at play behave, and how the passage of their leisure reflects their roles in society. He is entirely unconcerned with families or back-stories – there are no mothers or even fathers here to impose an arranged marriage, no cranky relations to indulge, no old ladies dallying optimistically with mirror and make-up box. The season is spring, and everybody in *Hyde Park*, even down to the precocious page and the biddable milkmaid, is young and sexually alert.

So, at the play's start, we are plunged into the middle of one love game while watching the start of another and the apparent climax to a third. Shirley employs a dramatic licence familiar in romantic comedy, in that his characters are unworried by financial problems and his women enjoy a freedom of choice and an equality of power beyond the usual boundaries of their patriarchal society. But this is London, not the sea coast of Bohemia, and in other respects the play is not romantic at all. Of the three love chases it seems set to follow, only one is successful – that of Fairfield and Carol, who belong to a tradition of bickering lovers which stretches from Shakespeare's Beatrice and Benedick to Congreve's Mirabell and Millamant and beyond. But Lacy and Mistress Bonavent at first appear to have celebrated their marriage at least three acts too soon – and then turn out not to be married at all. And if Trier and Julietta seem to anticipate the tradition of over-sentimental lovers embodied and parodied by Faulkland and Julia in Sheridan's *The Rivals*, this only serves to sharpen the jolt when Julietta spurns her suitor in the last act, apparently in favour of the reformed Lord Bonvile.

Social gradations are reflected in subtle differences in the characters' behaviour and their sense of sexual responsibility.

Mistress Bonavent, to judge alike from her circle of acquaintances and the confidence of her bearing, is clearly socially superior to her 'missing' husband, whose ungainly behaviour at the wedding signals his merchant status. Lacy, 'a man of pretty fortune', is genteel enough to have proved an honest suitor, in contrast to Bonvile, a 'sprig of the nobility', who finds it 'no shame . . . to love a wench' – by which he means to purchase her favours. Bonvile's dishonourable intentions towards Julietta thus put him in breach of the decorum which should govern his conduct as an aristocrat and a courtier – just as Trier breaches *his* decorum, as a man of honour, in misrepresenting his beloved as a 'lady of pleasure'.

Interestingly, Martin Butler suggests that Julietta is here meant to personify the integrity of 'the town', and her conversion of Bonvile to represent 'the court' accepting the responsibilities which are the corollary of its power. He also suggests that, for Shirley, Hyde Park itself represents 'a green world in urban London', and so is 'both country and town, nature and art'; and that this 'alternative nature' expresses the dual, town-and-country character 'of the gentry who frequent it and who are "cultivating" themselves' in their very pursuit of the social round. But despite the clear, eponymous importance of the park, it is, of course, the physical location only of the play's two middle acts: and in this, perhaps, Shirley is ironically tracing the passage so frequent in Shakespearean comedy: from court to country – and, inevitably, back again, with the characters reconciled and refreshed by their experiences. But again Shirley breaks the mould, for his Hyde Park is no pastoral Arden or mythic Athenian wood: it is a sort of tamed and *accessible* version of pastoral: a place in which to play games, whether of an amorous or an athletic kind. In this favoured resort of fashionable Londoners, to be 'refreshed' is to stroll down to Knightsbridge to visit Grave Maurice's convenient tavern – and most of the characters are clearly far from 'reconciled' at the end of the play.

The exceptions of course are the Bonavents, with the disguised, elusive but ultimately triumphant merchant returning to claim his own. Shirley relaxes one kind of dramatic tension very early in the action by revealing Bonavent's existence, but in doing so he heightens tensions of another kind. Thus, we know throughout most of the play that the 'marriage' of Lacy and Mistress Bonavent will prove to have been no less a 'game' than the goings-on in Hyde Park (and we are even reassured that the couple have not anticipated their marriage vows). Meanwhile, Bonavent, who could reassert his rights at any moment, is subjected to the humiliation of being forced to join in the dancing – a social grace in which he is clumsily unskilled. But while he bides his time, he knows that in this 'game' he holds all the trump cards. Even in the secret letter to his wife (which succinctly parodies every case history of a traveller restored), he is careful to note that it was a 'worthy merchant' who 'redeemed and furnished' him home – just as he and his class were increasingly called on to 'redeem and furnish' the finances of their supposed betters.

Although the play closes in expectation of the reconciliatory feast traditional to comedy, it leaves all the characters apart from the merchant and his wife in a state of suspension. The parallels between the dramatic loose ends and the prevailing uncertainties in Caroline society are surely to the play's purpose. Of course, from Shirley's standpoint the real 'climax' – the cataclysm of civil war, just a decade away – could not be anticipated; but beneath the deceptively simple, seemingly inconsequential surface of his play (designed with an art which, like Jonson's in *Bartholomew Fair*, conceals art) are many of the social tensions and uncertainties which brought that cataclysm about. This is a comedy, and so, despite the uncertainties, the tensions are conventionally relaxed: the 'court' learns to reform its manners and the 'town' to accept that 'country' values are best; but it is the 'city' that snatches the genteel Lacy's newly acquired property, both sexual and substantial, from under his very nose. No wonder that Bonavent is graceful enough to forgive the insult he has suffered and, with a mixture of generosity and enlightened self-interest, to invite everybody to supper. To Bonavent belongs the future.

The playwright's craft

FORM The play is clearly and distinctively transitional between, on the one hand, romantic comedy (with its pairs of lovers) and city comedy (with its satire on greed and social climbing), and, on the other, Restoration comedy of manners, with its character types drawn from the West End and its sharp focus on sex and social worth.

STRUCTURE The sandwiching of the scenes set in Hyde Park between those set in the domestic interior of Bonavent's house is reflected in the respectively public and private nature of the resulting encounters – Bonavent being ironically the only 'stranger' within his own four walls.

LANGUAGE The play is written in a blank verse so easy and casual as to be almost imperceptible. Mistress Carol has a vituperative flair which enlivens her scenes, as does Julietta in her fury with Bonvile, but the play's rhetorical force is far exceeded by its structural fluency and subtle, intermeshed plotting.

CONVENTIONS The disguise motif apart, the play anticipates conventions rather than recycling them: the characters of Venture and Rider thus foreshadow the fops of Restoration comedy – not yet full-blown, but clearly more concerned with boasting of conquests than their achievement. Given that actresses were not available until after the Restoration, there would also have been the unusual need to find no fewer than three boy actors able to play mature women rather than pert ingenues (assuming all are around the age of Mistress Bonavent, who has already been married for seven years).

STAGE PRACTICE The third and fourth acts set in Hyde Park (and indeed the bustling opening scene) would have involved quite a complex choreography of coming and going, meeting and overlooking, given that spectators sat on each side of the stage in private theatres, so that actors could only enter by the doors upstage – or, conjecturally, through the audience. The play would have been much better suited to the Restoration stage, with its two downstage doors on each side of the proscenium, and the added possibility of upstage entrances through the scenic vista.

In performance

The Master of the Revels issued his licence for *Hyde Park* on 20 April 1632, and it was probably first performed soon afterwards by Queen Henrietta's Men at the Phoenix (or Cockpit) theatre in Drury Lane. It was evidently still popular in 1639, when it was included in the list of plays acknowledged to be the property of Beeston's Boys, by then in occupation at that theatre. And we know that it was revived at least once during the Restoration, when Pepys in his diary records going to the first Theatre Royal in Drury Lane to see 'an old play of Shirley's, called *Hyde Park*, the first day acted'. He noted that 'horses are brought on the stage', but found it 'a very moderate play, only an excellent epilogue'. This production played before royalty on 14 July, but there is no record of subsequent performances until the RSC revival of 1987 by Barry Kyle at the Swan in Stratford, later transferred to the Barbican Pit. Kyle's updating to what Peter Kemp described as 'a Bloomsbury Group milieu . . . accords uncannily well with the very self-conscious, drily mocking nature of the characters'. As Mistress Carol, Fiona Shaw, 'as a kind of manic Virginia Woolf . . . hilariously brings out every last twitch and tic of the nervousness fuelling the brainy clowning'. Nicholas de Jongh agreed: Shaw 'revels in long-limbed gestural signs of nerves – hands smiting head, placating, tiptoeing and grimacing', while Alex Jennings, as Fairfield, 'greyly garbed in a mass of wintry costumes and tight collars, cannily allows a raging temper to break from his stiff young-fogeyish exterior'.

Richard Brome
A Jovial Crew

1641

Source

Brome may have been indebted to Middleton and Rowley's
The Spanish Gipsy (1623) for the broad outline of his plot, but
in its specifics it is his own invention.

The story

Oldrents, a wealthy but generous and well-loved landowner,
is worried by a fortune-teller's prophecy that his daughters,
Rachel and Meriel, will become beggars. His friend Hearty
attempts both to reason and laugh him out of his depression,
and Oldrents agrees to try to act merrily. His steward Springlove asks to be released that he may pursue the wanderlust
which overtakes him every spring, and join the company of
vagrants who have been sheltering for the winter in Oldrents'
barn. Rachel and Meriel, feeling oppressed by household cares
and their father's gloomy mood, persuade their suitors, Vincent
and Hilliard, that they should all make a trial of life with the
vagabonds; and Springlove, realising that this will literally
fulfil the prophecy and lift the old man's fear of their being
reduced to poverty, agrees to take them under his wing. Oldrents meanwhile has become compulsively jolly, and joins in as
the beggars, led by their hedge-poet Patrico, celebrate a new-
born baby while they prepare to depart. The volunteer vagrants
grow tired of their freedom after a single night's discomfort;
but neither male nor female runaways will admit as much to
the other, so they allow themselves to be tutored in the art of
beggary by Springlove. Vincent and Hilliard's high rhetoric
soon arouses suspicion and anger, while Rachel and Meriel
have to be rescued from the amorous clutches of Oliver, son of

the notorious Justice Clack. Clack's niece and ward Amie has eloped with his clerk, Hearty's nephew Martin, rather than go through an arranged marriage with the wealthy but lachrymose Tallboy, and the pair of runaways are given shelter by the vagabonds. But it soon appears that Amie is more attracted to Springlove than to the close and miserly Martin. Hearing that Hearty is at Oldrents' house, Oliver and Tallboy resort there in search of Amie, and are entertained by the eccentric servant Randall. As the beggars celebrate the hedgerow wedding of an eighty-year-old couple, Amie is told by Rachel and Meriel that Springlove is not what he seems, and she agrees to marry him; but the spurned Martin has betrayed her whereabouts, and the local watch arrive to take everybody they can catch into custody. Brought before Justice Clack, who is entertaining Oldrents and Hearty, they perform a play which re-enacts the misadventures just past – and Patrico reveals that the old man had once seduced his sister, whose child was none other than Springlove. All ends in reconciliation – but nothing more substantial than a 'miser's feast'.

The author and his work

Little is known of Brome's early life. He was probably born around 1590, and was in London by 1614, when he gets a mention in *Bartholomew Fair* as Jonson's 'man . . . behind the arras'. Whether this indicates that he was Jonson's servant or his protégé is unclear, but later the older man claimed that he had taught Brome how to be a playwright, and there remained a close affinity between the two, both personal and in terms of their dramatic work – though Dekker also laid claim to Brome as an apprentice, and Jonson' s satiric tone is certainly softened by Dekker's humane tolerance in Brome's comedy, in which genre he largely wrote. He worked for companies as low and ill-regarded as that at the open-air Red Bull, who in 1623 staged his first play, *A Fault in Friendship* (now lost, like his others for the company), and as fashionable as the King's Men at the Blackfriars and the Globe, where *The*

Northern Lass (1629), *The Novella* (1632), *The Weeding of the Covent Garden* (1632) and *The Late Lancashire Witches* (with Heywood, 1634) were staged. In 1635 he became the house dramatist for Queen Henrietta's Men at the private Salisbury Court, where among others *The City Wit* (1629), *The Sparagus Garden* (1635) and *The Antipodes* (1638) were seen. The company sued him in 1640 for breaching his contract by also writing for Beeston's company at the Cockpit, who staged *The Court Beggar* (1640) – until it was banned for a suspected satire on the King – and *A Jovial Crew*, which was his last play before the closure of the theatres upon the outbreak of Civil War. Brome died, apparently in poverty, in 1652.

The historical context

A vagrant was the legal description for any supposedly able-bodied beggar or vagabond, and vagrants were grouped with 'rogues' and 'sturdy beggars' to distinguish them from the more 'deserving' poor, who were unable to work by reason of illness or age. An act of 1572 prescribed whipping and piercing through the ear for a first offence, condemnation as a felon for a second and death for a third. This act also defined as vagrants 'masterless men' without land, peddlers, tinkers, jugglers and minstrels – though in also requiring that strolling players must obtain noble patronage to avoid being viewed as vagrants, it contributed to the regularisation of the theatrical profession by providing some security for those who obtained such patronage. The Elizabethan Poor Laws, consolidated in 1598 and 1601, at last recognised genuine unemployment, and placed responsibility for the care of the 'impotent poor' upon the parish: but asylum-seeking even in a neighbouring parish was forbidden, and those found wandering while searching for work were subject to being whipped until bloody before being returned to their place of birth. In giving Oldrents his name, Brome was reminding his audience that exorbitant 'new rents' were more commonly being extorted; and such 'rack-renting', together with the enclosure of common land, forced many reluctantly into a wayfaring life. So Justice Clack's threats were not without legal sanction, and Springlove's summer wanderings were less romantic than he makes them seem. As for the winter, shelter in a barn such as offered by Oldrents was not a likely respite for vagrants in real life.

The world of the play

Brome had written a number of city comedies – even, in *The Antipodes*, a topsy-turvy, anti-city comedy. But there is no trace of the city in *The Jovial Crew* (other than in the professions once pursued there by some of the beggars) and, of the two worlds which are given substance in the play, that of the beggars is not so much in conflict with the settled rural communities through which it passes as in a state of cold-warlike co-existence. Randall is a typical country-dweller in never having been further than twelve miles from his birthplace (V, i, 157) until the expedition to Clack's house; for while fashionable society enjoyed increasing freedom to travel, the rural gentry seldom took advantage of this – and the poor would neither have been able to afford it nor, indeed, been permitted the privilege without being outlawed as vagabonds. Housebound girls may have shared Rachel and Meriel's envy of the beggars' 'freedom', but would have been no less disillusioned by experiencing its harshness and pragmatic subservience.

Increasingly, the court was indulging in the manufacture of pastoral idylls to soften the buffeting of political realities, and at one level Brome's commonwealth of beggars is a timely corrective to that nostalgic cavalier fantasy, showing the wandering life as no escape from reality but a cruel existence in which women are subject to predatory rapists such as Oliver (who though restrained must still be propitiated). A courtier is no more than 'a great court beggar', and beggary itself apes the behaviour of the court, which begs 'by covetise, not need, / From others that which made them beg indeed' (I, i, 408–11). There is even a burlesque court masque, in which geriatric beggars become king and queen – for, as Vincent comments,

'Phoebus, we see, inspires / As well the beggar as the poet laureate,' to which Springlove adds, 'And shines as warm under a hedge-bottom as on the tops of palaces' (IV, ii, 136–9). And in the very last exchange of the play, before Springlove turns to the audience to solicit applause, Oldrents tells his new-found son that he will give him a daily blessing – 'Except it be at court, boy, where if ever I come, it shall be to beg the next fool-royal's place that falls' (V, i, 499–500).

Such tiny but cumulatively forceful barbs are scattered throughout the play. And there are less explicit reflections besides – Justice Clack thus resembles the King himself in holding that it is his prerogative to pass judgement before hearing the evidence, while the very name of Oldrents is a critique on the 'new rents' everywhere being demanded. So in presenting these contrasting ways of rural life to theatre audiences drawn from the proto-capitalist city and the leisured, fashionable town, it is not that Brome is afraid of commenting on the acute political contentions of the time; but his play transcends its satirical purpose (as did his master Jonson's) in creating alternative worlds which are fully realised and humanised by their very foibles and eccentricities.

These are interestingly balanced between the two domestic households of the play. Thus, Randall and Martin are both their master's trusted servant; but whereas the former is open about his temptations and resolute in avoiding them, the latter first succumbs, and then is too weak and miserly to enter wholeheartedly into his own deception. (Randall himself is a very Jonsonian creature – we could dispense with him entirely so far as the plot is concerned, but his regular off-the-wall interventions round out its reality.) Against Oldrents' determination to be merry, which becomes excessive and thus a humorous affectation, is set Tallboy's compulsive tendency to shed tears. To the first pair, Hearty serves as a proper model of moderate behaviour; and by contrast with the second pair, Springlove has a self-recognition which Tallboy never achieves, but which Oldrents recovers along with his daughters, his son and his self-knowledge in the final act.

Springlove returns to what is now truly his home, reconciled to a settled existence – as well he might be, having been promised 'a thousand pound a year to entertain your wife' (V, i, 473–4). But his former fellow-wanderers, with their complement of erstwhile lawyers, doctors, courtiers and soldiers, are left loose-ended and without resources (unlike the house servants of IV, i, who have been well provided for in Oldrents' mood of reckless generosity – which they appear concerned to emulate). True, the beggars have been granted 'free passage' by a drunkenly amenable Clack – but legally this entitled them only to find their way back to their places of birth, not to freedom to continue wandering (as they presumably intend), subject once more to abuse and arrest.

Apart from Springlove – and Patrico, who sits in authorial omnipresence over all – we never really meet the beggars as individual characters; and this is perhaps appropriate, given the communal nature of their existence. Of course, in comprising a commonwealth in a literal sense they are committing the economic sin of holding all in common, to exacerbate such moral sins as greeting the delivery of a child with a joyful birthing ceremony, careless of its paternity or bastardy, and such improprieties as finding a marriage between eighty-year-olds cause for celebration, not derision. And if we are tempted to take the moral high ground with Oldrents when he is offered his choice of virgin for the night (II, ii, 266–76), it is to discover that Brome is playing an ironic game with us – for the outrage registers as hypocrisy when we learn that Oldrents fathered Springlove on Patrico's hapless sister.

This revelation comes at the very end of the play, along with the knowledge that Oldrents' fortune is ultimately derived from his grandfather's fraudulent dealings. By this time, the only reconciliatory meal in prospect is a 'miser's feast', with the dishes set far apart, 'as if they fear'd quarrelling' (V, i, 271) – for we have moved from Oldrents' dwelling, with its old-fashioned hospitality, to the home of an unjust justice and his dissolute son (who assumes poor women's sexual availability as his father prejudges poor men's guilt), his miserly clerk and the self-pitying Tallboy. Brome gives us an aptly ambiguous climax to a comedy meant in part to take its audience's minds from the 'state disturbances' and 'alteration in a commonwealth' anticipated by Vincent (IV, ii, 90–4), but also in part to suggest that if national reconciliation were to be achieved, it would have to be based on real generosity not distorted justice, and that even those who afforded such generosity would need to recognise the past ills on which their present well-being might be founded.

The playwright's craft

FORM *The Jovial Crew* is at one level a comedy of humours, but has greater complexity in that Springlove, whose compulsive itinerancy would appear an affectation, is more self-aware than Oldrents, and is 'cured' by gaining knowledge of his own origins. The play begins to shape a quite new kind of humane comedy, cut short by the closure of the theatres.

STRUCTURE As suggested above, the essential movement is not from court to country and back, but from a warm and friendly domestic interior to the threatening outside world – and back to an altogether bleaker hearth.

LANGUAGE The play freely slips between blank verse and prose – not according to class or status, but as the balance tips between rhetoric and idiomatic speech. Brome draws extensively on the 'canting' language of the underworld, while one of the few marks of Rachel's individuality is her evident expertise in rural sports and games (I, i, 23–9). He also makes much use of catch-phrases and other verbal tics – for example, in the amateur beggars' hopeful parroting of 'Duly and truly pray for you' (III, i); in Oldrents' and his servants' insistence that 'he's no snail', which the Chaplain even renders into Latin (IV, i); in Clack's overriding 'Nay, if we both speak together . . .' (V, i); and in Tallboy's convoluted syntax: 'Would one of us two had never both seen one another' (V, i, 203).

CONVENTIONS Oldrents' acknowledgement of his paternity thanks to an *agnus dei* medallion is intentionally self-parodying – not least in view of Brome's tongue-in-cheek Prologue, promising a romantic comedy in which 'some impossibility / Concludes all strife' (lines 13–14).

STAGE PRACTICE When the beggars are (twice) 'discovered' carousing, the curtains of the discovery space would have been drawn to reveal them 'in their postures' (forming a tableau), from which they 'issue forth' downstage (I, i, 362, and II, ii, 167). Throughout, from these song-and-dance routines to the display of canting and the masque for the hedge-wedding, to the play-within-the-play in the final act, they serve as entertainers within the entertainment.

In performance

Although a quarto edition of *A Jovial Crew* was not printed until 1652, there seems no need to question its title-page claim that the play was first staged at the Cockpit (or Phoenix) in Drury Lane in 1741; and Brome's remark in his dedication that it 'had the luck to tumble last of all in the epidemical ruin of the scene' suggests that it was still being played right up to the closure of the theatres in September 1642. The play was also among the earliest to be revived after the Restoration, in January 1661, and among numerous performances in the following decades was one before the recently enthroned Willam and Mary in 1689. Its popularity continued into the new century, and it was acted every year at Drury Lane between 1704 and 1724. After 1760 competing comic-opera versions supplanted the original, which was lost to the live theatre until 1992, when the RSC revived the play at the Swan, adapted by Stephen Jeffreys under the direction of Max Stafford-Clark. Though wishing Brome's text had not been tampered with, Charles Spencer summed up: 'With its mixture of uproarious laughter, acute social observation and intimations of coming strife, this is a gripping and strangely haunting show.'

Chronology

Dates of plays, though often conjectural, usually derive from the complete chronological listing of all known plays in Annals of English Drama 975–1700 *by Alfred Harbage, as revised by S. Schoenbaum (London: Methuen, 1964). Plays included in the present volume are in bold type.*

1531	Henry VIII proclaimed Supreme Head of the Church in England
1532	Machiavelli's *The Prince*
1535	Suppression of the monasteries begins. Coverdale's Bible
1545	First Master of the Revels appointed
1547	Accession of Edward VI
1553	Accession of Mary I. *Gammer Gurton's Needle*
1558	Loss of Calais to the French. Accession of Elizabeth I
1562	The 'Thirty-Nine Articles' of the Church of England. *Gorboduc*
1566	Gascoigne's *Supposes*
1568	*The Marriage of Wit and Science*
1569	Last performance of York cycle of mystery plays
1572	Act for punishment of vagabonds
1574	Queen grants patent to Leicester's Men
1576	Last performance of Wakefield cycle of mystery plays. The Theatre and first Blackfriars open
1587	Execution of Mary Queen of Scots. Rose theatre built. **Kyd, *The Spanish Tragedy*. Marlowe, *Tamburlaine the Great***
1588	Defeat of the Spanish Armada. Lyly, *Endymion*. Porter, *The Two Angry Women of Abingdon*. **Marlowe, *Doctor Faustus***
1589	**Greene, *Friar Bacon and Friar Bungay***
1590	Peele, *The Old Wives Tale*. **Marlowe, *The Jew of Malta*. *Arden of Faversham***

1591   Peele, *Edward I*. Shakespeare, *Henry VI*

1592   Plague closes theatres for two years. **Marlowe,
          Edward II.** Shakespeare, *The Comedy of Errors*

1593   Daniel, *Cleopatra*. Shakespeare, *Richard III*

1594   Companies reorganised: emergence of the Lord
          Chamberlain's and the Admiral's Men. Shakespeare,
          The Taming of the Shrew

1595   Munday et al., *Sir Thomas More*. Shakespeare, *Love's
          Labour's Lost, A Midsummer Night's Dream, Romeo
          and Juliet*

1596   Second Blackfriars theatre built. Chapman, *The
          Blind Beggar of Alexandria*. Jonson, *A Tale of a Tub*.
          Shakespeare, *The Merchant of Venice*

1597   Shakespeare, *Henry IV, Parts One and Two*

1598   *Isle of Dogs* controversy. **Jonson, *Every Man in His
          Humour*.** Shakespeare, *Much Ado about Nothing*

1599   Essex in Ireland. First Globe playhouse built.
          Dekker, *The Shoemakers' Holiday*. Jonson, *Every
          Man out of His Humour*. Marston, *Antonio and
          Mellida*. Shakespeare, *As You Like It, Henry V, Julius
          Caesar. The Pilgrimage to Parnassus*

1600   Fortune theatre built. Heywood, *The Four Prentices
          of London*. Marston, *Antonio's Revenge*

1601   Essex's rebellion. 'War of the theatres'. Dekker,
          Satiromastix. Jonson, *Poetaster*. Marston, *What You
          Will*. Shakespeare, *Hamlet*

1602   Chapman, *May Day*. Shakespeare, *All's Well that Ends
          Well, Troilus and Cressida. The Merry Devil of Edmonton*

1603   Accession of James I. Plague closure of theatres.
          Royal patronage required for players. **Heywood,
          A Woman Killed with Kindness.** Jonson, *Sejanus*.
          Marston, *The Malcontent*

1604   Peace with Spain. Alleyn retires? **Chapman, *Bussy
          D'Ambois*.** Dekker and Middleton, *The Honest Whore*.
          Shakespeare, *Measure for Measure, Othello*

1605   Beginning of collaboration between Jonson and
          Inigo Jones on court masques. Red Bull built?

Gunpowder plot. **Chapman, Jonson and Marston,** ***Eastward Ho!*** Heywood, *If You Know Not Me, You Know Nobody*. Middleton, *A Trick to Catch the Old One*. **Marston, *The Dutch Courtesan*.** Shakespeare, *King Lear. A Yorkshire Tragedy*

1606   Day, *The Isle of Gulls*. **Jonson, *Volpone*.** Middleton, *A Mad World, My Masters*. **Tourneur, *The Revenger's Tragedy*.** Shakespeare, *Macbeth*

1607   Barnes, *The Devil's Charter*. Heywood, *The Rape of Lucrece*. **Beaumont, *The Knight of the Burning Pestle*.** Shakespeare, *Antony and Cleopatra, Timon of Athens*

1608   Chapman, *Byron*. Fletcher, *The Faithful Shepherdess*. **Middleton, *The Roaring Girl*.** Rowley, *The Birth of Merlin*. Shakespeare, *Coriolanus*

1609   Plague. King's Men begin probably begin playing indoors in winter, at the Blackfriars. Beaumont and Fletcher, *Philaster*. **Jonson, *Epicoene*.** Shakespeare, *Cymbeline*

1610   **Beaumont and Fletcher, *The Maid's Tragedy*. Heywood, *The Fair Maid of the West*,** *The Golden Age*. **Jonson, *The Alchemist*.** Shakespeare, *The Winter's Tale*

1611   **Beaumont and Fletcher, *A King and No King*.** Cooke, *Greene's Tu Quoque*. Heywood, *The Brazen Age, The Silver Age*. Jonson, *Catiline*. Middleton, *A Chaste Maid in Cheapside*. Shakespeare, *The Tempest. The Second Maiden's Tragedy*

1612   Prince Henry dies. Heywood, *The Iron Age*. **Webster, *The White Devil***

1613   Jonson, *A Challenge at Tilt*. Shakespeare and Fletcher, *Henry VIII*

1614   Hope and second Globe theatres opened. Fletcher, *Wit without Money*. **Jonson, *Bartholomew Fair*. Webster, *The Duchess of Malfi***

1615   The Overbury murder trial. Cockpit theatre built? Middleton, *The Witch*

1616 Deaths of Beaumont and Shakespeare. Publication of Jonson's *Works*. Jonson, *The Devil Is an Ass*

1617 Middleton and Rowley, *A Fair Quarrel*. Webster, *The Devil's Law Case*

1618 Execution of Ralegh. Fletcher, *The Loyal Subject*. Middleton, *The Mayor of Queenborough*. Swetnam, *The Woman Hater*

1619 Field and Massinger, *The Fatal Dowry*. Rowley, *All's Lost by Lust*

1620 Fletcher, *The Custom of the Country*, *The Double Marriage*

1621 Fortune burned down. **Dekker, Ford and Rowley, *The Witch of Edmonton*. Massinger, *A New Way to Pay Old Debts*.** Fletcher, *The Island Princess*, *The Wild Goose Chase*. **Middleton, *Women Beware Women***

1622 New Banqueting House in Whitehall opened. **Middleton and Rowley, *The Changeling***

1623 Spanish visit of Charles and Buckingham. 'First Folio' of Shakespeare's plays. Fortune theatre rebuilt. Middleton and Rowley, *The Spanish Gypsy*

1624 Death of Rowley. Middleton, *A Game at Chess*

1625 Accession of Charles I and marriage to Henrietta Maria. Plague closure. Death of Fletcher. Shirley, *Love's Tricks*

1626 Fletcher, *The Fair Maid of the Inn*. Jonson, *The Staple of News*. Massinger, *The Roman Actor*. Shirley, *The Maid's Revenge*

1627 Death of Middleton

1628 Ford, *The Lover's Melancholy*. Shirley, *The Witty Fair One*

1629 Start of Charles' eleven-year personal rule. Salisbury Court opened. Brome, *The Northern Lass*. **Ford, *The Broken Heart*.** Jonson, *The New Inn*

1630 Plague closure. Cockpit-in-Court opened. Brome, *The City Wit*

1631 Brome, *The Queen's Exchange*. Massinger, *Believe As You List*. Shirley, *The Traitor*

1632	Death of Dekker. Ford, *Love's Sacrifice*. Jonson, *The Magnetic Lady*. Massinger, *The City Madam*. **Shirley, Hyde Park, The Ball**
1633	Prynne's anti-theatrical *Histrio-Mastix*. **Ford, 'Tis Pity She's a Whore, Perkin Warbeck.** Heywood, *A Maidenhead Well Lost*. Shirley, *The Gamester*
1634	Deaths of Chapman and Marston. Brome, *The Late Lancashire Witches*. Davenant, *Love and Honour, The Wits*. Milton, *Comus*
1635	Brome, *The Sparagus Garden*. Killigrew, *The Conspiracy*. Shirley, *The Lady of Pleasure*
1636	Long plague closure, into 1637
1637	Death of Jonson
1638	New masquing house in Whitehall. Brome, *The Antipodes*. Davenant, *Britannia Triumphans*. Ford, *The Lady's Trial*. Shirley, *The Constant Maid*
1639	Ford dies. Brome, *The Lovesick Court*. Davenant, *The Spanish Lovers*. Shirley, *The Politician*
1640	Beginning of the 'Long Parliament'. Massinger dies. Last court masque: Davenant's *Salmacida Spolia*. Brome, *The Court Beggar*. Shirley, *The Captain*
1641	Heywood dies. **Brome, A Jovial Crew.** Killigrew, *The Parson's Wedding*. Shirley, *The Brothers, The Cardinal*
1642	Civil wars begin. Theatres closed from September
1643	*The Actors' Remonstrance* against their plight
1644	Interior of Globe dismantled
1647	Some public acting. Folio of Beaumont and Fletcher's plays published
1649	Trial and execution of Charles I. Commonwealth proclaimed
1650	Prince Charles in exile. Many playhouses by now pulled down
1653	Cromwell becomes Lord Protector
1654	Suppression of illicit playing
1660	Restoration of Charles II. Patents granted to Davenant and Killigrew to form theatre companies. Actresses permitted